THE JOHNS HOPKINS UNIVERSITY PRESS

THE DIRECTOR'S CIRCLE BOOK FOR 2003

The Johns Hopkins University Press gratefully acknowledges members of the 2003 Director's Circle for supporting the publication of works such as *Unconscious Crime*.

Alfred and Muriel Berkeley • Robert M. and Anne B. Evans

Alberta Gamble • Charles and Elizabeth Hughes

J. Kent Minichiello • Charles and Margaret M. H. Obrecht

Peter Onuf • Douglas R. Price • Anders Richter

Catherine and Andrew Schmidt • R. Champlin and Debbie Sheridan

C. John Sullivan and Family • Angela von der Lippe

Robert L. Warren and Family

�֍ JOEL PETER EIGEN ✤

UNCONSCIOUS CRIME

*Mental Absence and Criminal Responsibility
in Victorian London*

❖

THE JOHNS HOPKINS UNIVERSITY PRESS
BALTIMORE AND LONDON

© 2003 The Johns Hopkins University Press
All rights reserved. Published 2003
Printed in the United States of America on acid-free paper

2 4 6 8 9 7 5 3 1

The Johns Hopkins University Press
2715 North Charles Street
Baltimore, Maryland 21218-4363
www.press.jhu.edu

Library of Congress Cataloging-in-Publication Data

Eigen, Joel Peter, 1947–
  Unconscious crime : mental absence and criminal
responsibility in Victorian London / Joel Peter Eigen.
    p.   cm.
Includes bibliographical references and index.
  ISBN 0-8018-7428-9 (hardcover : acid-free paper)
    1. Insanity—Jurisprudence—Great Britain—History—
19th century.   I. Title.
  KD7897.E359 2003
  345.42′04—dc21   2003006215

A catalog record for this book is available from
the British Library.

FOR DEBBIE

CONTENTS

PREFACE

Anyone who places confidence in the notion that a person is presumed innocent until proven guilty is in for a rude awakening when he realizes how few courtroom defenses are available to maintain that innocence. If the criminal act was deliberately committed, one can only allege some form of provocation or plead the existence of a tragic mistake: "I honestly thought it was a stage knife." If the events surrounding the crime cannot sustain a defense based on either compulsion or error, the unfortunate accused must rely on a more drastic option; some form of mental distress propelled his hand or clouded his consciousness. But what options are open to the defendant who cannot even place himself at the scene of the crime? What courtroom defense is available to the person who was "missing" at the time?

Although it may seem natural to group all forms of mental alienation under the heading of insanity, the missing defendant presents the court with a distinctly different challenge. The conventional plea of insanity calls into question only the defendant's particular mental resolve: what he meant to do. There is little doubt that he had produced the physical act. But who (or what) commits the crime of a sleepwalker? What defense is open to the person in a seizure or to one who involuntarily responds to an automatic reflex? In an episode of sheer unconsciousness then, how does the law determine the author of the crime?

Tales of sleepwalkers wandering into the common law date at least to the seventeenth century, but only in the mid-1800s did the London courtroom meet an array of defendants who shared the jury's bewilderment that "someone could have done such a thing." As it happened, nineteenth-century automatons sauntered not only into London's courtroom, but into my survey of Victorian forensic psychiatry as well, quite unannounced. Midway through a study of medicolegal courtroom testimony, I began to realize that neither the newly arrived defense attorney nor the asylum doctor cum forensic psychiatrist had appreciated the distance between the array of mental states commonly associated with conventional insanity and the anomalous behavior of the missing defendant. Indeed, the only courtroom actors who recognized that something new had emerged were the nonprofessionals, the members of the jury, whose innovative and totally unprompted verdict "not guilty on the grounds of unconsciousness" signaled the arrival of a new class of defendants, commonly described in medical texts as "doubly conscious" and in contemporary literature simply as mesmerized.

But where exactly did the missing defendant fit with prevailing legal and philosophical thought regarding volition and criminal responsibility? I mentioned the unexpected discovery of the unconscious defendant to Nigel Walker, author of the seminal volume *Crime and Insanity in England*, which had inspired my earlier research on the origins of forensic psychiatric testimony. As he had earlier supplied invaluable guidance in illuminating the origins of common-law notions of insanity, Nigel proved once again to be the source of all things forensic and philosophical, encouraging me to consider the role that consciousness had played in John Locke's definition of the person—and by extension—the common law's attribution of legal responsibility. To punish a person for an act undertaken while asleep, the seventeenth-century essayist had written, was "no more of Right" than to hold one twin accountable for his brother's act. The legal issue that sat at the heart of these mid-nineteenth-century trials was not therefore the actor's intent, but whether the person on trial was the same *person* who committed the crime. The focus of the research therefore expanded to consider the Victorian era's evolving conceptions of unconscious states of being and the psychological possibility that a mentally absent person could pursue purposeful activity.

A visiting fellowship offered by Cambridge University's Institute of Criminology during the year 1996–97 enabled me to survey the array of defenses available to nineteenth-century defendants in the London courtroom. In addition to the resources of the University Library's Hunter and Macalpine collection on the history of psychiatry, I was able to take advantage of the encyclopedic resources of the Wellcome Trust Centre for the History of Medicine, and to continue a rewarding association with the late and dearly missed Roy Porter. Together with members of a cohort of researchers in the history and sociology of medicine, I gratefully acknowledge an overwhelming debt to this singular scholar and mentor, whose own encyclopedic knowledge of the social world of medicine has inspired an entire field of study. I was fortunate that year to meet medical historian Michael Neve, also of the Wellcome, who remains a vital sounding board and patient listener to my ideas about the twists and turns in the history of forensic psychiatry. Also during that year I became acquainted with legal historian Martin Wiener, whose writings on social policy and law have alerted today's students of legal evolution to the pride of place that volition enjoyed in Victorian criminal justice policy. I am pleased to acknowledge the guidance Marty has given me in historical methodology and the location of archival sources.

A second sabbatical leave prompted me to accept the kind invitation of the fellowship of Pembroke College to return to Cambridge to compete this research. My host at Pembroke, fellow criminologist Loraine Gelsthorpe, provided intellectual sustenance and friendship throughout the year, and it is to her and to the members of the Senior Parlour that I gratefully acknowledge many kindnesses and stimulating conversations. I doubt that a finer, more welcoming society exists at any university. While auditing Neil Manson's superb survey on "the unconscious before Freud," I met the Australian psychiatrist Michael Salzberg, with whom I shared particular interests in the legal and cultural implications of epileptic seizures. Our after-class discussions developed into weekly dinners that helped us both frame the separate, though parallel projects we were pursuing, and also served to cement a wonderful friendship. I was also blessed with a continuing association with legal historian Rose Melikan of St. Catherine's College, who provided unstinting encouragement in the craft of writing and strategies for coping with its various demons. Hers is also a friendship I treasure.

I further want to acknowledge a summer stipend awarded by the National Endowment for the Humanities that allowed me to return to Cambridge between the two sabbatical leaves to complete data collection. Social scientists who are historically and theoretically inclined have come to look to the Endowment for support, and gratefully acknowledge the vital role of research funds in enabling them to ask the sort of questions that traditional, quantitative scholarship often overlooks. Together with the Endowment, the Provost's Office at Franklin and Marshall College has provided generous resources, both financial and spiritual, and I thank the college's Board of Trustees for understanding the irreplaceable role of academic scholarship in ensuring that faculty members as well as their students will be actively engaged in learning.

I owe a debt also to scholars and friends both in England and America who have listened patiently and offered insights at crucial moments in the research. Robin Williams, Erica Haimes, Caroline Mason, Marcia Dewey, Roger Smith, Michael Clark, Helen Krarup, and Phyllis Freeman have provided continuing guidance and welcome encouragement. At 59 Maids Causeway, Yvonne Garrod offered generous hospitality and friendship throughout, and I thank her warmly. Kathy Clark and Pippa MacCallister skillfully helped to prepare the manuscript, and Gladys Topkis, as always, provided invaluable guidance for clearer diction and coherent organization. Above all, I want to thank my editor, Jacqueline Wehmueller, for her guidance, sound judgment, gentle prodding, and support throughout the stages of this project. On a personal level, I am pleased to thank Richard F. Summers for offering valuable insight, and patient, good counsel when it was needed most. Maurice and Judy Kaplow continue to provide a haven both physical and spiritual, and a bond that only grows stronger with the passing years. As always, my sister Mikki Eigen Rocker provided the greatest source of inspiration, helping to keep the memory of our parents alive and their many lessons in living, vital. There only remains to thank my colleague, Scott Lerner, whose support, enthusiasm for this work, and insight never flagged. It is rare that two colleagues willingly share their writing with each other—knowing full well what the other will do to it—and I treasure both the trust and the friendship that sustains that bond.

This work is dedicated to the memory of a valiant woman whose love of family and friends knew no bounds. Her steadfast belief in the importance of my research often served as a beacon in the darker days; I miss her encouragement more with each passing year, and in many ways, the loss only grows deeper. Deborah Rocker Klausner met life face-forward, asked no sympathy for the cards she'd been dealt, but rather inspired those in her circle to seize the possibilities of life. Her indomitable spirit infuses all who knew and loved her with her own unique sense of purpose and drive.

UNCONSCIOUS CRIME

INTRODUCTION

❖

SHORTLY AFTER SHE SET OUT her daughter's pajamas and placed a hot-water bottle in her bed and a glass of milk on the bedstand, Mrs. Cogdon picked up an axe, reentered the bedroom, and struck the now-sleeping girl twice in the head. Details of the fatal night had to be explained to the bewildered and distraught mother because all she could remember of the assault was her terror at seeing a Korean soldier attacking her beloved Pat. As it happened, there was no Korean soldier in her daughter's bedroom, just as the previous night Mrs. Cogdon had been mistaken about the poisonous spiders swarming over Pat, prompting her to swat the imagined insects violently off her daughter's face. Eventually indicted for Pat's murder, Mrs. Cogdon did not plead insanity, despite the ready evidence of hallucinatory episodes. Indeed, medical witnesses who testified on her behalf conspicuously sidestepped the psychological implications of the deadly insects and menacing soldiers she had imagined which, to the nonmedical observer at least, certainly suggest some degree of unconscious hostility toward the daughter. In the end Mrs. Cogdon simply pled not guilty to the murder charge. Her narrative of the events surrounding Pat's death met no opposition from the prosecutor or, apparently, from the jury, whose members returned an outright acquittal. Given a defendant who never denied wielding the axe and who refused to raise a plea of insanity, how are we to understand the jury's finding of blamelessness?

The particular question facing the jury in *The King v. Cogdon*, an Australian case heard in 1950, was not how deranged, deluded, or distracted the accused was at the time of the crime.[1] Those were the questions for an insanity trial; the law's criterion for exonerating culpability

1

in the face of madness was well known, if not always easy to put into practice. Mrs. Cogdon presented the court with a different legal defense, one that carried no authoritative case law for its solution. Defendants who alleged the existence of sleepwalking, amnesia, or fugue states in which they were "not themselves" asked the courts to determine who, precisely, had committed the crime. In the Cogdon trial, medical witnesses mentioned each of these states of suspended consciousness; Pat's assailant was in effect found not guilty because the crime was not hers at all. The Mrs. Cogdon who lovingly filled the hot-water bottle and warmed the glass of milk was clearly in a state of altered consciousness at the moment the axe was wielded.

She *was* sufficiently conscious to maneuver her way around the house, to remember where the axe could be found, and to direct the lethal blows in order to immobilize the soldier in the shortest amount of time. What sort of altered consciousness allows for such purposeful activity on the part of a person described as "asleep"? Pat's death, after all, was not the result of random battery; Mrs. Cogdon had not *bumped into* her daughter—striking her in some flailing action—while roaming aimlessly about the house. Someone had dreamt about soldiers, sought out the axe, and struck the sleeping girl. If the criminal act did not "belong" to Mrs. Cogdon—as the jury's outright acquittal appeared to proclaim—what relationship did the murderous assassin bear to the mother who, as the defendant's husband testified, "absolutely adored Pat"? Was she, in effect, a *Mrs. Hyde*?

Novelists, moral philosophers, social scientists, and clinicians specializing in mental aberration have long questioned whether the unity of the self was more an article of Western faith than a demonstrable reality. Evidence of wildly exaggerated mood swings, "uncharacteristic" feelings and behavior, and extreme episodes of "otherness" such as sleepwalking and hypnotic trance have long prompted speculation about the possibility of a second self, or indeed of multiple selves inhabiting the same body. The challenge such a conception of *splitting* poses to contemporary intellectual and religious thought is considerable, but nowhere is the debate as consequential as for the common law. Precisely because sleepwalkers, posthypnotic subjects, and other *entranced* persons experiencing altered states of consciousness reveal no history of mental impairment (in their "host state," they manifest little if any confusion), the common law's traditional way of approaching impaired mental function—as a variant of insanity—fails to address their crimes. Persons described as dissociating or in fugue states manifest no failure to understand what they're "up to"; rather they are bystanders to the crime if awake at all. By their lack of agency—by not being the author of their crime—they do not resemble the delusional person, for example, who believes himself compelled to act. They are instead far removed—literally, a person away—from both the contemplation and the execution of a crime that quite clearly belongs to someone else.

Only in the late twentieth century, and then only in Western legal systems, has the possible existence of multiple selves reached a comprehensive diagnosis in the category of Multiple Personality Disorder (MPD). American courts in particular confront a host of peculiar, almost risible criminal justice riddles. Could a twin personality raise a writ of habeas corpus if incarcerated for the actions of its wakeful other? Are the police obliged to advise all resident personalities, *in seriatim*, of their Miranda rights before the lot can be taken into custody? If a witness suffers from MPD, must all persons *inside* be sworn?[2] There is then, of course, the overriding question of criminal responsibility. If the accused had been effectively unconscious when another personality committed the crime, how can a jury apportion responsibility between—or *among* —the personalities residing in the one defendant standing trial? Confronted with defenses of "multiplicity," some American juries have considered dissociation to resemble conventional states of delusion and delirium and have chosen to acquit on the grounds of insanity. Some judges have ruled that it would be unfair to hold the "host" personality responsible for behavior of which he or she was unaware, or from which he was unable to refrain. Still other jurists wonder whether the best way to proceed is to prosecute (only) the "alter in control," to examine all the resident personalities on the witness stand, or simply to ask the host what he or she understood about the nature of the action.

Today's jurors could hardly be blamed for throwing up their hands and asking, "What are we to do when confronted with medical evidence alleging that a hidden personality may have actually committed the crime?" The question that confronts today's medical historian though is somewhat different: When and where did ideas of splitting, of multiplicity, of fugue states evolve and how have common-law courts reacted to a defense of "nonresponsibility" based not on insanity but on the curious state of being *missing* at the time of the crime? What sort of testimony did the juror draw upon to make sense of this extraordinary state of being?

Looking for Historical Clues

Jurors and medical historians are not, of course, the only persons perplexed by the alleged presence of multiple personalities. Just as there have been novelists, moral philosophers, social scientists, and *mad-doctors* actively consumed by questions of fragmented selves and fractured consciousness, so have there been works of fiction, scholarly treatises on the mind, and medical texts that have explored the notion that a hidden self lay dormant just below the conscious surface of the subject's personality. Certainly, Freudian notions of the unconscious come immediately to mind, wherein long-repressed instinctual impulses manifest themselves in seemingly innocuous slips of the tongue or in more menacing forms: in paralysis and other hysterical symptoms. Literature as well has proffered images of hidden selves, often in opposition to the host personality, throwing up an evil, in contrast to a moral, self.[3] Such novels have been the subject of extended analysis, as have Freud's views of repressed memories and long-delayed emotional reflexes. However, medical reports of doubled personalities, of second selves emerging periodically, predate Freud by almost a century. Fictional renderings of a secretly hidden twin, graphic as they may be in depicting identity transformation by drinking a potion or gazing at one's increasingly grotesque image, fit the needs of the literary genre, not necessarily those of medicolegal history. For the purpose of examining the law's response to multiple selves and the realities of splitting, we would need the *trial* of Dorian Gray, or the *plea* of Dr. Jekyll, and we would need these in the form of a courtroom, not a literary, narrative.

Fortunately for the legal historian, there is available a curious set of pamphlets known as the *Old Bailey Sessions Papers (OBSP)* that, beginning in 1674 and continuing until the early twentieth century, report courtroom testimony of every trial at the Old Bailey, London's central criminal court.[4] These trial narratives of the Old Bailey's sittings (the "sessions") were taken down in shorthand, transcribed and printed nightly, and sold on the street within days of the trial. Although written for nonlawyers, they carried the imprimatur of the Common Council for the City of London, which ordered their publication. That the *OBSP* were intended for a lay audience adds to their utility for historical reconstruction of trial testimony because today's readers can hear the contemporary language of "nonlawyerly" London, particularly in pivotal questions asked of witnesses and especially in the occasional summation given by the judge. Over time, the Old Bailey trial narratives grew increasingly more comprehensive in reporting courtroom dialogue; nineteenth-century readers revealed an insatiable curiosity for trial detail fueled by "a rich mixture of prurience and moral outrage."[5]

For the purposes of legal history, the drawback of relying on a publication designed for general readers is that the publisher probably deleted the more technical discussions of criminal law practice and doctrine. Fortunately, legal innovations can often be grasped through judiciary comments and the objections made by defense attorneys that are picked up in the trial narrative, often, apparently, without the recorder's awareness that a significant departure in common-law thinking was in evidence. There is also the question of the trial narratives' comprehensiveness: because the *OBSP* are silent on some matters does not mean that one can confidently conclude the issues were *not* raised in court. Happily, one can supplement the trial narrative with newspaper accounts. The *Times of London*, for example, maintained a complete index of criminal trials, and other city newspapers were likely to report the events surrounding the more unusual crimes and innovative defense strategies. In addition, contemporary law and medical journals provide a context to gauge the fit between trial testimony and the professional commentary published in these two practitioners' publications.

One further refinement in court reporting that occurred between 1843 and 1876 helps to assess the significance of a courtroom innovation in trial procedure. Beginning in the mid-nineteenth century, the publishers of the *OBSP* nominated ten to fifteen trials each year (out of approximately ten thousand) to highlight under the rubric "Index to the Points of Law and Practice." Thumbnail descriptions of specific cases and their unusual forensic elements are offered, with an eye to alerting the reader to an apparent departure in legal thinking reflected in a singular verdict, or to unfamiliar issues raised in judge-jury dialogue. Such attention to changes in legal practice and the introduction of novel forms of defense suggest that the eighteenth century's general reading public appears to have metamorphosed into a legally savvy, well-educated Victorian consumer attuned to, and hungry for innovations in courtroom drama. Avoiding both the salacious and the macabre, "indexed trials" address an array of thorny legal riddles, prominent among them the question of when to call specialists to the stand and the proper scope of issues for expert testimony. Then as now, the fear that men of skill and unique experience might twist and frame courtroom evidence—and in the process displace the jury's function—served as a flashpoint between law and the emerging specialty of mental medicine.

The *OBSP* had proven their utility to my earlier study of the origins of medical testimony bearing on questions of mental derangement between 1760 and 1843.[6] These dates bracket the first trial in which a medical witness testified at the Old Bailey about insanity as a medical disease and the formalization of the insanity plea during the trial of Daniel McNaughtan. At the end of this celebrated trial, the House of Lords asked the trial judges to formulate criteria that future courts could employ when considering a plea of insanity.[7] That McNaughtan was the third political assassin, or would-be political assassin, since 1800 to be acquitted on grounds of insanity may have accounted for the urgent request for a formal set of criteria, which have become known as the McNaughtan Rules.

There was a further reason for judicial anxiety about insanity acquittals: an increasingly expansive universe of derangement that medical witnesses brought into the courtroom to support their opinion of the accused person's lack of accountability. Three years before McNaughtan's trial, a "lesion of the will" was said to have rendered Edward Oxford blameless for firing two pistols at Queen Victoria.[8] Other less notorious offenders at the Old Bailey were described as suffering from a *moral insanity,* a derangement not of the intellect but of the "moral sentiments": how one "ought to feel" toward others. One of the defining elements of moral insanity was a "will out of control," an insistent, irresistible force that propelled the afflicted into criminal violence. Daniel McNaughtan's derangement was attributed to a political delusion, and yet he too was described by medical witnesses as helpless when in the throes of the "black spot on his mind . . . nothing short of a physical impossibility would prevent him from performing any act which his delusion might impel him to do."[9]

When seen against the backdrop of the marked increase in the number of criminal trials in which medical witnesses were testifying and a qualitative shift in testimony that spoke to a derangement not just of the human mind but of the human heart as well, the McNaughtan Rules—the criteria defining the accused's failure to understand the nature of the crime and the difference between right and wrong—represent an effort to restrict the medical witnesses to commenting on the *knowing* faculties.[10] Such disputed medical diagnoses as "irresistible impulse" and "moral insanity"—states suggesting a thoroughly conscious volitional chaos—were left conspicuously out of the picture. By stressing the mind's cognitive faculties, the McNaughtan Rules affirmed the common law's traditional construction of the forensic *person:* a rational, purposeful being capable of perceiving the consequences of his acts.

As long as the court was presented with deluded, confused, and delirious defendants, the McNaughtan Rules could be employed to prosecute the allegedly insane. And as long as the court was presented with medical testimony framed in terms of intellectual incoherence and distraction, the testimony of mad-doctors and other self-described specialists in mental medicine presented no fundamental challenge to the common law. On those occasions when the language of the medical man departed from the court's conceptions of "legally relevant" madness, when the defendant was said to manifest a derangement not of intellect but of moral feeling, the reaction from the bench could be sharp and swift. "Do you conceive this is really a medical question at all which has been put to you?" an Old Bailey judge asked archly of medical witnesses positing the existence of a moral insanity a few years before McNaughtan.[11] The 1843 Rules had been implemented to forestall the reintroduction of the "lesion of the will" and the "irresistible impulse" and to focus on cognitive rather than volitional faculties. And that, as far as the English judiciary was concerned, was that. Or was it?

To gauge the law's ability to circumscribe medical testimony, I returned to the *OBSP* and examined the courtroom testimony given in insanity trials for the ten years following the McNaughtan verdict. The news that early forensic-psychiatric witnesses were effectively muzzled with regard to moral insanity and volitional derangement would have come as a surprise to the jurors in the 1847 case of *Regina v. Ovenstone.* Driven to despair by a legal action brought by George Crawley, a creditor, John Ovenstone sought out Crawley in his office and shot him in the jaw. Indicted for felonious assault and causing an injury dangerous to human life, Ovenstone was visited in prison by John Conolly, chief physician to the Hanwell Lunatic Asylum and a frequent medical witness in insanity trials.

Conolly's prison visit doubtless alerted prison surgeon Gilbert McMurdo to pursue his own conversations with the prisoner, as McMurdo had been charged by his employer, the Corporation of the City of London, to converse with defendants suspected of contemplating a plea of mental derangement. McMurdo's appearance in an early-nineteenth-century insanity trial was almost as predictable as the thrust of his testimony in the Ovenstone trial. As he advised the jury in almost all his previous trips to the witness stand, he had "not observed anything to lead him to believe [the defendant] is of unsound mind." Then, in an uncharacteristically generous nod to the emerging specialty in mental medicine, he added, "I know the senior physician at Hanwell, he is a man who is looked upon in the profession in every way as a man highly gifted, he has had very large opportunities for judging of this question, and of course his opinion would be worth more on such subjects than that of a person like myself."[12]

John Conolly lost no time picking up on this remarkable concession. Referring immediately to the one thousand patients under his care and to his work on "Diseases of the Mind," the superintendent of Hanwell moved to establish his familiarity with the prisoner's state of mind: "I have known numerous cases where pecuniary losses and domestic afflictions have so operated upon the mind as to deprive it of reason— I believe a great many cases of moral insanity arise from pecuniary losses or domestic afflictions. I do not believe him [Ovenstone] to have been unconscious of the act he committed, but I believe him to have been under an impulse which he was not in a state of mind to resist—he had lost control."[13]

Although Conolly "imagined" that the prisoner could not distinguish right from wrong (the McNaughtan criteria), the thrust of his testimony concerned unaccountable impulses. His testimony drew heavily on medical writing that, by the 1840s, had begun to disparage the tradition of treating cognition as the sole consideration for an insanity acquittal. Ironically, the first medical term to gain prominence in insanity trials—delusion—had left its own idée fixe among jurists: without the presence of a predominant and prepossessing idea, judges averred, there was no insanity.[14] Medical writers, however, objected to the law's exclusive reliance on delusion as the requisite condition for nonresponsibility, arguing that it was not circumscribed error that prompted the delusional to crime but a derangement that "implicates the moral affections, the temper, the feelings and the propensities, [affecting] the moral character even more than the understanding."[15] To affirm this belief in the professional literature was one thing, to express it in court quite another.

Disappearing Defendants: Methods and Sample

While medical writers complained about the law's misguided reduction of insanity to delusion and jurists maintained that only cognitive impairment would exempt a perpetrator from criminal responsibility, courtroom combatants seem not to have noticed that their debate
was growing increasingly irrelevant to a cadre of mentally aberrant defendants who refused to stay confined in their post-McNaughtan categories. This population of mentally wayward defendants presented the
court with an array of afflictions that departed qualitatively from delusion, delirium, and mania. Instead of the familiar delusional murderer,
the Old Bailey juror met a sleepwalking knife-wielding nursemaid. The
conventional delirious ranter was replaced by a methodical, purposeful,
yet "morally vacant" juvenile poisoner. The place of the insensible, in-
coherent defendants was taken up by an asylum patient possessed of
twenty thousand spirits that interrupted him while he was testifying
in court, trying to mislead him about a date critical to the murder trial.
Even the politically inspired assassin was replaced by an articulate and
poised defendant who changed places with a manic, religiously inspired
Other, while giving his own defense.

How could either the medical specialist or the jurist respond to descriptions suggesting that the person on trial was not in fact the person who committed the crime? After all, it was one thing to consider a
defendant insensible or out of his wits, but how could one apply the
legal criterion of "knowing right from wrong" to a defendant who, although at some level conscious of what he was doing, could still be described as "missing inside himself"? How was it possible for a person to
engage in nefarious activity and yet retain no memory of the behavior
and the sentiment that animated it?

Confronted with the unexpected appearance of these missing defendants, I searched the contemporary medical literature to find similar tales of suspended consciousness and of actions taken for which no
trace of memory remained. These accounts begin in 1817 and reach their
most complete expression with Eugène Azam's 1876 publication of a
case study of Félida X, European medicine's first fully described case of
doubled personality.[16] I decided therefore to extend my search through
the *OBSP* for further cases of "unconscious crime," and eventually discovered that 1876 also marked the introduction of an intriguing French
medical term directly into Old Bailey testimony. *Vertigé épileptique*, a

nonconvulsive form of epilepsy, was described as rendering the defendant's actions "automatic." It signifies the first use of a medical term to address the likelihood of thoroughly unconscious behavior.[17]

Certainly the question of vague or cloudy consciousness had been part of medical (and lay) testimony from the beginning of the nineteenth century, although it had always been coupled with some form of delirium or insensibility. Now in 1876, the state of unconsciousness was given a berth of its own, separate from the familiar species of insanity. Indeed, medical witnesses expressly denied that the defendant was insane at all.[18] Also in 1876, a verdict of "not guilty on the ground of unconsciousness" was recorded for the first time in the London courtroom, prompting the judge to announce his intention to write to the Home Secretary to clarify his thinking on the issue, and the publisher of the *OBSP* to distinguish this anomalous verdict by including it in that year's "Index to the Points of Law and Practice."[19]

I therefore selected 1876 as the terminal year for case collection, reasoning that the years between the articulation of the McNaughtan Rules—ostensibly restricting insanity to cognitive disorder—and acquittal "on the grounds of unconsciousness" should provide insight into the Old Bailey's evolving response to defendants whose professed states of fractured or suspended consciousness departed significantly from traditional notions of mental impairment. Just how divergent these states of being were from the law's conception of insanity was made abundantly clear by the jury's explicit reference to unconsciousness as the reason for the acquittal. Medical witnesses speaking in support of a *sane* unconsciousness in this trial and in one five months later were giving voice to a different conception of involuntary behavior.[20] Although the accused were "absolutely unconscious" of what they were doing, their condition was not "characteristic of insanity in the slightest way." Not deluded, not deranged, not delirious in the slightest, the defendant's action was involuntary because an *automaton* had committed the crime.

The effort to identify the specific trials featuring unusual states of suspended consciousness meant that all testimony given in this thirty-three-year span had to be scrutinized, because a guilty verdict or a simple acquittal could easily mask testimony that explored the defendant's dubious "authorship" of the crime. Even insanity acquittals had to be read carefully, because some had resulted from directed verdicts, in which the judge stopped the trial, saying, "It is quite obvious that [the prisoner] did not know what she was about." A comprehensive reading of all cases delivered to the Old Bailey by the grand jury is therefore required to ensure the inclusion of all trials that explored extraordinary states of mind, not only those that resulted in insanity verdicts or those precluded by the finding that the defendant was unfit to be tried.

Between the years 1843 and 1876, 198 defendants—approximately eight to ten per thousand defendants per year—put forward a defense of aberrant mental state at the time of the crime. (Appendix table A.1 gives the categories of offenses over time.) One-quarter of these prisoners were found unfit to stand trial, the *OBSP* reporting simply, "Upon the evidence of [prison surgeon] Gilbert McMurdo [and later John Gibson] the prisoner was declared unfit to plead." McMurdo's appearance in no fewer than seventeen trials in the second quarter of the nineteenth century begs the question of the mad-doctor's entrance into the criminal courtroom as an exercise in empire building on the part of medical practitioners eager to establish cognitive dominance in the courtroom.[21] Whether one looks to the regular employment of prison surgeons to converse daily with pretrial defendants and report their observations later to the court, or to private physicians "desired by the Solicitor of the Treasury to attend" a particular trial—a post-McNaughtan innovation—it was the court's administrators, not the Royal College of Physicians, who were responsible for the growing reliance on medical testimony in cases of extraordinary mental state. Indeed, one could well argue that the evolving use of specialists in mental medicine was a truly defensive move. Suspicion that the prison surgeon or other court-appointed medical men might testify in court prompted defense attorneys to secure medical experts of their own. The practice spiraled to the point that, by 1843, medical witnesses were present in three of four trials in which the prisoner's mental state was at issue.

That legal and administrative changes produced medical participation in the criminal trials, however, is only part of the history of forensic psychiatry. Of arguably greater importance is the content of the testimony and the influence of the medical witnesses' ideas. But evidence of influence is tricky. A range of factors—detectable as well as recondite—can affect a jury's verdict in historical courtroom narratives. Certainly one would find it daunting to account for any jury's reasoning in today's verdicts, even with all the opportunity at one's disposal to gauge the jurors' reaction to the demeanor and testimony of any particular witness. Estimating the influence of historical contributors must therefore be a hazardous undertaking, especially because verdicts suggest more than they actually reveal. An acquittal on the grounds of insanity, for example, can hardly be attributed to the specific aspects of a mad-doctor's testimony. Similarly, a conviction might reveal only that the judge "leaned against" the defendant in his case summary and instructions to the jury, or, even more tellingly, that he permitted the prosecution to present "rebuttal" testimony to lessen the impact of the defense witness's (innovative) testimony.

While not ignoring the obvious value of verdicts—not least for the defense attorney concerned with the attractiveness of an acquittal to prospective clients—the significance of innovative medical testimony may best be gauged by scrutinizing the tone and direction of courtroom testimony and the specific comments made by the bench. Recent histories of nineteenth-century medical testimony have employed a variety of sources—most often law reports or medical texts and journals—to examine the emergence of new medical descriptions and diagnoses of aberrant behavior, and the medicolegal dialogue they generated. The present research supplements this rich history with the dialogue that emerged in the courtroom itself. One can capture the language of medicine and law in a variety of ways, but I believe that without exploring the day-to-day forensic examination and cross-examination of medical claims to expertise, it is difficult to appreciate the significance of the courtroom's role in shaping the dialogue between these two powerful professions and the negotiation that rendered medical testimony a legal resource. The history of forensic psychiatry is, after all, the history of law. Any inference historians and sociologists of medicine hope to draw from medical writings and legal commentary must take account of how medical insight was proffered in the cut and thrust of examination and cross-examination.

Martin Wiener's recent work on the changing language of courtroom defenses in the Victorian era is a case in point. His review of courtroom records suggests that the law's evolving efforts to shape fundamental defense claims alleging provocation, drunkenness, and insanity revealed the judiciary's determined effort to engineer ever more stringent levels of prudence and heightened standards of impulse inhibition.[22] My own review of the post-McNaughtan Old Bailey reveals that even though consciousness was familiar to the courtroom before the McNaughtan verdict, this key consideration for assessing the accused's intention took on an increasingly expansive meaning once the defendant was described as "missing," not merely deluded. Originally employed as a synonym for a lack of awareness, unconsciousness eventually expanded to include a state of mental life inaccessible to the waking person. Similarly, delusion, a term traditionally associated with circumscribed error and impelled action, became associated with a "disintegration of the personality," as delusory beliefs came to resemble resident spirits with a memory all their own.

Hovering over the introduction of new forensic-psychiatric terms—and the new meanings given to traditional ones—is the overarching question of how the court chose to receive this testimony. The long-familiar tension between the judiciary and the emerging specialty of mental medicine hardly abated after the imposition of the McNaughtan Rules, but it comes as a surprise to learn that, far from circumscribing the medical expert, the newly articulated criteria actually created an expanded opportunity for medical men to comment on material they heard in the trial itself. The obvious threat such medical inference posed to the "job description" of the juror became the focus of rancorous debate in successive trials, with little acknowledgment paid to previous judicial decisions or expressed opinion. As in so many areas of contentious courtroom debate, the issue of proffered impairment had to be fought anew on a case-by-case basis. The progress of the law, as Lawrence Stone reminds us, is not linear. Historians of medicine in particular have recognized that the status and significance of forensic-psychiatric evidence were negotiated continually at every trial. Over time, however, one can glimpse the absorption of clinical terms and innovative meanings given to familiar forms of behavior, as they become the focus of courtroom deliberation. And it is for this reason that the *OBSP* have proven invaluable. In courtroom dialogues, in instructions to the jury, and in innovatively worded verdicts, one begins to suspect the emergence—or, more precisely the disappearance—of a particular sort of defendant.

Wondering about *Who* Is Inside

Prisoners in the Victorian courtroom who debated unseen spirits while they were testifying, who suffered amnesia after the crime or lapses in consciousness while committing it, who sleepwalked through an offense or exhibited fits of temperament so out of character that their own spouses could hardly recognize them presented the Old Bailey with a qualitative departure from the "traditional" insanity trial. One can only wonder with what wistful nostalgia courtroom personnel must have looked back to the relatively straightforward days of delirium and delusion in the early years of the century. Someone—or *something*—very different had wandered into the Victorian era's Old Bailey and would eventually find its way into the twentieth-century American courtroom in the form of splitting and associated fugue states.

Although nineteenth-century defendants were not characterized as possessing (twentieth-century) multiple personalities, there is the unmistakable presence of persons describing the alleged criminal episode in terms of an unknown self. There is also evidence that the Old Bailey was a forum increasingly hospitable to the assertion of such suspensions in human agency. Both medical witness and judge could express reasonable doubt that the defendant—though not insane—was yet not "master of his actions." In the end, the trial narratives reveal the Old Bailey to have been no less credulous to claims of unconsciousness than the surrounding popular culture, which had long entertained the possibility of trance states and hypnotic spells. What distinguished the court's response to "unconscious" behavior were the very real legal consequences that attended testimony speaking to "self-management without self-knowledge."

Ultimately, the Old Bailey was asked to decide the criminal responsibility of a defendant who failed to rise to the law's conception of the Person: a sentient being capable of maintaining a continuous awareness of who he was. It was precisely this state of constant consciousness that the "missing" could not maintain. Amnesia, absence, sleepwalking, possession, and "automatic fits" would challenge fundamental Western beliefs that consciousness linked thought to act, and hence responsibility to assault. Medical writings might speculate on the possibility of automatic behavior, but only the court could exonerate the behavior of an automaton. The trials discussed in the following pages have been selected to illustrate the courtroom dynamic that introduced doubt into the individual's capacity to remain a constant person, an anxiety that took on special urgency once it was suggested that an unknown part of the self could be responsible for the most uncharacteristic criminality.

ONE

DOUBLE CONSCIOUSNESS
IN THE NINETEENTH CENTURY

❖

*F*ROM MESMERISM TO SOMNAMBULISM, from animal magnetism to hypnotism, from autonomous mental reflex to autonomous behavioral excess, nineteenth-century London was awash
in a host of altered states of consciousness that was itself maddening.
Beginning with Franz Anton Mesmer's eighteenth-century claim to
have removed the regulatory power of the will, medical practitioners
and salon hypnotists alike exploited the possibility that an idea "suggested from the outside"—that is, not from a person's own consciousness—could produce behavior beyond the individual's control and even
awareness. Given the Victorians' well-documented preoccupation with
the will and the era's paramount goal of fostering an ethic of self-
mastery among all British citizens, such morbid fascination with unconscious and uncontrollable behavior reminds one of someone with an
abject fear of snakes who, upon entering a zoo, makes his way immediately for the reptile house.

In the Victorians' case, mounting anxiety over nonregulated behavior coexisted with, and in its own way perversely stimulated, a seemingly insatiable appetite for demonstrations of unconscious states of
being. The predominant paradigm for framing an episode of "absence"
was the *trance:* an induced state of being in which the patient (or "client"
or "subject") was suspended somewhere between consciousness and
sleep. The ostensible purpose of putting the subject in a trance was to
investigate the hidden secrets of the mind, particularly the possibility
of decoupling reason and choice from subsequent behavior. Whether
induced by mesmerism or hypnotism, the trance "beheaded the will."[1]
As the mesmeric "operator" and the hypnotist manipulated the subject'

sensory organs and introduced "outside" ideas to the brain and spinal cord, the subject's voluntary control over thought and reasoning was effectively suspended.

Of course, any observer of mesmeric or hypnotic states was also aware that voluntary control over thoughts could also be suspended internally. Dreams revealed bizarre, outrageous, and personally horrifying ideas that could pass through one's mind without an ability to "correct" or, indeed, even interrupt noxious associations and accompanying emotions.[2] Beyond mere dreaming, sleepwalking graphically revealed the extent to which ideas could not only possess the mind but also lead to physical motion, with the dreamer's conscious self powerless to intrude upon the impelling idea. The power of such an idea to rouse the sleeping person and produce movement captivated—and sometimes horrified—the onlooker. Although the peregrinations of sleepwalkers could sometimes appear as "blind" wandering, European folklore suggested that their movements were anything but directionless. When mesmerists referred to induced trance as "artificial somnambulism," they were therefore appropriating not only a culturally resonant image of strangely unconscious states of being but goal-directed behavior as well.[3] Whatever the express purpose of the nocturnal odyssey, however, one question remained regarding the actions undertaken in a state of artificial or natural somnambulism: How was such determined action possible with external senses held in abeyance? Who or what guided the behavior of the automaton?

Demonstrating that involuntary reflexes could steer human functioning did not, of course, require the parlor theatrics of hypnotic spells or mesmeric trances. Respiration, digestion, and circulation proceeded not only without conscious will but also without any awareness at all. It was, in part, the Victorians' effort to explore the range of involuntary reflexes that produced the parlor demonstrations—and, indeed, scientific investigation—designed to examine whether human behavior was governed by autonomous body mechanisms or by the actor's own will. But even as mid-nineteenth-century medical writers presented human functioning in an increasingly biological framework,[4] the person at the heart of this Victorian inquiry was not automatically relieved of moral responsibility for actions undertaken in a suspended state of being. The will might not have had an organic "home" in the schema of reflexes, with the inculcation of proper habits and attitudes, the will could be purposefully inhibited.[5] By sheer force of will, the individual could conform himself to the prevailing normative code.

Seen in this light, the effort to investigate how one might introduce and channel sensory stimulation for desired behavioral effect was no mere salon divertissement into the fantastic, for all the entertainment it provided as an after dinner diversion. In the world of academic science, physiologists pondered how "entranced" individuals experienced sensory impressions and consequent action "entirely bypassing volition." Beyond the "silent" physiological processes of respiration and digestion, medical authors considered a range of human activity unattended with awareness. Women who gave birth while unconscious demonstrated the autonomy of contractions; sleepwalkers who negotiated complicated and dexterous near-acrobatic feats revealed motor processes totally bereft of conscious decision making.[6] These examples revealed the work of autonomous reflexes, given a conceptual home in Carpenter's "*Ideomotor* principle of action" in which ideas introduced "externally" bypassed the actor's volition, leading directly to behavior.[7] It is little wonder, then, that the well-documented Victorian passion for order, discipline, and authority lent an urgency to mapping out the universe of "autonomous" activity, and the possibility that the purposeful inculcation of proper habits could serve as the effective counterweight to unruly automatic reflexes.

There was, however, a ghost in the sleepwalker. Existing studies of Victorian mental medicine and the era's obsessive preoccupation with self-control depict the unconscious states of sleepwalking, epilepsy, and absence as periods in which the person had been somehow "switched off," leaving no room for purposeful activity. Nineteenth-century medical tracts, however, described unexpected and uncharacteristic behavior in ways that have received far less attention from today's medical and legal historians, although every major nineteenth-century effort to describe observed states of suspended consciousness included its features. In mesmerism and epilepsy, in somnambulism and hypnotism, one meets the mysterious specter of the double: an alter presence that manifested behavior and attitudes sharply discrepant from, and often in direct opposition to, the "host."[8] Somnambulism was not mere unconsciousness, but "a new life, returning at unequal intervals . . . a new character [with] a separate conscience."[9] The sleepwalker revealed not one soul asleep, but one physical body housing "two souls." Animal magnetizers claimed to see a client's mesmeric *self* emerging, "an influential personality . . . when awakened she had been transformed. . . . The mischievous, playful, authoritative mesmeric subject was replaced by a shy servant girl."[10] And hypnotists reported a secondary "ego" that emerged into the foreground—the subject's ego was pushed aside as the hypnotist gained access to another person.

This unexpected emergence of a second self was not confined to somnambulism, hypnotism, and animal magnetism. Epilepsy, conceived today to be restricted to convulsive muscular attack, revealed to nineteenth-century writers a transformation in the afflicted's personality. In her "natural state . . . [the] patient is quiet, modest, unabusive, showing amiable dispositions. In her new state, she is mischievous, sometimes impudent, and runs around the house looking for an opportunity to do harm."[11] That a person in an epileptic fit was not herself was hardly a novel observation; that the epileptic appeared to be someone else was very much news. The delusional person, so familiar in the eighteenth and early nineteenth century, appeared by the mid-1800s to be not merely captive to an idée fixe but to be someone with "an altered persona." Even profound delirium suggested not (just) confusion, but a new temperament: "No two manners could have differed more."[12] It was the markedly disparate nature of two personas occupying the same person that struck the clinician's attention; the host personality was reserved and inhibited, the alter was animated and vivacious.[13]

The Emergence of the Medical Double

The first term to surface in mental medicine to denote the remarkable dividedness in persona was double consciousness, coined by physician Samuel L. Mitchill in 1817. Mitchill reported the case of Mary Reynolds, a young servant girl who awoke from a deep sleep to reveal a memory "as a *tabula rasa;* all vestiges, both of words and of things, were obliterated and gone. It was found necessary for her to learn everything again." On *re*awakening, Reynolds was ignorant of all that had transpired, including all the new information and skills she had acquired in her second, animated state. According to Mitchill, she was "as unconscious of her *double* character as two distinct persons are of respective separate natures."[14] A similar report surfaced the following year of a person with sharply discrepant personality states: "she appeared as a person might be supposed to do, who had two souls, each occasionally dominant, and occasionally active, and utterly ignorant of what the other was doing."[15] Writing of a third case five years later, H. Dewar, an Edinburgh physician, took issue with Mitchill's term, double consciousness, preferring in its stead double personality or divided consciousness. These terms, Dewar argued, better described a sleepwalker when doubled states revealed two trains of thought "dissevered from each other." Dewar described a young woman who could only remember events specific to her second state when she found herself in subsequent episodes of "wanderings." As Dewar recounted, in these states of doubled personality she inhabited the role of an Episcopal clergyman, baptizing three of the household children, and of a jockey at Epsom Downs, riding the kitchen stool around the room, "but without being awakened." She was eventually brought to herself by having her hands immersed in cold water.[16]

As argued recently by Ian Hacking, the meaning of consciousness conveyed in the above examples conforms closer to Dewar's use of "personality" or character than with mere mental awareness.[17] Mary Reynolds and others who went periodically missing were not "doubly aware" of their state of being; rather, they manifested two distinct behavioral selves, neither one cognizant nor conscious of the other. Dewar's preference for the term double personality revealed a contemporary preference for interpreting the two states in behavioral terms, rather than as strictly mentalist "splitting." But beyond debating the most apposite term to capture the essence of these alter selves, there remains the precise nature of doubling itself. Clearly, doubled consciousness was not a matter of mere mood swings. Described as "two spiritual personalities in the same individual" or "two identities residing in the same person," double consciousness suggested a transformation rather more thoroughgoing than waking up one day and not feeling oneself (or one self). Unfamiliar moods and acts can certainly be perceived as being "out of character," but double consciousness required something else: a trance. In this state of suspended being, one experienced an intervening period of unconsciousness or confusion, most often coupled with amnesia.[18] "One identity is laid aside, with all the remembrances connected with it, but another is put on, and with the new identity a new memory acts in concert."[19]

But forgetting could extend further. Beyond actions undertaken when in the suspended state, beyond the skills and learning acquired when the subject was not himself, there was the very real danger of forgetting one's own personal identity. In the second half of the nineteenth century, J. Crichton Browne wrote of the doubly conscious as persons whose two different natures—whose two different trains of thought— in effect gave the appearance of two separate human beings. Personal identity, Browne argued, is after all something more than consciousness: it is the constant awareness that one is the same person from one moment to the next. "For amongst the most fundamental principles of the mind is the conviction that man continues to be always himself, that he is at any given moment the same person as he was the moment before and that he has always been since he came into existence. This belief, in fact, is the very essence of mind, and arises necessarily out of the succession of momentary conscious states, just as corporeal identity springs out of a succession of material atoms endowed with certain vital functions."[20] When persons in their "abnormal state" fail to remember faces from the past or are unable to associate names and sounds with events of their life, it is not because they are suffering amnesia. These memories quite literally belong to someone else's life.

It must be admitted at the outset that anyone who has never lived through an episode of "divided identity" would find it very difficult to imagine what it feels like not to be oneself. To bridge this gap in experience, Browne provided vivid illustrations of stage actors so submerged in a theatrical character that they exclaimed, "I cannot get out! I cannot get out." Mrs. Siddons, the great nineteenth-century actor, "had not merely assumed a character, but lost her own in the creation of the poet." At the end of a performance, the French tragedienne Rachel "could not doff either the character or the madness of Ophelia."[21] He supplemented these theatrical examples with accounts of "doubly conscious" persons who express fears of not being able "to get back into myself again." Personal identity could literally disappear; "the me [could be] annihilated." In his vivid accounts of *lost* persons, Browne described double consciousness as more than a succession of subjective states: the individual had quite clearly divided into two separate beings.[22]

Before the publication of Eugène Azam's case history of doubled personality the second being had not entered the literature as a fully integrated, coherent self.[23] Similar to cases of doubling written earlier in the century, the patient, Félida, manifested wildly different temperaments, periodic memory loss, and heightened sensory perception in her second personality, a phenomenon sometimes described as "clairvoyance" by medical authors. But Azam went to great lengths to distinguish Félida's *dédoublement* (or *amnésie périodique*, or *dédoublement de la vie*—he left it to his reader to decide the most appropriate descriptive term) from earlier cases of ordinary doubling. Unlike some patients with double consciousness, Félida was not conscious of "being" two personalities. Unlike sleepwalkers, she was not "asleep" but enjoyed her "full intellectual powers." Unlike the delirious person who might seem to inhabit two worlds, Félida's second state is not confusion but a complete existence: she is "perfectly rational." This is a second—and full—personality, not an episode of suspended consciousness, sleepwalking, or trance.[24]

Azam further distanced Félida from persons with earlier incarnations of doubling because she did not forget as they did. Félida failed to remember events not because of delirium or unconsciousness but because nothing existed in her memory of the experiences of the other self. She was not even aware that nothing existed. As Azam explained, she was not capable of surmising or speculating about the gaps in her experience as one might do with a book in which pages are missing. Readers can always read forwards and backwards, in hope of constructing a coherent narrative. But the "plot" of *dédoublement de la personnalité* is not continuous; it is perfectly discontinuous, for only one memory can exist at a time. Félida could not "remember" a debt incurred or an inheritance received because these events did not happen *to her*.

In time, through experiences with other people, she began to understand that someone else inhabited her body. "I am obliged to resort to a thousand subterfuges for fear that I shall be taken for an idiot," she explained to Azam. One such story is particularly vivid. On her way home one afternoon in a coach, Félida "felt that period which she calls her [normal state] coming on. She was drowsy for a few seconds, without the ladies who were with her in the coach perceiving it, and awakened in the other state absolutely ignorant [of] why she was in a funeral coach, with persons, who according to custom, were speaking of the qualities of the deceased, whose name she did not know. Accustomed to these situations, she listened. By skillful questioning she succeeded in making herself acquainted with the circumstances, and no one could suspect what had transpired."[25] The remarkable element of this story is the self-conscious awareness she maintained, both about her condition and about the censure she would invite if those in her intimate circle knew of it. Her careful management of self-information reminds one of delusional patients who know enough to circumnavigate delirious shoals to appear sane to their examiners—hoping to be released from an asylum—but not enough to counteract their obsessive fears or beliefs.

For Azam, the fact that Félida remained completely "amnesic" of events that transpired in the other personality's life carried explicit implications regarding the legal significance of her state. Although he openly conceded that dédoublement's resemblance to other acknowledged states of "nonresponsibility" such as insanity, epilepsy, and somnambulism was a question "difficult to solve," he was unequivocal about the importance of amnesia. If the accused "cannot remember an accomplished act, though it may be recent, [he or she] cannot be *compos mentis,* as it is understood in law."[26] The clinician did not elaborate, although contemporary experience supports his contention that a person with complete amnesia would be very difficult to bring to trial. Such a defendant could neither advance a rationally based plea nor assist his counsel in preparing a defense.

Beyond the practical difficulties of prosecuting someone for a crime he cannot recall, amnesia ultimately speaks to the status of the alter self as a person. One question continually surfaces in the literature about the "doubly conscious": to what extent are there two distinct persons inside, and to what extent is the *état seconde* not really a second self at all but a suspended state of consciousness in which sensory stimulation and associated ideas have radiated automatically into action, unmediated by the mind's faculties of judgment and volition? This is no idle philosophical query. If the second state is merely a state of unconsciousness, the forensic construction of a person—an intentional being who chooses to engage in action—is profoundly challenged. The possession of a separate memory appeared to affirm the first reading: a separate person with her own history of experience and an awareness of what she was "up to." But being two different persons might also mean that one could not possess a continuous knowledge of right and wrong from one day to the next (or from one *person* to the next). Without such knowledge— without a capacity to know that one's acts were legally transgressive— one could not act with intent, with the choice to do evil. Harmful, even fatal assaults might have taken place, but without the actor's consistent and continuous consciousness that he was doing wrong, a crime had not occurred.

Amnesia therefore held the key. A perfectly encapsulated memory— inaccessible in moments when the subject was not himself—argued for the existence of two separate persons. A failure to maintain constant memory of one's identity also implied the failure to remember why something was wrong. Both sets of memory loss would come to bedevil the nineteenth-century Old Bailey courtroom.

From the Clinic to the Courtroom

Double consciousness, memory loss, and the possession of an alter personality were not, of course, the only states of mental aberration that confronted the Victorian courtroom; indeed, they were often confounded with evidence of bizarre forms of distraction long familiar to the court. From the first recorded acquittal on the grounds that the defendant was not of "sound mind" (1505) to the formalization of the insanity plea after the trial of Daniel McNaughtan (1843), English common law struggled to articulate the level and form of mental derangement that would denote the extent of impaired consciousness sufficient to remove criminal responsibility.[27] "Like a mad bullock more than anything else" may not have been a medical witness's preferred characterization of the insane, but "wild beasts" took their place alongside various other culturally resonant images—"out of her wits," "his brain was *turned*"—that were routinely invoked by eighteenth-century neighbors of the accused to describe the wild histrionics and verbal pandemonium of the putative mad person.[28] Indeed, as long as "mad bullock" imagery prevailed in the courtroom, medical witnesses functioned in a very limited expert capacity; with madness "spectacularly on view," who needed nature's unambiguous legibility to be read by a credentialed expert? Only when insanity became a more recondite condition, capable of hiding or attaching itself to a submerged idea or prepossessing fear while the rest of mental functioning remained intact, would the mad-doctor cum forensic-psychiatric witness distinguish his testimony from that of the neighbor.

The first term these specialist witnesses employed to distinguish their testimony from the layperson's observations was delusion, which described an essentially submerged derangement that could be revealed only when the trained examiner "pulled" the appropriate thread. As medical specialists explained in court, when the accused was in the throes of delusion, his conscious awareness of the nature of his act—of the natural consequences that would follow an assault or a theft—was thrown into doubt.[29] The deluded could be unconscious of the legal wrong they were committing—overcome as they were with religious zeal—or unconscious of the personal harm they would cause themselves—so insistent was the devil that "you must and you shall kill your child."[30] Lapsed or suspended consciousness was therefore very much a part of the pre-McNaughtan insanity trial, although it was rarely mentioned by name. It was instead the natural course of delirium or insensibility that implicated one's ability to remain aware of one's surroundings.

By the 1830s, a profoundly mistaken belief was only part of the reason for finding the accused's actions involuntary. No longer (simply) faulty understanding or a preoccupying fear, delusion took on a volitional prong as mistaken beliefs and impelling, insistent ideas assumed a will of their own. The coupling of delusion with an irresistible force reached memorable expression in the McNaughtan trial: "I mean that black spot on his mind . . . if the delusion impels him to any particular act, the commission of that act is placed beyond his moral control."[31] It was this component of delusion, the loss of moral control, that suggested that for all his "understanding" of his behavior, the delusional person was no longer the master of his acts.

That a person could be capable of involuntary action while still conscious of the wrong he was committing was a conception of madness that caused the most heated debates between jurists and the burgeoning profession of mental medicine. For the court, consciousness necessarily implied the retention of self-control; indeed, the law required the effort to conform one's behavior to the dictates of law. To entertain the image of the accused as a mere bystander to his crime—or worse, as the helpless agent of an impulse swamping his will—was too much to ask of the court. Mental derangement that clouded reason was one thing; mysteriously impelling impulses were quite another.[32]

But suppose the accused had not been a mere bystander or a hapless, helpless agent; suppose she had been absent from the scene of the crime? What was the common law to do with a defendant whose action appeared methodical and purposeful but who was herself missing at the time of her crime? Suppose any of the persons described in the reports of doubled consciousness had not wandered into the kitchen to ride an imaginary horse but into their children's room to administer poison in the guise of a pudding? Would the law look upon these acts as deluded and excusable, or as voluntary and culpable?

To punish someone when awake for something done while asleep was no more right, John Locke had argued in 1690, than to punish one twin for his brother's crime.[33] Questions surrounding the existence of discontinuous, perhaps doubled selves, and the legal issues that accrued, clearly precede the mid-1800s by almost two centuries. It was the essential link that conjoined consistent consciousness to personal identity that intrigued Locke. "[A]s far as this consciousness can be extended backwards to any past Action or Thought, so far reaches the Identity of that Person."[34] Locke's notion of the person was strongly shaped by forensic considerations, applying only to "intelligent Agents . . . [where] personality extends it *self* beyond present Existence to what is past, only by consciousness, where it becomes concerned and accountable." And in the end, it is consciousness that justifies God's sentence: rewards or punishments were merited because one was conscious of having done an act.[35] As Mary Douglas has observed, Locke's original theological rubric provided the secular law courts with "a coherent, unitary self," capable of appreciating the demands of moral principles. The issue was not one of proving the existence of such a unitary self, or person: this forensic construction of the person was "intellectually, juridically and morally necessary."[36] Whether legal fact or courtroom fiction, the basis of Western notions of individual responsibility required the existence of a conscious, consequence-perceiving person for matters of assigning criminal responsibility.

Locke's explicit conjecture about the possibility that different consciousness attended a sleeping and a waking self served to frame the debate about consciousness and culpability that would return to English forensic debate two centuries later. "But if it be possible for the same Man to have distinct incommunicable consciousness at different times, it is past doubt the same Man would at different times make different Persons. . . . [This] is somewhat explained by our speaking in *English* when we say that he *is not himself*, or is *beside himself*. . . . The *self* same Person was no longer in that Man."[37] The term "incommunicable consciousness" does not refer to mental impairment or derangement; delirium, "irresistible impulses," and mania are in no way invoked. The common law had traditionally looked to impaired consciousness as a sign that the mental element required for crime was missing. Locke, on the other hand, explicitly left consciousness intact, yet missing: "the self same Person was no longer in that man." The state of functioning evoked above spoke not to deranged mental contemplation but to the physical doing of the act. If different points in time witnessed the emergence of different persons, the lack of a consistent self meant that one could not be sure who committed the crime.

Such questions of "authorship" were not at issue in insanity trials. That Daniel McNaughtan stalked and shot the man he believed to be the prime minister was never in question. No one at his trial—certainly no medical witness—alleged that the Glasgow wood turner was not the person who did the shooting, sleepwalking his way to Robert Peel's residence with a loaded pistol. When the question of involuntary behavior entered trial testimony, it was in the context of an impelling persecution delusion: one that "destroys moral liberty" and "carries a man quite away."[38] He may have been thrust into crime by his delusion, but he was hardly unaware of having shot someone.

Compare McNaughtan, or any putative insanity defendant, to persons in an epileptic fit, a sleepwalking trance, or a period of absence when understanding and feeling have become so divided that they seem to belong to separate persons. The only confusing element for the defendant was how anyone could possibly consider that he or she had committed such an atrocious deed. To add to the defendant's disbelief, the victim is often a loved one—a child, spouse, or grandparent—and witness after witness attest to the care and affection habitually shown the now deceased relative. Contemporary medical authors actively engaged both the criminal features of such states of suspended consciousness and the vexing forensic questions they raised, but could only speculate on the court's reaction. Alfred Swaine Taylor, author of the Victorian era's most widely cited forensic texts—in and out of court—pondered "how far a person should be held responsible for a criminal act perpetrated in that half-conscious state when the individual is suddenly roused from sleep," but he offered no answer.[39] Taylor would have to wait twenty-five years for a reply.

"A Crime of Which I Am Unconscious"

I thought it was a thief in the house. I heard a noise by the side of the bed. I said "Joseph," I thought then it was the porter. I got no answer—I took the looking glass and hit her and broke it—I took the candlestick and hit her till I broke it [and] then I took the bottles and battled with her half an hour, and when the lights came on I found the woman dead.[40]

The woman was Cecilia Aldridge. One must concede at the outset that her murder was not the most promising context in which to raise the defense that the perpetrator was "half unconscious," a state induced by a frightful dream. That Jacob Spinasa had taken some liquor shortly before falling asleep in the arms of Miss Aldridge left the unfortunate impression that the attack was occasioned by delirium tremens rather than by guiltless hallucinations. There was also the thirty-minute interval to account for in which the prisoner pummeled his victim with every available implement at hand. Surely even the most generous allowance for a netherworld that spanned sleep and full arousal would last seconds or fractions of minutes, not fractions of an hour. Further, the unfortunate setting of the killing—a notorious London brothel—did not enhance the credibility of the prisoner's claim to innocence. And finally there was the brutal attack: the prisoner's hand bitten by the victim in a vain attempt to save her life, with clumps of his hair found clutched in her rigid grasp. One can only empathize with the defense attorney on being presented with such a case. Standard courtroom defenses were not thick on the ground.[41]

After recounting details of the stuporous condition that allegedly preceded the fatal assault on Miss Aldridge, the court summoned to the stand Dr. Hess, the physician who had been called to the scene immediately after the victim's body was found.

DEFENSE ATTORNEY: Without suggesting that the man was in a state of insanity, or anything of that kind, is it not perfectly consistent with your knowledge of medical science, that persons in a sane state, who go to sleep in a drunken state, and have distempered dreams and so forth, may be suddenly agitated by hallucinations and delusions, and still not be in a state of what you would call insanity?

DR. HESS: Such things have happened.

JUDGE: What things have happened?

HESS: That persons suddenly waking up have committed some act under delusion or hallucination. May I explain? Such persons, in first awakening from sleep, are reckless and have committed some act of which no one would have thought them capable beforehand—they have been suddenly afflicted with the most absurd illusions and delusions, without there being any permanent mental disorder. . . . A man being afflicted with a powerful and impressive dream may awake under a delusion, having been perfectly sane before, and be perfectly sane immediately afterwards.

DEFENSE ATTORNEY: [Reading from Dr. Taylor's chapter entitled, "Hallucinations and Illusions," which the author associates with insanity] I will pause there to ask you, supposing, for instance, that a man had a dream in which he believed that the evil spirit, the devil, was in the room, might that operate upon his mind in a sleeping state in such a way to impel him on awaking to do acts that he would not have done if he had been awake and had his reflecting powers [been] perfectly at his command?

HESS: I should rather put it this way . . . I agree with Dr. Taylor when he says, "These states of mind are dependent upon a disordered state of mind." I shall not quite follow you in saying that a diseased state of mind like a diseased state of the body, may exist for a very brief period and be succeeded by a perfectly healthy state. . . . I concur with the passage of Dr. Taylor that "illusions often occur during the act of suddenly waking from sleep, giving rise occasionally to serious questions involving criminal responsibility."

The prosecutor immediately seized upon the "suddenly waking" element in Dr. Hess's testimony in an effort to neutralize the well-known medical author's words regarding the "serious questions involving criminal responsibility" that attended hallucinations. He asked the witness, "Did you ever know of a case of a man fighting with a woman for half an hour under an hallucination?" Dr. Hess responded unambiguously, "No."[42]

Conceding that this case was "in some respects shrouded in mystery," Judge Baron Channell proceeded to sidestep the defining elements of that mystery—the prisoner's wakeful confusion, his hallucinatory fear, a motiveless attack on a (relative) stranger—to highlight the only issue he believed relevant to the jury's deliberation.[43] Was this a case of murder or manslaughter? Was there evidence of murder aforethought, or did the killing result from a provocative argument that turned into a deadly struggle? In the end, one suspects that the twenty-to-thirty-minute physical struggle persuasively militated against a finding of either wakeful confusion or involuntary manslaughter. With no insanity defense as such put before them, and no judicial instructions regarding how a hallucination could lead to involuntary action, the jurors responded to their limited options by returning a conviction for murder. Of course, one has no indication how the case might have concluded if the prisoner's hallucination had been a matter of mere seconds rather than many minutes. Jacob Spinasa would certainly not have been the first defendant to find sympathetic jurors after raising the specter of a hallucination, but he would have been among the first defendants at the Old Bailey to claim innocence for "a crime of which I am unconscious."[44]

For purposes of medical history, however, it is not the jury's verdict that is of enduring interest so much as what the medical man said about the defendant's condition: the place Spinasa's particular distraction occupied in the professional gaze of nineteenth-century mental medicine. Dr. Hess's refusal to speak of dream-induced violence as a form of derangement independent of an existing insanity is anything but an exercise in diagnostic hair-splitting. Although he freely admitted that dream-related hallucination could give rise to "serious questions involving criminal responsibility," he insisted upon linking any such unconscious attack to existing mental pathology. The prisoner had no previous contact with a medical specialist, however, and no recorded history of previous hallucination.[45] When Dr. Hess substituted his own quote from Taylor's familiar *Medical Jurisprudence,* one is reminded that the Old Bailey could witness medical men refusing to follow the lead of an activist defense attorney, sometimes to the prisoner's obvious detriment. The medical witness chose to cite his own medical authority, not the attorney's. And that medical authority, in this witness's opinion, precluded the finding of substantive impairment without diagnosable mental distraction.

Medical men throughout the Victorian era disagreed with one another both in and out of court, although most of contemporary literature would lead one to suspect that the rivalry for professional dominance between medicine and law consumed the specialists in mental medicine.[46] Courtroom narratives of the actual trials, however, reveal that neither profession maintained a monolithic stance regarding the role of expert testimony at the Old Bailey. Defense attorneys often sought to use medical men to secure an acquittal; prosecuting attorneys used them hoping to effect the opposite result. Judges, as it turned out, assumed no visceral posture regarding the assertion of medical opinion, except on those occasions when the testimony appeared to fly in the face of (the judiciary's) common sense.

Nineteenth-century medical men have not obliged contemporary historians with abundant materials to enable a reconstruction of the ongoing professional conflicts within medicine, although one can glimpse basic differences regarding specific issues: for example, whether intellectual impairment must attend any form of insanity.[47] In terms of the particular direction medical testimony took, one assumes that the various allegiances medical witnesses brought into the courtroom—and into the prison cell to interview the prisoner—stemmed in large part from the particular school of medical psychology to which they sub-scribed.[48] One can also assume that medical men contracted by the government to interview prisoners believed to be contemplating an insanity plea conceived of their role as one of unmasking "counterfeited" madness, and that they would testify to that effect in court. This does not mean, however, that medical men privately retained by defense attorneys revealed the countervailing sentiment: an ever-ready diagnosis delivered to support an acquittal.[49] Clashes between judge and medical witness associated with the assertion of expert forensic-psychiatric opinion were just as frequent as the defense attorney's evident frustration with a medical witness who could subvert the strategy of a prisoner's defense, as was so clearly in evidence in the trial of Jacob Spinasa.

Unconsciousness at the Old Bailey

Introducing unfamiliar diagnoses into medical testimony—the proffering of unusual renderings of the mind—is therefore bound up with the ongoing tensions of the trial itself. Since 1760 there had been a functioning role for the mad-doctor, and a division of courtroom labor that permitted specialist opinion to enter Old Bailey deliberations. London's central criminal court had long grown familiar with madhouse practitioners describing extraordinary states of being that rendered the prisoner, in their opinion, so profoundly confused that a "will to harm" —a choice taken to commit a crime—was beyond imagining.[50]

Examined on a trial-by-trial basis, the initiation of medical testimony exploring states of absence, unconsciousness, and "crimes of an automaton" at first represents to the historian of law a subtle variation in the generic insanity trial. Only over time does one perceive the shift in courtroom testimony that depicted the accused's actions as so uncharacteristic that the prisoner was indeed not himself. Sleepwalking at first resembled the familiar state of delirium, but the truly delirious were confused most of the time: the somnambulist's daily life was perfectly coherent. Epileptic fits might remind the horrified observer of nothing so much as generic apoplexy or a full frenetic mania, but when the epileptic fit had *gone off,* the afflicted was "quite himself again." The medical witness's task had therefore grown increasingly complex. He was no longer trying to argue the forensic relevance of terms suggesting a "lesion of the will" or a "paroxysm of mania." He was instead drawing the juror and defendant into an increasingly narrow circle in which persons with no history of observed mental derangement could be capable of the most horrific acts in moments when they were not "themselves."

The first sign that medical testimony was presenting a significant variation of the typically insane—the delirious, manic, insensible offender —can be seen in accounts of the defendant's failure to understand how he could have committed such a crime. This was usually phrased as the prisoner's inability to remember what he had been "about," his inability to "give [an] account of himself for at least ten days to a fortnight," the observation that he seemed "perfectly oblivious to the crime."[51] As one prisoner testified, "I did not know where I was till I *came to* in the cab." This was the comment of someone who did not know he had committed an act, let alone a crime. Medical witnesses described such defendants accordingly as "lost," "vacant," "wandering," or "like a man in sleep." When prisoners were able to acknowledge that they had engaged in some activity, they stared unknowingly at the medical practitioner who tried to remind them why the act was wrong ("He did not understand that he had committed a crime") or of the tenuous nature of the position he was in ("He always spoke of it as a thing which would pass away").[52] Of this prisoner, the witnesses testified, "his mind was obscured to the moral nature of the act," suggesting not defective intelligence or delusion, but an inability to integrate thought with moral consequence.[53] Without the two joined together, it was difficult to consider the crime as an intentional act—as purposefully chosen behavior—for all the seeming sanity of the prisoner.

There was also, to be sure, medical interest in impulsive crime, in "homicidal insanity" and "homicidal monomania."[54] It would be a singular, highly suspect inquiry into Victorian psychological medicine that found medical witnesses reluctant to entertain the possibility of blind impulse and impaired self-control. Certainly medical men at the Old Bailey had no difficulty describing a defendant as having "no control over his action" or acting in the throes of an "irresistible impulse." But here as well, it is the inexplicability of the action, the lack of discernible reason, and the missing pathological medical history that put the "blind" in blind impulse. "He seems quite unable to give any account of why he did it, any more than it was done by another person," said one witness of a defendant who was blind to his own connection to the crime.[55] Forensic-psychiatric diagnoses of homicidal insanity and monomania were employed in court to account for a crime for no reason: "a sudden, violent act from an inadequate motive." Such impulsive crime underscored the witness's belief in a lack of agency: the prisoner was not "answerable" for the crime.

Within the context of testimony asserting a defendant's inability to know what he was "about," his failure to understand the moral harm of his act, and the ready invocation of irresistible impulses and automatic reflexes to account for inexplicable, ultimately self-injuring behavior, the explicit and frequent mention of "unconsciousness" by the post-McNaughtan medical witnesses found a ready resonance. One was "unconscious of the act," "unconscious of [the] delivery," "unconscious of what I was saying to him," and "unconscious of the wickedness of the act."[56] Of course, simple "awareness" or "appreciation" could be substituted for some of the ways that consciousness was invoked, but a reading of the testimony in the context of what it meant to act with intention suggests an unfamiliar context for so conventional a term. Absent, "missing," and "a black cloud over his senses" were invoked by medical (and some lay) witnesses to describe the person's state of unconsciousness at the scene of the crime. When the states of otherness are combined with "nonconvulsive epilepsy," with dreamlike behavior, or with active tales of possession, the full implication of medical testimony that explored the questionable authorship of the accused's crime grows evident: "a person attacked with epileptic vertigo is unconscious while he is committing the act . . . not insensible . . . they do acts automatically . . . they act as mere machines."[57]

But where was the defendant during the episode of automatic behavior? How did the Old Bailey respond to the specter of such "missing defendants": absent from the scene of the crime, or sleepwalking their way through a murderous assault? Is the common law's response discernable in jury verdicts, in courtroom questioning—"Do you mean to tell us after [he gave] his reasons for killing Mr. Waugh, that he did not know killing was contrary to the law?" (asked three times of a medical witness)—or in the judge's explicit instructions to the jury?[58] How did courtroom dialogue resonate with or depart from elite professional opinion, expressed in medical texts by medical editors eager to affirm medicine's growing expertise in matters mental?

I have selected five Victorian trials heard at the Old Bailey between the years 1843 and 1876, through which to examine the variations in unconsciousness that defendants could be said to manifest as well as the medical testimony that tried to make sense of such unusual states of being. Each of the following five chapters begins with a particular type of splitting or fragmenting of consciousness, and then draws on a number of related trials of the period to explore the courtroom dialogue this particular form of distraction generated. The five trials are those of a prisoner who not only defends himself but reveals an alternate self to the jury while testifying; a twelve-year-old boy who knew how to procure arsenic but not, apparently, why adding it to the family sugar bowl was wrong; an "absent" young woman accused of murder whose fits inspired the judge to ask a witness whether it was the defendant or the fit who (or that) struck him; a witness to a murder who is interrupted while testifying by spirits of the Queen, Luther, and Calvin, which attempt to substitute their memory for his; and finally an automaton described by medical witnesses as completely "unconscious" of having cut off her daughter's hand.

What unites these cases and the supplementary trials with the episodes of sleepwalking and trance reported by Mitchill, Dewar, Mayo, and Browne is not the explicit courtroom mention of a double or an *état seconde*. No *Sybils* wandered into the Victorian courtroom, at least none who were spotted in the Old Bailey in the middle years of the nineteenth century. Instead, defendants prosecuted in London's central criminal court shared with the sleepwalking patients in the medical literature the defining elements of amnesia, variations in temperament in stark opposition to the familiar personality, and, most trenchantly, unaccountable—indeed, unimaginable—behavior. Ultimately, what coupled the Old Bailey prisoner and the case-study patient was a "discontinuous" life. As oppositional as Dorian Gray was to his portrait, as morally disparate as Jekyll was to Hyde, the depravity of the *unconscious* murderer was described as bearing no relation to the "kind and affectionate" friend and parent that one meets over and over at the Old Bailey, staring in bewilderment as the prosecutor describes his or her moral obloquy to the jury.

Today's reader of the *OBSP* begins to wonder whether the supposed discontinuity reveals different persons, or irreconcilable emotions within the same person. Most of the crimes described appear to have been premeditated, all involved victims and defendants well known to each other, and most featured the use of a lethal weapon or poison, suggesting a deliberate choice of means to effect a specific, envisioned end. If this defendant was "missing" at the time of the crime, the perpetrator was certainly no stranger to the victim. Over the years 1843 to 1876, it is the concept of the unconscious itself that underwent the greatest change in court. Originally merely the repository of forgotten knowledge and innumerable connections among ideas, the unconscious took on a new function, storing the resentments and hostilities not expressed within the victim and the offender's day-to-day interaction. Examining the account of the pre-Freudian unconscious as it emerged at the Old Bailey, one might well wonder if the crimes so shocking to the defendant were really so inexplicable after all.

TWO

"Do You Remember Cardiff?"

✢

$\mathcal{I}$ N July 1854, Ann Howell of Cardiff brought a libel action against James Benyon for publishing an account of his alleged seduction of her, which effectively dashed Howell's prospects of marrying Mr. Hughes, a Baptist minister. When the libel case came to court, Benyon enlisted the services of a London-based attorney, Hardinge Stanley Giffard, whose relentless cross-examination of the plaintiff—designed to show "that an improper intimacy had existed between her and the defendant"—eventually elicited her confession that she had indeed spent the night in a public house with Mr. Benyon.[1] The young woman appeared to grow faint at this admission, prompting a call heard in the courtroom to open the window to give her air. One of the spectators, Hugh Pollard Willoughby, grew increasingly exercised at the sight of the attorney's unchivalrous treatment of Miss Howell, and when he leaned forward to tell Giffard of his displeasure, the attorney turned around and made a rude gesture, adding suggestively, "We shall soon come to the rig!" Willoughby was so taken aback by what he perceived to be a homosexual advance that six months later he followed Giffard back to London, walked into the Old Bailey, and shot the attorney in the face.

It is true that there had been a libel action in Cardiff six months before the murderous assault. It is also true that Miss Howell had swooned under the press of intense cross-examination. And there seems little doubt that Hugh Pollard Willoughby had aimed a loaded pistol (with another in reserve) at Hardinge Stanley Giffard, firing at close range. But whether Willoughby had ever been in the Cardiff courtroom at all is anybody's guess, because the shooting victim had no recollection of seeing him or speaking to him, and he certainly had no memory of trying to seduce him. That Willoughby's presence at the earlier trial could not be satisfactorily proven in the case of *Regina v. Willoughby* was the least of the jury's problems.[2] In this trial for attempted murder, jurors could not be sure which Hugh Pollard Willoughby was facing them in the dock: the poised prisoner who deftly examined the medical witnesses himself or the religiously obsessed, bible-thumping ranter with whom he alternated.

By the time the defendant had begun to unravel, the jury had grown familiar with Willoughby's singular behavior. On the opening day of the trial, the defendant, a man of "gentlemanly appearance and of good family," walked into the court with a document that appeared to be a legal brief and declared his intention to conduct his own defense, thereby dismissing Mr. Clarkson, the attorney engaged by his family. He also requested that several witnesses from the libel trial at Cardiff be served with a subpoena, a request that was summarily denied by the judge, who also let Mr. Clarkson stand as defense attorney.

Prosecutor Ryland opened the case against the defendant, reminding the jury that Willoughby stood indicted on two serious charges: assault with intent to murder and assault with intent to commit grievous bodily harm. The defendant, he continued, "a minister of the established church, a gentleman of education and position, and connected with a somewhat high and certainly most respectable family," stood indicted for an offence "committed under very extraordinary circumstances."[3] Anticipating a likely defense of mental derangement, the prosecutor alerted the jury that their task would be to consider whether the unfortunate gentleman at the bar was suffering from a condition of mind that rendered him not responsible for his crime. Following this opening statement, he called the victim of the shooting to the stand.

HARDINGE STANLEY GIFFARD, ESQ.: I am a barrister, practicing in this Court, and on the Welsh Circuit. On 18th September last, I was in this Court, in the discharge of my duty; I was sitting in the end seat of the Counsels' table; I had just concluded a case for the prosecution, and was reading another brief—my eyes were directed to the table—the prisoner came up to me—I did not observe him until he was close to me—he said, "Do you remember Cardiff?"—I then turned my face towards him, and he jerked up something which I afterwards ascertained to be a pistol, close to my cheek, and fired it—the explosion of the powder made me stagger back for a moment, and I felt a smart rap on the cheek, which I presume was the powder—I do not think there was any wadding—I think it was only the powder; a small circular hole was cut in my cheek by the explosion—the skin was broken. I did not at the time find an injury inside my mouth; but some days afterwards I found that the explosion . . . had lacerated the inside of my mouth.[4]

Still acting as Willoughby's defense counsel, Mr. Clarkson cross-examined the victim: "Do you remember ever to have seen this unfortunate gentleman before the occasion when, in last July, you were at Cardiff, on your circuit?" After testifying that he could not recall seeing Willoughby or having any communication with him "either directly or indirectly," Giffard then commented on the events surrounding Miss Howell's fainting, believing at the time that any request to give her air came from her attorney.

DEFENSE ATTORNEY CLARKSON: In consequence of any application, by whomsoever it was made, to the learned Judge, for air for the witness, did you turn around in an angry manner, either to Mr. Willoughby, or anybody else?

VICTIM GIFFARD: No, certainly not—I did not by any intimation, or sign, or motion of my body or hand, seek to intimate to the prisoner or anybody else, any act of indecency on my part, or that of anybody else.

Clearly outraged by Giffard's forceful denial, defendant Willoughby interrupted his attorney's cross-examination and "with great warmth" discharged Clarkson on the spot. "Mr. Clarkson is not my counsel, he is only retained by my family [soon to figure prominently in Willoughby's conspiracy narrative]; and he shall not act for me." Asked by the judge if he intended to repudiate Clarkson, the prisoner replied, "Most certainly I do." He was dismissing Clarkson because of the particular defense the attorney was about to make, in flagrant opposition to Willoughby's instructions. As there was no reason to conclude at the time that the defendant was anything but *sui compos,* the judge observed that he failed to see how Clarkson could act for the defendant against his expressed wishes. Not to be dismissed without being heard, Clarkson countered that he had once before found himself engaged by friends of a defendant against the defendant's wishes, and that trial judge saw fit to let him proceed in that capacity. This judge failed to see the logic of such an action. As recorded in the *OBSP,* "If a man appeared and pleaded not guilty, and said he desired to conduct his own defense, no one could be thrust upon him as Counsel against his will, if he was *sui compos*, he clearly had a right to decide for himself."

Although the defendant was certainly agitated and angrily objected to the courtroom procedure, it nonetheless bears keeping in mind that the judge had twice pronounced Willoughby to be of sound physical state. This most recognizable of "gentlemanly" defendants was articulate, precise, and composed. Although he was about to embark on a progressively elaborate—and in time, bizarre—interrogation, Willoughby's questions were those of a persistent examiner, not of a vertiginously spinning madman. That he was examining witnesses at all serves as a reminder that defendants a century earlier could be left to question witnesses themselves; defense counsel was not a standard feature. In the event, the role of examiner and cross-examiner often fell to the judge. Defendants rarely entered directly into courtroom dialogue except for their statement to the jury, the "Prisoner's Defense," uttered at the end of the trial.

With the nod from the judge, Willoughby gathered up his brief and turned toward his alleged victim, still on the stand.

WILLOUGHBY: Do you not recollect, during the cross-examination of Miss Howell, when you saw what an interest a gentleman behind her took in the trial, turning around to him and saying with a violent motion of your arm, "We shall soon come to the *rig*"?

GIFFARD: No, I did not [and, refusing to comment on the mysterious nature of the "rig," he returns to Clarkson's previous question]. I believe there was some question put, as to whether Miss Howell had slept in a public house; but I cannot now recollect the cross-examination.

Frustrated by the witness's refusal to be drawn, Willoughby opened a new line of questioning, invoking the name of his brother, Sir Henry Willoughby, to construct a supposed conspiratorial link between him and the victim's father-in-law. Receiving no satisfaction here either, he returned to the threatened intimacy between Giffard and himself.

WILLOUGHBY: Did you not, in point of fact, labour in every possible way to stab to the vitals this young woman when fainting, by insisting to the Jury that I had been guilty of an unnatural offense?

GIFFARD: No, I did not insinuate to the Jury anything about you.

WILLOUGHBY: Did I not direct you by my motions to state your case against me to the learned Judge [at Cardiff], Mr. Justice Williams?

GIFFARD: I have already said that I did not see you; the black cap [that Willoughby alluded to in an earlier question—the black cap that a judge donned when announcing a sentence of death] was not brought forward, nor a second black cap—there was no black cap produced at the assizes at all—I did not then strenuously implore your forgiveness in the presence of Mr. Justice Williams—you did not say "No, no, no!"—nor did I implore the forgiveness of the Court, the Jury, the Magistrates, and the gallery for a considerable period of time when you said to me, "Do you remember Cardiff?" I did not know the meaning of the phrase at all."[5]

And with these adamantine denials, victim Giffard left the witness stand.

That the victim—shot at close range in the face—was able to give any denials at all deserves comment. As an eyewitness testified, "I heard something of an explosion and at the same time I heard the explosion I heard something rattle . . . against one of the partitions in the Court . . . underneath I found a pistol ball." Apparently the pistol had not been loaded well, and when the gunpowder ignited, the ball simply dropped out of the gun. Giffard had in fact been shot—but shot with black powder. Of course, that Willoughby was singularly inept at loading the firearm in no way mitigated the seriousness of an indictment for attempted murder, although it did render the account of the crime scene somewhat farcical. Still, he was on trial for carrying two loaded pistols into the courtroom with the intent to shoot the attorney, and it was *that* resolve that concerned the remaining, and pivotal witnesses.

Gilbert McMurdo was certainly no stranger to the Old Bailey; his presence in trials that turned on the prisoner's alleged mental condition had long been a predictable element in the Victorian insanity trial. What could not have been foreseen was his being called to *argue* the defendant's insanity.[6] The prisoner had not entered an insanity plea; indeed, it was Willoughby's suspicion that his attorney was laying the groundwork for such a defense that prompted him to "repudiate" Clarkson's help. Willoughby's defense turned on the question of provocation; insanity undermined rather than supported such a plea. One can well imagine the "warmth" with which Willoughby listened to the following exchange.

GILBERT McMURDO, ESQ.: I am surgeon of the gaol of Newgate, and have been so for many years. I have had many cases of insanity brought before me—since the day the prisoner was committed to Newgate I have continually seen and conversed with him—I happened to be in the prison immediately after he was taken there, and I saw him—I am of the opinion he was then, and is now, of unsound mind.

JUDGE: Are you of opinion that he is of unsound mind so as to be incapable of distinguishing between good and evil?

McMURDO: His case is peculiar—your lordship is aware, quite as much as I can be, that many persons of unsound mind are particularly shrewd upon many points, and that unless you have the thread given you, you cannot draw out of them just cause to form your conclusions. I had some information given me, and I conversed with the prisoner, and the observations he made, the accounts he gave me, and his reasoning upon them, were all such as to cause me necessarily to form the conclusion [that] he is labouring under a most horrible delusion; a settled delusion, which renders him perfectly of unsound mind at this moment—I believe he has been labouring under an entire delusion with reference to this matter.

JUDGE: Have these delusions any reference to the matter now under inquiry?

McMURDO: Certainly.[7]

With the last question and the succinct reply, the judge managed to lodge Willoughby's florid delusion squarely in nineteenth-century medicolegal reasoning.

A Fateful Delusion

It seems a certain justice that it was the judge who inquired about the significance of delusion to the defendant's behavior, because it had been a legal—not a medical—voice that had introduced and then affirmed, the critical nature of delusion in questions of criminal responsibility. In the celebrated trial of James Hadfield for the attempted assassination of George III, attorney Thomas Erskine (eventually to become solicitor general) argued that although the defendant had purchased a gun, made his way to the Drury Lane Theatre, and patiently waited for the King to acknowledge the audience's singing "God Save the King" before aiming his pistol at the Royal Box and shooting, he was in fact insane. This was no easy defense to mount, because criminal law recognized only a *total* want of understanding and memory—*a total insanity*—as grounds for acquittal. Erskine argued instead that the true essence of insanity was delusion: a false and resolute belief that no contrary evidence could shake loose in the mind of the deluded.[8]

But there was more to courtroom jurisprudence than establishing the mere presence of delusion; one needed to demonstrate a necessary link between fatal error and the criminal deed. The delusion had to be of the right sort. Erskine had little difficulty complying with this stricture: Hadfield believed that only his own death at the hands of the state would reenact Christ's execution and precipitate the Second Coming.[9] The force of the belief propelled him to the attempt on the King's life, precisely because it was a capital crime. Although there would be many more defense attorneys who would follow Erskine's lead and incorporate delusion into a courtroom strategy, few defendants would be able to say that they chose their crime *because* of its punishment: a state execution. In fact, few putatively insane defendants would allege that they chose their acts at all.

Originally associated with a profound intellectual error, delusion eventually assumed the dynamic of an insistent, compelling force that led the hapless true believer into crime. Certainly Daniel McNaughtan's trial is well remembered for the blind force of the defendant's delusion that the prime minister was out to get him: "nothing short of a physical impossibility would prevent him from performing any act which his delusion might impel him to do." The haunting specter of McNaughtan's delusion was its resemblance to a "lesion of the will" or an "irresistible impulse" in that conceptual error seemed to carry a spur to action all its own. The word *impulse* did not have to be uttered by the McNaughtan medical witnesses: the implication was sufficiently clear. If the judges called to the House of Lords thought they were circumscribing delusion's focus to exclude volitional chaos by employing the standard of "*knowing* right from wrong," it was a vain hope. And if they thought that knowing an act to be wrong served as a natural curb to putting oneself in legal jeopardy, they were to learn more on that score, too. As noted jurist James Fitzjames Stephen pointed out in 1883, Hadfield knew his act was wrong.[10] Indeed, that was why he chose it. In electing to sacrifice himself for the common good therefore, Hadfield exposed the ambiguous nature of the "wrong" in "knowing right from wrong": an act could be legally transgressive and yet be morally creditable.

Whether it carried its own autonomous spur to action, and whether the "wrong" in knowing right from wrong needed further parsing, the essence of delusion was that it precluded measured judgment regarding the nature of one's acts. Whatever Willoughby might have understood about the consequences of aiming the pistol at Giffard, could anyone in court accuse him of "calm judgment," given the elaborate seduction and conspiracy plot that lay behind the events of the Old Bailey shooting?

When the judge asked Gilbert McMurdo if the defendant's delusion had reference to the current indictment, few in the court could have doubted that all the medical witness had to do was give his assent for the perfect "Hadfield link" between delusion and act to be forged.

As it happened, there was at least one courtroom participant who questioned the prison surgeon's perceptions. Although McMurdo was sometimes compelled to justify an opinion of a prisoner that he derived exclusively from prison interviews, he had never before faced cross-examination when he had discerned and reported the presence of an "unsound mind," and certainly never from the putatively mad defendant himself. Instead of a skeptical and inquiring defense attorney probing the limit of his training in mental medicine, McMurdo faced a prisoner bent on examining in detail the grounds for the surgeon's diagnosis. The medical man's refusal to comply with the defendant's set theatrical piece is signaled by his insistence on referring to Willoughby in the third person.

WILLOUGHBY: What observations do you allude to which induce you to say I am of unsound mind?

SURGEON McMURDO: The prisoner related certain events which he considered had taken place in public, such as we cannot conclude did occur, and he reasoned upon them—he has continually referred to those circumstances which he related to me, and he has said (relating to what he considered the Judge had done), "If they were not done, then I am stark mad; I am under a delusion; they either did happen, or they did not, if they did not, I am under a delusion, and I am mad; it is no use my talking to you."

WILLOUGHBY: Do you consider me to be of unsound mind in any other respect?

McMURDO: His unsoundness of mind is to such extent upon this point, that I should consider him of unsound mind on any point, supposing he were to do an act where his correctness of conduct [were] to be called into question.[11]

Although relegated to the status of a courtroom bystander, former defense attorney Clarkson followed the progress of the trial, taking the conclusion of McMurdo's testimony as an opportune moment to inform the court that Forbes Winslow, noted alienist, author, and medical witness at the McNaughtan trial, was in attendance. Winslow's acquaintance with the defendant predated the alleged assault by five years, so he was well positioned to affirm that the defendant had indeed suffered from a history of mental distress. Seizing the opportunity afforded by Winslow's presence, the prosecuting attorney expressed his willingness to examine him, and the judge agreed, although it was clear he was on untested ground. The defendant, of course, had no intention of calling on Winslow's services, for the simple reason that he had no intention of pleading insanity. Although it was not unheard of for the prosecution to subpoena prison surgeons and for private practitioners to cast doubt upon defense claims of derangement, it was certainly unusual to marshal the government's subpoena power to seek and impose an insanity plea on a reluctant defendant. Even so, it was not at all clear how the court could compel the testimony of a medical practitioner whose appearance in court could not have been anticipated by the prosecution.

The novelty was not that Winslow would be testifying in a trial in which neither side had issued a subpoena for him—that was also true in McNaughtan's prosecution, when Winslow simply offered his services to the Old Bailey, in part, one suspects, to advertise his recent publication. In the Willoughby case, he had no book to promote, and would be questioned to support a plea by a defendant who was actively rejecting it. The judge mused that "the object of any prosecution was merely to discover the truth"; that was, after all, why it had been "the duty of the prosecution to call Mr. McMurdo." And though it was not a parallel duty to call anyone acquainted with the defendant, "Counsel for the prosecution might [examine] any person who had an opportunity of knowing the state of mind of a prisoner, when that state of mind fairly arose, as it did now, as the question in the inquiry."

DR. FORBES WINSLOW: I am a physician. I have for many years had my attention called to the question of insanity—I have seen and conversed with the prisoner, with the view of ascertaining the state of his mind—I first saw him in Paris in 1849 or 1850, at the request of his family . . . his having left England suddenly, pending a commission of lunacy issued by Lord Chancellor Truro—he was under various delusions respecting his family—I then considered him of unsound mind—I saw him again the 19th [i.e., the day after the shooting] and again on the 24th in Newgate— I considered him of unsound mind on both occasions—I have been in court during the whole of this trial.

JUDGE: What is your medical opinion of the state of his mind on 18th September last?

WINSLOW: I have no doubt that he was then insane—from what I knew of him before that time and since, and having heard what took place on the 18th September, I have not a doubt that he was then of unsound mind.

WILLOUGHBY: Did not you tell me you would be of the opinion that I was not labouring under a delusion if my statements were corroborated by [Cardiff Judge] Mr. Justice Williams and others?

WINSLOW: I mentioned to you that if you could establish to my satisfaction that the circumstances you alleged actually occurred in Court, they would be facts and not delusions, and that of course would considerably modify my opinion—you then said Mr. Justice Williams was in a position to establish all the facts.

WILLOUGHBY: Not all the facts, the leading facts—did I object to see you?

WINSLOW: Not at all . . . nor to answer any of my questions—I believe the impression you have upon your mind with regard to the conduct of Mr. Giffard, and the case in Cardiff, to be a delusion. If those things can be proved to be facts, then, of course, they would not be delusions. You told me that your brother had deprived you of your property for the last twenty years, and that Mr. Morris, your solicitor, had forsaken you at the last moment—you told me if that was a delusion, you must be mad—I asked you if it would not be better to plead insanity, in order to avoid being transported—I endeavoured to persuade you that you were under a false impression; and I said, with a view of comforting you, that it was quite possible in the course of time that these impressions might be removed.[12]

Thus ended the case for the prosecution, and as it turned out the case for the defense as well. Composed and articulate, Willoughby had been able to elicit from the witnesses to the shooting the obvious care he had taken to ensure that no one but Mr. Giffard was injured, and, no doubt inadvertently, the near unanimous belief that he was fatefully deluded regarding every material element at issue in this trial: the events in Cardiff, his circumstances in Paris, Giffard's designs on him. Although pointedly direct and rigorous in his questioning, Willoughby was nonetheless measured in his treatment even of his supposed arch nemesis. Especially persuasive was his logic: delusion and the "facts proved" could not occupy the same stage. Either he was mad or he was wronged.

The question of "either-or" that emerged in his long and convoluted Prisoner's Defense, however, was one not so much of delusion or sanity but rather *which* Hugh Pollard Willoughby was speaking at any given moment. Shortly after he began his summation, the jury was aware that there were cracks in Willoughby's person.

Gentlemen of the Jury, it is now my painful duty, unassisted by Counsel and without legal help, to call your attention to the defence which I shall make to the charge for which I am indicted; namely, for feloniously and maliciously shooting at and discharging . . .

Here, the *OBSP* note, "The prisoner suddenly broke off and said, 'people seem to be hissing me.' Upon being assured that this was not the case," he returned to his oration mid-sentence.

. . . a loaded pistol at Hardinge Stanley Giffard, with intent to murder him, and before I do so, I implore you to weigh carefully and dispassionately all the circumstances bearing upon the question which you are called upon to try, in order that you may arrive at a just and righteous conclusion, as to whether there was [preconceived] malice in this act which is necessary to constitute the offense of murder.

Although seeming to steady himself after hearing the hissing sounds provoked by his careful delineation of the legal requirement for a finding of murder, the well-spoken defendant began to recede in the background as the subject of his brother, Sir Henry Willoughby, suddenly surfaced in his defense. Requesting that ladies seated in the courtroom might withdraw, he opened up an entirely new line of defense, providing further reasons for his estrangement from his family and the flight to Paris. Sir Henry Willoughby "had shown to me **** [presumably referring to an intimate body part too indelicate to print] and I had banished myself from my country for the last six years, in order to avoid these frightful exhibitions, and still more frightful consequences." No one, however, would believe him when he recounted the tale of this trauma when he was confined in Newgate. Indeed, the chaplain convinced him not to repeat the tale of his brother's behavior when the case came to court. Upon reporting these events, the defendant raised his arm for emphasis "exclaiming two or three times, '*bum, bum*.'"

After this enigmatic expression, Willoughby returned to the distress Miss Howell had suffered from Mr. Giffard's cruel cross-examination, prompting her to plead with him, "Do not be so hard, I wish to speak the truth." On seeing her fainting, "I suggested that the windows might be opened, and a cup of water be given to her," and the judge complied. From that moment, however, "Mr. Giffard commenced every possible outrage against all public decency," and, as the *OBSP* report, "The prisoner here entered into the details of alleged indecent gestures and motions on the part of Mr. Giffard." Willoughby continued,

Mr. Giffard continued grinning, and after a short time the black cap, that emblem of death—yes gentlemen, two black caps—were brought forward; Mr. Giffard then implored my forgiveness, then that of the learned Judge, then that of the Jury, then that of the public collectively, and myself individually. I nodded and said "No, no," and I submit to you, gentlemen, supposing I state the facts correctly, but only upon that supposition, I submit to you, that had I then taken the law into my hands, this indictment would fall to the ground.[13]

When speaking of Cardiff, Willoughby's knowledge of the law was considerable, alluding to a defense of provocation that would indeed negate intent. He realized the dubious grounds he had for alleging overwhelming compulsion to avenge a perceived insult six months after the alleged assault. As it was, the common law would not have recognized an obscene gesture or even an indecently voiced assault. Only a forceful physical blow was recognized as justifiable grounds for retaliation.[14] Realizing the meager grounds he had for an affirmative defense of provocation, Willoughby reminded the jury of his solicitous consideration for the safety of innocent bystanders, which was remarked upon by the courtroom bystanders, and the fact that the pistol must have been aimed "obliquely" to cause so little damage to the victim. Had he pressed the pistol at Giffard's face, "The ball must have gone into his head." Even the amount of gunpowder used was barely enough to launch a fatal shot. Quoting an eyewitness, the defendant continued, "I heard an explosion, not so loud as I should expect from a pistol loaded with ball." Also, "the ball was not flattened," further proof that the ball might have fallen out; and the charge of powder was small.

Appearing to conclude his remarks, Willoughby addressed the jury:

Gentlemen, I have thus attempted to state, very imperfectly, the unhappy circumstances which led me to discharge the pistol at Mr. Giffard. I apprehend with the greatest deference, under the correction of their lordships, that the question in point of law for your consideration is simply this—Was a loaded pistol (recollecting that the ball might have fallen out) fired at Mr. Giffard with the felonious and malicious intent of murdering him against the statute? I presume, in deep humility, that it will be for you to say—though alas! I have no law books, nor any assistance whatever—whether that [preconceived] malice, which is necessary to constitute the offense of murder, can be identified [with the] grossly beastly conduct of

Mr. Giffard, in which excitement I unhappily continued until the pistol was discharged at or near the person of Mr. Giffard?

After advising the jurors that they should commit him to Bedlam if they could detect "the slightest false premise in any of the questions which I have put today to Mr. Giffard," the defendant abruptly broke off his parsing of the legal code and, overwhelmed by brimstone bellowing up from the Hebrew Bible, exclaimed "[M]ay the flames which may now be burning on the known site of Sodom and Gomorrah scorch me to a cinder, and may I fall 'like Lucifer, never to rise up again,' never to hope again, in the pit which is the bottom."

What was the jury to make of this sudden emergence of apocalyptic vision? Following the display of a soul tormented by threatened fires from hell, Willoughby just as abruptly returned to his defense, reminding the jury that in Cardiff he had been "a passing traveler . . . to take the part of a sinking maid," and was in turn the pawn of attorney Giffard, "attempting to stab [him] in the vitals by falsely insinuating to the Jury [what jury?] that I had been guilty of a crime that ought not to be mentioned—when his own bestialities were so crying and insulting to the court." Finally he pleaded: "Restore me to my liberty and teach that family clique [and here, once again Willoughby fades from view]

> to know and to feel that the star of my destiny shall not wax pale, through their dark, their crafty, their torturous, and their wicked machinations, that the day of his deliverance has arrived to the "prisoner of hope"—to him who, as far as Cardiff is concerned, has been "more sinned against than sinning"; and that doubtless there is a God whose name is Lord Jehovah, that judgeth iniquity.[15]

It required no special medical training or experience in prison interviews to find and pull the thread that would unravel Willoughby's florid delusions. There was no moment in the trial—let alone in his behavior at the crime scene and later in Newgate—when the force of his beliefs was not apparent, though their status as a delusion became manifest only after the shooting. During the examination and cross-examination of witnesses, his composure and judgment were unexceptionable; indeed, a latecomer to the trial might well have been unable to spot the accused during the case. The defendant's unity as a person, however, began to unravel once he began the Prisoner's Defense, first with a sudden pull signaled by "people seem to be hissing me," then later with his unexplained punctuation of *"bum, bum,"* and finally the fabric completely unwinding as the threatened bestiality of Giffard overtook him and the scorching fires of Sodom and Gomorrah—an unambiguous biblical allusion to pederasty—engulfed his soul.

This was not the Hugh Pollard Willoughby who calmly but deliberately waited until Giffard had concluded his Old Bailey trial, approached his desk, and shot him in the face. And this was not the self-possessed advocate who extracted from seasoned medical witnesses the admission that if his version of the facts proved true, his beliefs would be anything but delusional. Old Bailey juries had certainly heard ranters before in the form of defendants displaying the ravages of religious monomania and delusions of persecution.[16] But the London courtroom had never before experienced ranting from a defendant who, only moments earlier had sparred adroitly with renowned courtroom witnesses. This stark alternation between two distinguishable personas in the same body existed in medical lore and folk myth; it had never before been seen at the Old Bailey. And there is little doubt that the defendant would have wished that it had not been seen at all. His only hope of convincing the jury of the truth of *his* facts lay in presenting a coherent, composed narrative.

It was precisely this image of uncontrollable, nonresponsible behavior that lay at the heart of the judge's instructions to the court. As reported in the *Times of London,*

[H]aving observed upon the extraordinary nature of this inquiry, [the judge] said he apprehended the jury could entertain no doubt that, supposing the prisoner to be of sound mind and understanding when he fired the pistol close to the face of Mr. Giffard, whether it was loaded with ball or not, he must at least have intended to do him some grievous bodily harm. He thought, therefore, that the real question they would have to consider was the state of the prisoner's mind at the time, and whether the evidence satisfied them that he was labouring under delusions and was not responsible for his actions. The learned judge then called the attention of the jury to what the prisoner represented to have occurred in the court at Cardiff, and said that even if witnesses had been called to prove that such occurrences really had taken place in an open court of justice, their veracity might almost have been doubted; but as it was it appeared to be quite clear that the whole matter was a delusion, and that nothing of the sort could possibly have occurred. The jury would consider, however, all the circumstances of the case, and if they felt no reasonable doubt that the prisoner was not of sound mind when he committed the act, it would be their duty to acquit him on that ground.[17]

Although the rise of the defense bar throughout the late eighteenth and early nineteenth centuries had doubtless lessened the extent of judicial influence during Old Bailey trials, instructions such as these remind today's readers of the *OBSP* that the judge's words were the last that juries heard and could significantly direct the flow of verdict deliberations. This influence would be meaningful even when the judge's instructions were far from prescriptive; one can only guess at a juror's reaction to an instruction that included the phrase "as it was, it appeared to be quite clear that the whole matter was a delusion [i.e., the perceived homosexual advances]; and that nothing of the sort could have possibly occurred." Whether it was the judge's unequivocal reading of the defendant's mental state, or their own conclusions drawn from the perplexing, alternating defendant's persona, the jurors required only minutes to return a verdict of not guilty on the grounds of insanity.

Willoughby's jury was not the first to acquit on the grounds of insanity over the forceful objection of a defendant, nor was his the first trial to take delusion seriously. It was, however, the first post-McNaughtan trial to witness a dramatic split in the delusional person's courtroom behavior. Willoughby's final speech displayed more than an inability to correct a false belief; there was a disintegration of self into artful questioner and religious ranter. Fears of eternal damnation took over, much like a possessing Other, crowding out his own powers of judgment and self-restraint. Like a piece of cloth unraveling, Willoughby seemed to go missing—to disappear inside himself—in a fit of religious mania. One can only wonder at the jury's reaction to this fateful transformation. Who was the person who appeared in the final moments of the trial? What relation did he bear to the calm, deft questioner who so adroitly conducted his own defense?

Willoughby as Precedent

Although the jury responded to Willoughby's antics with a finding of insanity, which may seem unproblematic given his Old Bailey theatrics, the verdict was at best an imposed compromise. The defendant had not asked for such a finding; indeed, he had dismissed his attorney rather than see it put forth. In the jury's eyes, he was both far too pitiable to convict and far too dangerous to acquit. Willoughby had wandered into the uncharted territory of one defendant evincing two persons. How could the jury be sure which Hugh Pollard Willoughby would surface at any given time? *Regina v. Willoughby* could look to no earlier case for a binding ruling; instead, it appears to have set a precedent of its own.

Five years after Willoughby entered Bethlem, an Old Bailey court cited Lord Chief Baron's unusual decision to admit medical testimony in support of a plea that a defendant assiduously rejected. James Moore's contempt for the world of madhouses and the very label of insanity had grown from bitter experience; he had been released from a House of Correction only to find that he was being sent to an asylum. Except for his delusion about having an engine trapped inside his stomach, asylum administrators eventually believed him a good candidate for release, particularly as "his conduct towards his wife was very affectionate." Five days after his release he beheaded her.

Like Willoughby, Moore began his trial by dismissing his defense attorney, having taken particular exception to the attorney's referring to him as a "wretched man" in the first question asked of the first witness. "I was never wretched," the defendant exclaimed; "even in the worst of my days I was always happy." And, again like Willoughby, Moore tried to expose the flaws in the medical witness's inference of his insanity.

DEFENDANT MOORE: Have you seen anything in my behavior in any way to show I was not in my right mind?
DIVISIONAL SURGEON OF POLICE: I do not know what is inside of you.[18]

The surgeon might better have answered, "I do not know *who* is inside of you." The memory of the killing clearly belonged to someone else, most likely to the unnamed persons the defendant believed murdered his wife in a plot to send him back to the asylum. James Moore certainly had no memory of the killing; by his account he was missing from the crime scene. With no defense plea alleging insanity and a defendant objecting to its very mention, Justice Baron Bramwell found himself in the identical position that the Chief Baron had occupied a few years before. As the *OBSP* report,

> Mr. Baron Bramwell, after referring to the case of *Regina v. Willoughby*, suggested that if any witnesses were in attendance who could give evidence as to the real state of the prisoner's mind, they might be called by the counsel for the crown; he did not intend to lay down that course as a general rule, but in a case of this nature, there could be no objection to such a course.[19]

The prosecution then called to the stand McMurdo's successor to the position of surgeon to Newgate prison.

JOHN ROWLAND GIBSON: I spent an hour and a quarter with him the first night he was in gaol, and I have seen him daily since—in my opinion he was not of sound mind—I have had conversations with him about the crime itself. I asked him whether he did not feel much concerned by it— he said no, he felt no concern at all, he believed it was a plan to put him again into the lunatic asylum.

The defendant indeed used this alleged plot to anchor his defense to the jury, again maintaining that he had nothing to do with the brutal killing: "I should like to know in what I am deficient that I am not in my right mind . . . why should I have [the engine] passed into my inside to be made a plaything of?"[20] It remained a mystery to James Moore how anyone could have thought him capable of killing his wife, why he was not believed, and why he should be returned to an asylum. "Evidently displeased" by the verdict and the disposition, Moore "seemed anxious again to address the jury [but] was removed from the bar."[21]

The trials of Hugh Willoughby and James Moore present today's historians of law and medicine with as many interpretive challenges as they doubtless presented to contemporary courtroom participants. Murder and attempted murder were not unusual crimes, but they were the most serious offenses tried at the Old Bailey, the former carrying a possible death sentence. Mary Ann Moore had been killed in a domestic assault, which raised the stakes even higher since, as Martin Wiener has recently argued, Victorians were taking an increasingly punitive stance toward domestic slayings. Husbands or partners who hoped to elicit empathetic solidarity from the all-male jury by pleading some form of provocation met judicial instructions that considerably narrowed the grounds for such a defense.[22] Of course James Moore did not plead provocation, nor in fact did he plead insanity. In his own words, he was not home when the brutal murder took place, and that may well have been his one true statement. An outright acquittal would have followed if the jury had believed his claim of innocence. His insanity acquittal doubtless reflected the jury's believing the medical witness. In a curious way, the jury also believed the defendant: he was telling the truth as far as he knew it. The assault belonged to somebody else.

The Enduring Significance of Delusion

From failure to correct an error of judgment to failure of memory, from an inability to control one's actions to an inability to maintain a constant self, delusion retained its significance in Victorian criminal trials even as it embraced the phenomenon of a second self unknown to the defendant. That delusion was beginning to serve as sufficient evidence of insanity is clear from legal writings and judicial questions asked of medical witnesses. "Has he any delusion at all?" was becoming a question commonly asked by judges of medical witnesses regardless of the focus of their testimony. Sensing a too-ready attempt to reduce all insanity to delusion—and particularly to the notion of a circumscribed error in belief, leaving all the faculties perfectly coherent—some medical witnesses went to inordinate lengths to avoid inferring the presence of delusion.

In 1854, the same year as *Regina v. Willoughby,* two of England's most eminent medical men testified in an Old Bailey trial, revealing decidedly different opinions regarding the centrality of delusion to insanity. Although Luigi Buranelli's obsessive fear that he was passing urine through his anus had nothing to do with his killing Joseph Latham, his defense attorney endeavored to establish the presence of the delusory fear as an incontrovertible sign of a seriously deranged intellect. His plea was supported by John Conolly, asylum superintendent at Hanwell, and the one medical witness who could rival McMurdo in the frequency of his appearances at the Old Bailey. "[A] man cannot be of sound mind, and have an absolute delusion," Conolly unequivocally asserted.[23] His opinion was contradicted, however, by a rebuttal medical witness, a prosecutorial strategy that would become a matter of contention between judge and defense attorneys as the court turned its attention to the vexed nature of expert testimony. Noted author and lecturer Thomas Mayo interpreted the defendant's obsession with his fistula to be

> an exaggeration . . . generally traced to some trifling foundation—I certainly do not consider that persons exaggerating in that way can be properly classed with those of unsound mind; you would extend a very dangerous excuse if you did.
>
> DEFENSE ATTORNEY M'ENTEER: You only saw the prisoner one day, I believe.
>
> DR. MAYO: Only once—I have heard all the evidence here today—I should not consider if a man thought his bed was swamped with water that would

be a delusion. . . . I conceive it quite natural, quite conformable with the laws of hypochondriasis, that he should go on exaggerating to any extent.

M'ENTEER: [W]ould you consider it had ever arrived at a delusion?

MAYO: Well, that is the fallacy of delusion; there is no end.

M'ENTEER: Although it was repeatedly shown that there was not a drop of [urine] in his bed, and that delusion being still persevered in, day after day, [he] was not under delusion?

MAYO: I do not consider incoherency an element in making up delusion—inconsecutiveness is nearly the same thing—I should not consider inconsecutiveness and incoherency as tending to create a morbid delusion: there must be something beyond it.

M'ENTEER: I will just read a passage from the work of a gentleman whom I am sure you must have a very good opinion of (*reading from page 26 of Dr. Mayo's own work*): "In dealing with the grounds which I have recently considered, for imputing insane delirium—namely, the presence of inconsecutiveness of thought in cases of certain delusions—how does the medical witness conduct his inquiry and arrange his evidence? [H]e makes, or he ought to make, each of these elements throw light on the other—where incoherency and inconsecutiveness exist there is little difficulty—continual inconsecutiveness I believe involves the presence of morbid delusions, that is sure to produce them." Do you agree with that?

MAYO: [having just chosen to characterize the defendant's ideas as "inconsecutive" rather than delusional]: Yes, inconsecutiveness and incoherency, when continued are pretty sure to have delusion with them—I do not believe [there is] in the evidence given here proof of inconsecutiveness of the character in the conduct of this man. . . . I saw not that amount of disorder of thought, or any such extent of error in the succession of ideas, which would amount, in any fair reasoning or observation, to insanity; that takes in inconsecutiveness and incoherence too.[24]

In addition to reminding future expert witnesses to be always conversant with their own publications, Dr. Mayo's testimony reveals that professional differences regarding law and medicine were just as likely within the medical fraternity as they were between the bench and the witness box. This was especially true when prosecution attorneys after the McNaughtan trial called medical witnesses to reply to defense witnesses, although McMurdo's frequent appearance for the prosecution ensured such differences, even when no medical men were called in rebuttal.[25]

Beyond the glimpse his testimony provides into the evolving dynamic of courtroom treatment of expert evidence, Mayo's language is noteworthy for introducing the term "inconsecutiveness" directly into the trial narrative. Delusion as conspiracy, as a spur to action, as a profound error in belief so circumscribed that no other intellectual idea could be entertained, was well familiar to the Old Bailey juror. When a physician or a surgeon attested to the existence of a delusion, and a connection was drawn to an indicted crime, the status of the delusory fear for the question of criminal responsibility was evident in the likelihood of an acquittal. Mayo's use of the term added a different and particularly salient element, given the common law's construction of criminal responsibility. It was consistency of consciousness that linked the individual to his act, making him a human, culpable agent.[26] Traditionally, to assert that the accused was deluded had been to argue that he was not conscious of doing wrong, that, like Hadfield, he was fatefully wrong about the consequences of his act. Saying that the deluded were profoundly confused did not amount to saying they were "missing" at their own crimes. They had not become someone else; they stayed themselves, if lamentably unknowing.

"Inconsecutiveness," on the other hand, belonged to the language of inconsistency and suspended consciousness, of amnesia and trance. Hugh Pollard Willoughby alternated between his coherent and manic selves; James Moore had no recollection of killing his wife for all the blood inexplicably splattered over him; Thomas Mayo's testimony coupled delusion with alternating states of consciousness. That two of the three accused felons defended themselves against both the criminal charge and the inference of insanity further distanced them from the *defendant's* behavior. It was in the end very fitting that Willoughby and Moore each played the role of examiner in his own trial. The person described in the medical testimony was a source of curiosity not only to the jury and judge, but to the defendants as well.

⚔ THREE ⚔

"I Mean She Was Quite Absent"

❖

*I*T IS NEVER A GOOD IDEA to poke one's head out the front door at 5:00 A.M., glance furtively from side to side, and then retreat into the house immediately upon seeing a policeman. This is bound to arouse suspicion. It is further unwise to carry bundles of clothing out to the street and suddenly throw them back into the house at the sight of the same constable. Better by far to walk straight to the cabstand as planned and disappear through the early morning mist. Had Mary Ann Hunt kept her rendezvous with cabdriver Henry Mapleston and ridden with him to the railway station, she would have been miles away from Adam Street, Marylebone, long before the unpleasant odor drifting from the back kitchen alerted the remaining boarders that all was not well with her roommate, Mrs. Stowell.

Now, fifteen minutes after abandoning her plan for a quick exit, Mary Ann Hunt found herself trying to hold fast the door that Police Constable Battersby was forcing open with the weight of his shoulder. Once inside, he confronted her with his suspicions: "Had you been an honest woman you would have taken one of those *cabs* in the street, and not have watched until the policeman was out of sight." After learning that the suspicious girl lived with an old woman—and supposing that the bundles of clothing belonged to the woman—he announced his intention to speak with the woman directly. When Mrs. Stowell did not answer his knock, the now suspect Mary Ann Hunt explained, "She is as deaf as stone." Finally succeeding in extracting a key from another boarder, the policeman entered the room where Mary Ann Hunt and Mary Stowell cohabited. Crumpled on the floor with her head under the wood stove, a cord wound several times around her neck, and a pool

55

of blood running from her head to the center of the room was Mrs. Stowell. Clearly, it was not deafness that had kept the old woman from answering Constable Battersby's knock.

This grisly discovery might have taken hours if not days had Mary Ann Hunt not fed the policeman's curiosity by trying to thwart his search. First alleging that no key could be found to the locked door, she next lied about the route through the alley. When the policeman expressed his intention to continue, she offered him half a crown for "something to drink." Saying, "this looks blacker still," he doubled his efforts to search the house, prompting the suspect to ask if she could visit the lavatory. After several minutes, the policeman forced open the door to the toilet and discovered the suspect twisting clothes around her neck, "I supposed attempting to strangle herself." All these actions proved critical in a trial that would turn on the defendant's capacity to know right from wrong and conclude with the judge's donning the black cap of death. It would be hard indeed to imagine a more daunting challenge for the defense attorney, faced with a client who had initially attempted to flee the scene of the murder, next tried to bribe a policeman to suspend his search, and, when all else failed, sought to kill herself before the inevitable discovery of the battered body.

Two months after the killing, Mary Ann Hunt entered the courtroom at the Old Bailey and listened as the prosecution addressed the jury. This was a case, the jurors learned, that would require "the most serious consideration at their hands . . . the substantial defense set up was this, that the prisoner was in such a state of mind at the time that she was not criminally responsible for her acts."[1] After recounting the events that surrounded the victim's brutal killing, the prosecuting attorney urged the jurors to consider the prisoner's state of mind in light of the witnesses he would produce to "state that they had never observed anything in her proceedings to induce them to believe that she was not in a sound state of mind." At this point, of course, jurors could expect to hear witnesses on either side of the case presenting contrasting views of the prisoner's level of functioning. What they could not have expected was testimony that called into question Mary Ann Hunt's presence at the crime, and a direct question from the judge asking witnesses to distinguish between the defendant's intentional actions and the autonomous effects of a convulsion.

True to his word, prosecutor Bodkin did not stint on producing friends and coworkers of the prisoner who had observed no sign of mental waywardness. In fact, they presented the picture of a vengeful, surly young woman. "I heard the prisoner say to the old lady that she would *do* for her—she repeated that over different times—that alarmed me, so that I fetched Mr. Hayman, the landlord . . . I heard the prisoner call the old lady an old hypocrite, and I heard the old lady say to the prisoner that she was the first lodger she had ever had, and she would be the last." Little did Mrs. Stowell know how prophetic her words would be. Sensing the damage such testimony could inflict, defense counsel Clarkson asked, "Where were you when you heard the prisoner say, 'I will *do* for you?'" "Upstairs [the witness, a Miss Nisbet, responded]—my window was open—it's my belief that the voice was the prisoner's—I believe it was her voice—I am not certain of it." Now it was the prosecutor who feared that the threat was quickly losing its potency for the jury. He reminded the witness that "you had your window open?" to which Miss Nisbet replied, "Yes, it was the room immediately over the back room [where the two women lived]—I have not the slightest doubt whatever that it was the prisoner's voice I heard." Following further testimony that explored the strained relationship between the victim and the accused, the prosecutor concluded this segment of the trial by asking Susanne Nisbet, "Are you sure it was on Monday [the day before the killing] that you fetched Mr. Hayman [the landlord]?" She replied simply, "Yes."

Defense attorney Clarkson could do little to minimize the threat or to cast doubt upon the witnesses who named the prisoner as the antagonist, but he managed to open his preferred line of inquiry when the prosecutor called a neighbor of the prisoner to testify. "I never detected anything peculiar in her manner or way of talking—on the Monday and the Tuesday when I saw her—her manner was as usual, but she looked paler than on ordinary occasions." Seizing on the proximity of the day of the crime to this neighbor's observation of Hunt's physical debility, Clarkson began the following line of questioning:

DEFENSE ATTORNEY CLARKSON: Did you know that the prisoner had been affected with an irregular discharge and was ill in consequence at times?

ANN SMALLBONE: She once made an observation to me that she had an obstruction of that kind, but she afterwards told me that she had a renewal—I believe it was first of all on the Sunday week before the deed was discovered, and likewise on the Tuesday morning, the day before it was discovered.

JUDGE: When was it she told you that she had an obstruction in a certain respect?

SMALLBONE: . . . [S]he told me on Sunday week that she had had a return of this matter, and on the Tuesday [the day of the killing] that she had a return of that illness . . . a return of the periodical complaint.

CLARKSON: And that was the occasion when you observed her to be so much paler than usual.

SMALLBONE: Yes, I observed her to be very pale on the Tuesday, more so than I had ever done the day before.[2]

Prosecutor Bodkin could obviously see where this was going, so he called to the stand the cabdriver, who provided a detailed account of the prisoner's methodical plan and fee negotiation to travel to Adam Street in the early morning hour. The cabdriver's story would have even greater effect once the coroner testified, putting the time of Mrs. Stowell's death at the same hour of his conversation with the defendant. When he told her the fare to the railway, she had protested, "You must take me for less than that, I have only got two or three bundles." Probably feeling emboldened by his witness's detailed report of the prisoner's self-possession in the early morning hours, prosecutor Bodkin broached the subject of the accused's mental and behavioral condition, as attested to by persons who had known her in shared employment.

WILLIAM SMITH: I am butler to Mr. Robert Gillespie, of York-place, New-road. I have known the prisoner seven or eight years—during that time I did not observe anything in her mode of talking or in her conduct different for ordinary, natural people.

It is not clear why the prosecutor asked the following question, perhaps to try to define the issue of "fits" before the defense attorneys introduced this loaded term. In any case, the prosecutor appears to have made a classic courtroom blunder: he asked the witness a question without knowing the answer ahead of time.

PROSECUTOR BODKIN: Do you know whether she had any fits during that time?

SMITH: Yes, two or three dreadful fits—I have seen her in them, and a dreadful palpitation of the heart—I can scarcely tell what kind of fit it was—it took four men to hold her, it was so violent. I was myself one of them—it required strength to hold her down—she used to be rather delirious after these fits—she seemed quite to lose herself—I mean she was quite absent.

Seizing on this last word and repeating it in his next question, the defense attorney hoped to underscore its significance in capturing the image of a woman who had taken leave not only of her senses, but of herself.

DEFENSE ATTORNEY BALLANTYNE: For how long after the fits did you observe this state of absence?

SMITH: It might have been half or three-quarters of an hour—except when my attention was attracted to her by those fits I did not notice her manner particularly—she seemed a very good, kind-hearted person indeed—every body that knew her while she lived at Brighton used to speak of her with the greatest praise.

Prosecutor Bodkin then called Ann Jones, another acquaintance of the prisoner, to attest to the defendant's manifestly ordinary behavior and conversation. He was no doubt dismayed by the defense attorney's use of her testimony to reinforce testimony regarding the defendant's customary genial nature.

ANN JONES: I never noticed anything extraordinary in her conversation or manner—she always conducted herself well in my presence—I never saw her in a fainting fit—the last time I saw her was on the Monday before the old woman's death.

DEFENSE ATTORNEY CLARKSON: Am I to understand, when you say that she seemed on that Monday to be as you had seen her, that she was a kind hearted, good, amiable person in whom you detected nothing particular?

ANN JONES: Yes—I never had my attention called to the prisoner more than to anybody else—I do not pretend to form any judgment upon any ailment with which she was afflicted.[3]

The defense attorney did not need the witness to draw any inferences regarding menstrual obstruction; there would be two medical specialists who would later offer a professional rendering of Mary Ann Hunt's fits following her reproductive ills. Even without expert medical opinion underlying its significance, attorney Clarkson knew the folk wisdom that surrounded a woman's behavior during even "normal" menstruation. As one contemporary Victorian described it, "[while menstruating] a woman is undoubtedly more prone than men to commit any unusual or outrageous act . . . it is not improbable that instances of feminine cruelty (which startle us as so inconsistent with the normal gentleness of their sex) are attributable to mental excitement caused by this periodic illness."[4] Women's psychology, throughout the mid- to late nineteenth century, was most often linked to reproductive processes, and Mary Ann Hunt's psychology would prove no exception. What was unusual in her trial was the novel combination of irregular menstrual discharge with periods of absence: discontinuous episodes of functioning that could span thirty to forty-five minutes. The defense team deftly educed the contrast between these violent upheavals and the kindhearted person everyone described. As the final lay witness presented by the prosecution eventually concluded, "She was a harmless person, not given to violence of any kind."

Hoping to counter the jury's image of just how gentle this prisoner could be, the prosecutor led the coroner, William Crofton Moat, through an agonizingly grim description of the victim's "most dreadful injuries: . . . six ribs broken on one side, eight on the other; lungs literally crushed; cord tied around her neck and an accompanying wound produced by the assailant's knuckles forced so violently against the throat that the windpipe was broken." Although obviously brutal, the fatal attack was apparently not drawn out, prompting defense attorney Clarkson to inquire, "You say the injury you found on the ribs of the deceased might have been inflicted in about a minute and a half?" (implying that the violent attack resembled the sudden outburst already imputed to the defendant). Mr. Moat replied, "It might have been done instantaneously—I think that one person could stop the circulation of the air-vessels of the wounded person by a string, by the fists, or by the knees, and at the same time, break the ribs on both sides of the body—it could have been done by sitting on the body and squeezing the throat—that is quite speculation—you asked me to imagine how it was done and I have done so." It was a question from an unexpected quarter that brought the coroner's testimony to an end.

JURY: Was it possible for the deceased to have fractured her ribs from any fall or accident?

MR. MOAT: Quite impossible—I should think—I am firmly of the opinion, as a surgeon—that external violence from another person operated to produce these fractures.[5]

The final expert witness for the prosecution was, as always, prison surgeon Gilbert McMurdo. He had been instructed by the court to pay particular attention to Mary Ann Hunt "with a view to ascertain the state of her mind." McMurdo's appearance and inferences were familiar to the Old Bailey: "I have not noticed anything which in my judgment justifies an inference that she is otherwise than of a sound mind—she has complained to me of symptoms of certain inconveniences, which led me to put further questions as to her condition, and my belief is that she is pregnant." Hunt's defense attorney wasted little time questioning the prison surgeon's credentials with regard to women experiencing menstrual difficulties.

DEFENSE ATTORNEY CLARKSON: You have no doubt had considerable experience with reference to the diseases of women?

MR. McMURDO: I have had some—I am aware of disorders, more or less mischievous, arising out of irregularity of menstrual discharges—the interruption or temporary stoppage of the discharge sometimes affects the brain—I have not known of women becoming permanently mad from the state of disorder—I have known of their being so for a considerable time—I have read of permanent derangement of intellect arising from that cause in combination with others—the instance of temporary derangement arising from that are frequent.

JUDGE: Do you follow the question, that temporary insanity is a frequent consequence in that matter?

McMURDO: I must accompany my answer with an explanation. I should not term it insanity, but that the mind was not acting as it had before, that it was not sound during that time.

Mr. Clarkson's next question of McMurdo managed to incorporate the touchstone images of insanity, but using the phrase given by the prison surgeon: "Have you not known frequent instances of what is called unsoundness of mind, by which I mean, derangement of intellect, so that a person would temporarily, be incapable of responsibility, arising from that cause?" McMurdo responded:

McMURDO: No, I have not known frequent instances—I have read of some circumstances of the mind being deranged by the interruption of the secretion—I have known . . . hysterical fits [to] require bleeding—I have not known insanity, preceded by hysterical fits or convulsions, continuing for a period of years and increasing in these years. I should expect that a long continued attack of epileptic fits would affect the mind, but [not] hysterical fits . . . I should say when the patient was not affected by that interruption, that she would be in a perfect state of mind, although low and desponding . . . of course with continual attacks, the brain would become worse—as far as I can ascertain I think she is from three to four months gone in pregnancy—in some cases of stoppage of the periodical discharge there is a slight discharge, and in other cases it is entirely stopped—I have known instances where there has been none, and in those cases the health is generally exceeding interrupted, bodily as well as mentally—generally speaking, a sudden discharge after an arrest of that kind is the result of mental excitement or bodily fatigue—I do not practice as an accoucheur.

Prosecutor Bodkin: During the time your attention has been directed to the prisoner, has she been attacked by any hysteria or fit of any kind?

McMurdo: She has not, to my knowledge, nor have I observed any tendency to such an attack.

Bodkin: Supposing a person, after some interruption, to have had a resumption of the discharge [and] was pursuing their ordinary calling . . . down to nine o'clock of the evening . . . according to anything you have met with in practice, or read of, would you expect that in the course of the night following, at nine o'clock, a paroxysm would come on and deprive the party of her intellectual faculties?

McMurdo: I should not.

The judge at this point brought the examination of McMurdo to a close with a reminder to the jury that the prison surgeon might be speaking beyond his expertise.

Judge: Have you had experience in cases of insanity arising from irregularity in respect of that function?

McMurdo: I do not myself practice as an accoucheur, and am not likely to have these cases brought under my immediate notice—I am speaking from cases . . . under my notice attended to by others, and from books— I have had under my eye for short intervals cases of temporary derangement of the faculties of the mind, arising from irregularity in respect of that function—in those cases healthful action of the brain generally returns simultaneously with the healthful action of that function—I consider the one as the consequence of the return of the other.[6]

The defense attorneys could hardly have hoped for a more favorable resolution to the prosecution's side of the case. Through careful cross-examination, they had been able to document the prisoner's changed physical appearance on the night of the old woman's death, her history of violent fits associated with suppressed menstruation, and a "kindhearted" demeanor sufficiently gentle to earn the approbation of her intimates. Prison surgeon McMurdo, a practiced and familiar figure at the Old Bailey, had been obliged to acknowledge a limit to his expertise, reinforced by the judge himself.

Witnesses for the Defense

In many ways, character witnesses called by the defense attorneys continued the delicate strategy of presenting the prisoner as a "kind, humane person" who could nonetheless exhibit frightening, violent fits following episodes of suppressed menstruation. As an acquaintance testified, "I found her on the floor in the kitchen, quite insensible . . . she required two or three men to hold her, the fit was so violent—I found her in the fit between eleven and twelve, she was not perfectly sensible until four o'clock in the morning—she was sensible for a short time, but relapsed." To underline the esteem in which this witness held the prisoner, the defense attorney asked: "I believe you have come a very great distance at very great inconvenience," and was well rewarded with the response, "Yes: the prisoner bore a very good character for humanity and kindness of disposition, and her manner of expressing herself, even to the poor woman [Mrs. Stowell] was kind in the extreme—as far as I had an opportunity for judging, she was a kind and humane person."

Another character witness's description of the prisoner's sudden fit in which "she attempted to strike us" prompted an intriguing question by the judge:

JUDGE: Do you mean that the convulsive action nearly struck you, or that she had powers of mind about her, and intentionally struck you?
WITNESS: She was violent towards the parties round, struggling—in struggling she struck us.[7]

The judge's query focusing on intention went to the heart of attributing criminal responsibility: human agency. If it were possible to become dissociated from one's action—commonly referred to as "automatic" action—such fits would carry crucial importance in trials that turned on the question of precisely what it was the accused meant to do. Mary Ann Hunt had not been *confused* by this person's motivation in approaching her, nor had she been deluded about his designs. If it was in fact a convulsive action that did the striking, the person known as Mary Ann Hunt was not the perpetrator of the assault.

Completing the list of coworkers and fellow residents who could attest to Hunt's kindly demeanor and violent fits, the defense case closed with two medical witnesses of its own. Neither had visited the prisoner in gaol—indeed, neither had ever met her. They presented their own credentials to the court: a basis of familiarity with the prisoner's general case that McMurdo lacked.

William Verrall: I am a surgeon, practicing in Brighton—I attended the prisoner's brother at two different periods—his complaint was delirium on both occasions—I have never attended the prisoner professionally. I have attended many cases of suppressed menstruation—I am senior surgeon at the Lying-In Institution—that is an infirmary in which all the diseases of women are treated—fits of different character are frequently the consequence of suppression of the menses—I believe that a continuation of those fits for a number of years might contribute to a permanent injury to the brain—I have heard the whole of the evidence in this case— I should describe the fits from which the prisoner is said to have suffered as hysterical fits—a person would not have a fit without the brain being affected—I have known persons suffering from these fits arising from the same cause, who have lost their reasoning powers for short periods while under the influence of the fit, and for a short period of time afterward while the brain is recovering itself—I do not believe that a person would be able to distinguish what she was doing, or the circumstances surrounding her, during the fit—if there was such a predisposition [to insanity] in a family, any exciting cause would be likely to produce insanity.

The following question, if asked by one of the defense attorneys, would strike one as slightly leading in its implication. Used by the prosecution, the word innumerable sounds a bit sarcastic, and the response was doubtless unwelcome to the questioner:

Prosecutor Bodkin: I suppose in the course of your experience, your attention being particularly directed to the diseases of women, you have met with innumerable cases of women suffering more or less inconvenience from an obstruction of this kind?
Surgeon Verrall: I have—it is a complaint to which very many young women are subject—during those fainting fits the patient would be quite insensible, and incapable of any determinate [that is, planned or *intended*] action—persons are very violent in some cases of hysteria but equally incapable of determinate action.[8]

The prosecution's attempt to place the prisoner's act in a time frame that coincided with the restoration of regular menstrual activity was similarly unsuccessful, prompting the witness to declare that "the first discharge did not relieve the system, or nature would not have brought it on again so soon—I can give no opinion as to whether the attacks of hysteria or faintness would be indicative of greater intensity of the obstruction or the reverse." Hoping to rescue the witness from testimony that was fast becoming impenetrable, the defense attorney asked a final question that stressed the cumulative, not the transitory, nature of the impairment.

Defense Attorney Ballantyne: Supposing the prisoner to have been enduring fits of the kind described, arising from the obstruction of the menses for the last fourteen years, do you believe that that would have a material effect upon her constitution and upon her mind?

Verrall: I do—it would weaken the powers both of the body and mind, and that without reference to the particular attack.

The final medical witness to appear for the defense was a surgeon who had treated Mary Ann Hunt's brother for delirium tremens. Like the preceding witness, Surgeon Richard Rugg attested to the prisoner's vulnerability to insanity, given the taint of the family's predisposition. In describing Mary Ann's particular distraction, however, he gave an opinion that stretched beyond the medical characteristics of the ailment, engaging the ultimate legal issue at the heart of the prosecution.

Surgeon Rugg: I have heard the evidence that has been given in this case, with reference to the fits and the obstruction of the menses—there is no doubt that its continuation for a long time might affect the brain—and that affection of the brain might be exhibited by melancholy, or violent excitement. I have a person laboring under such an obstruction [that] she is obliged to be put under restraint—I should say during the period of that excitement, they would not be capable of knowing what they were doing, and *would not be answerable for it* [emphasis added]. [D]uring that violent paroxysm they have a greater hatred to their immediate friends than to other people. I have known females of a naturally kind and humane disposition who have exhibited symptoms of ferocity under such circumstances—it is a very common symptom.

Prosecutor Bodkin: If I understand you, assuming the brain has been so far acted upon to induce mania, those are the consequences.

Rugg: Not in all cases of course—I should think it very likely under excitement—these are the consequences that would very possibly follow.[9]

And this, stated Mr. Ballantyne, was the case for the prisoner.

It was not, however, the case for the prosecution. Breaking with all
tradition that would have relegated him to the role of a cross-examiner
in this phase of the trial, Prosecutor Bodkin announced his intention to
call a medical witness in rebuttal. Defense attorney Ballantyne objected,
arguing that the proper time for doing so had passed and that it was
"not now competent to them to give fresh evidence in contradiction of
the prisoner's case." The question of rebuttal witnesses would surface
again later in the century, with a judge ruling that the evidence "should
have been offered in the first instance, as the tendency of some portion
of the examination of the witnesses for the prosecution appeared to raise
the issue."[10] In the trial of Mary Ann Hunt, however, the judge ruled
that the evidence was admissible, giving the following reasoning: "[T]he
learned Judges (in answer to the questions submitted to them by the
House of Lords after the trial of M'Naughtan) expressly stating, that
after all the witnesses had been examined, and after all the facts had
been stated, persons of skill might be called upon to give their opinion
whether, assuming the facts disposed to be true, the accused was sane
or insane at the time."[11]

One could certainly share the defense attorney's surprise at such a
tendentious reading of the McNaughtan Rules. Clearly the judges appearing at the House of Lords were giving their assent to the use of
medical experts to comment on lay perceptions of derangement. They
would hardly have endorsed the calling of medical witnesses to set in
context the observations of other medical witnesses. Such an interpretation would produce interminable trials, as each side called witnesses
to refute the other side's experts, resulting in an endless spiral. The only
"new" evidence put before the jury by the defense attorneys was the testimony of the two surgeons. One wonders if Mr. Rugg's arrogating to
himself the capacity to aver that the women in such a state of excitement "would not be answerable" for their actions led to the unorthodox
interpretation of McNaughtan, one that would not be shared by other
members of the Victorian bench. The following prosecution medical
witness was called.

Alexander John Sutherland, M.D.: I have had considerable experience in diseases of the mind—I have lately turned my attention to that

exclusively—I was desired by the Solicitor of the Treasury to attend [this trial]—I have particularly attended to the evidence of the witnesses called on the part of the prisoner—assuming that all the facts spoken by the witnesses are literally true, they do not, in my judgment, indicate any unsoundness in the prisoner; not in any degree whatever, in my opinion.

DEFENSE ATTORNEY BALLANTYNE: You mean to infer that the prisoner has all those powers that nature gave her, in a perfect state?

SUTHERLAND: I mean she is not in a state either of insanity or unsoundness of mind—I believe it has not been affected in any way by disease. [In answer to a question regarding his lack of first-hand contact with the defendant] . . . of course it is hardly fair to say so, because I have not examined her in person—I can only form an opinion from what I have heard—I could still only give an opinion if I had examined the party, but it would of course be more satisfactory—I received directions from the Government at ten o'clock this morning to attend here—I am the son of a gentleman who has the management of a large lunatic asylum—I have known insanity produced by defective menstruation and by hysteria consequent upon it . . . I have known persons whose disposition has been naturally very mild and humane, to become almost ferocious under those attacks—they are sometimes incapable of judging between right and wrong; but those sort of cases are usually accompanied with delusion—the continuation of hysterical fits arising from imperfect menstruation for fourteen or fifteen years is not calculated to affect the brain—epileptic fits are—in epilepsy the patient bites the tongue, foams at the mouth, and goes to sleep immediately after the fit—in hysteria the brain is secondarily affected from the *uterus.*

PROSECUTOR BODKIN: [Apparently to defuse the issue of Sutherland's slight knowledge of the accused by offering him a chance to address it again] You have been asked whether, in order to form an opinion of the present state of mind of the prisoner, it would have been more satisfactory for you to have examined her personally; you say it would?

SUTHERLAND: Yes—I do not require any physical examination to form a judgment upon the facts which have been deposed to by the witnesses . . . according to the descriptions given by the witnesses, I believe the fits to which the prisoner has been subject to have been hysterical fits.

Asked specifically if "her brain is in any degree injured," Sutherland replied that it was not, having been acquainted with "innumerable instances in which [obstructed menstruation] had produced no such effect." Continuing in the fine Old Bailey tradition in which an attorney's adroitly crafted question could render the witness's answer almost superfluous, the prosecutor asked, "Have you ever known, or read, or heard of a case . . . in which a woman, apparently in the possession of her senses at about nine o'clock on one night, and apparently in her senses the following morning, between four and five o'clock, making preparations for a journey, had in the interval been seized with an attack which deprived her of her intellectual power and caused her to commit a violent crime?"[12] It only remained for the physician to deny ever knowing of such a case or having read of a case "exactly parallel to it," and for the judge to sum up the present case for the jury. He advised jurors to determine first if the prisoner was the person who had caused the death of the deceased, and if so was she in such a state of mind to render her accountable for her acts. At twenty minutes to midnight the jury retired.

A trial that lasted fourteen hours in court required only twenty-five minutes for deliberation. Finding the prisoner guilty of murder, jurors nonetheless strongly recommended mercy, not because of her physical frailty—which had been amply demonstrated by her fainting midway though the prosecution's case—but "on account of her previous good character." The judge was not moved. Placing the black cap of death upon his head, he stated that the prisoner's crime "was so dreadful that he could not hold out the slightest hope of a commutation" of the sentence of death. He then asked Mary Ann Hunt if she had "anything to say in execution of her sentence." In a faint voice she replied, "I believe I am in the family way."

Although condemned prisoners could take the opportunity to address the court with all sorts of pleas for mercy, "pleading the belly" was the one comment that automatically mandated further inquiry. For at least seven centuries, English women had served on exclusively female juries to determine if a prisoner was "quick with child or [with] a quick child."[13] Matrons only were called to such service, jurists reasoning that they alone were experts on matters of childbirth. The practical result of finding a condemned woman "quick with child" was a stay of execution, possibly leading to a pardon, once the outrage surrounding the initial verdict subsided. Given the possibility of this reprieve, it is not surprising that the Jury of Matrons could be plagued with corruption, erring, when it did, on the side of the prisoner. And given the harshness of the eighteenth- and nineteenth-century penal code, it is not surprising that such "biased" practice took its place next to other jury contrivances such as down-valuing the price of stolen goods or returning convictions of manslaughter rather than murder.

Mary Ann Hunt has the distinction of being one of the two last women whose plea of pregnancy was submitted to a Jury of Matrons and one of the unfortunate convicted women who were *not* deemed a fitting recipient of such a jury's "pious perjury."[14]After retiring to the prison with the defendant, the matrons returned to the court a half hour later. Like the all-male jury, the Jury of Matrons, it seemed, had a low tolerance for ambiguity. When asked whether the prisoner was quick with child the forewoman replied that Mary Ann Hunt was not.

JUDGE: You say that she is not quick with child—that she has not a living child within her?

FOREWOMAN: That is our verdict. We are all of that opinion.

JUDGE: Let the prisoner be removed. The law must take its course.

Women, Biology, and Crime

The singularity of Mary Ann Hunt's prosecution and conviction stretches beyond her treatment by the Jury of Matrons. In the years following the McNaughtan acquittal, Hunt was the only woman sentenced to death as a result of an unsuccessful defense based on mental absence. She was not, however, the only woman to enter an Old Bailey trial indicted for murder. In fact fatal assaults were fast becoming the most common crime committed by women proffering an insanity plea. In the years between 1843 and 1876, some fifty-six women pled a form of mental derangement at their trial, thirty-two of them in cases of murder. (Appendix table A.3 gives the distribution of indictments.) Another fourteen pleas emerged in cases of grievous assault. Property crime (stealing, forgery, publishing a libel) accounted for only 16 percent of the crimes committed by allegedly deranged females. While it may seem logical to associate personal assault with psychological impairment, the history of criminal insanity in England since the midpoint of the eighteenth century reveals a different association: two-thirds of insanity defenses—for both men and women—grew out of prosecutions for theft.[15] Although personal crime represented half of all insanity trials near the midpoint of the nineteenth century, as late as the 1830s it had constituted only a third of the cases. This relative distribution of property to personal crimes was also seen in "sane" criminality.[16] In the first half of the nineteenth century, 72.3 percent of all female offenders at the Old Bailey were prosecuted for some form of larceny. How then to account for the sudden predominance of personal crimes in the third quarter of the century?

The answer lies, one suspects, in the dramatic reduction in the number of crimes that carried capital sanction. Before Parliamentary activity in the 1820s, 1830s, and 1840s shortened the reach of the "Bloody Code," some two hundred or more offenses, most of them concerning property theft, were punishable by death. Indeed, death was mandated for the purloining of goods worth over thirty shillings. There was every reason to plead any sort of defense in such a dramatic circumstance: extreme poverty, dire family need, or quite simply "being out of one's wits." The modern insanity trial did not, therefore, evolve out of notorious cases of political assassination or even a surfeit of grisly, brutal murders. When eighteenth- and early-nineteenth-century jurors heard an insanity plea, it was most often in a case of stealing tankards from a pub, linen from a shop, or sovereigns from a pocket. And it was altogether likely that the fingerprints on the purloined sovereign belonged to a woman. Considering the severity of the sanction associated with these thefts, it comes as little wonder that women should be proportionately represented in the "property category" regarding insanity trials. It is also apparent from courtroom testimony in the eighteenth and early nineteenth centuries that women suffered from the same forms of mental distress as men: melancholia, delusion, and insensibility. All this was to change, curiously, with the abolition of death sentence statutes in the second quarter of the 1800s.

Of the initial two hundred or more capital statutes still on the books at the beginning of the seventeenth century, only fourteen remained in force after 1839.[17] The preponderance of property offenses had vanished, leaving only various types of arson (of Her Majesty's ships, of buildings of trade, of a building "any person being therein"), embezzlement, and destruction of religious buildings to carry a possible death sentence. Personal crimes were clearly in the majority in the list of revised capital crimes: buggery, rape, assault, property offenses that resulted in wounding, and of course murder. With shoplifting, pickpocketing, and domestic theft no longer carrying capital sanction, there was little reason to plead insanity because such a plea, if successful, avoided a death sentence only at the cost of indeterminate incarceration (in Bethlem Hospital before 1863 and Broadmoor thereafter). As fewer women indicted for theft pled mental derangement, the percentage of women raising insanity pleas in personal crimes grew proportionately. By the end of the third quarter of the nineteenth century, indictments for assault and murder prompted more than four of every five insanity pleas entered by female defendants. Of these personal crimes, infanticide predominated; even among the general category of assaults, the victim was almost sure to be a child.[18] The association of child murder with female defendants also ushered in a qualitative change in how women's psychology and its relation to women's unique biology was explained to juries.

Since at least the publication of Robert Burton's *The Anatomy of Melancholy* (1621), the secret to women's psychological frailty was sought in their peculiar constitution: "those vicious vapours which come from menstruous blood . . . troubling the brain, heart and mind."[19] Hysteria had in fact been linked to reproductive organs earlier in the century by Edward Jordan in *A Briefe Discourse of a Disease Called Suffocation of the Mother* (1603), which resurrected ancient theory that proffered derangement attendant to a wandering uterus.[20] In 1673, William Harvey lent considerable authority to the theory of the uterus's Grand Tour: "No one of the least experience can be ignorant what grievous symptoms arise when the uterus either rises up or falls down or is in any way put out of place, or is seized upon spasm."[21]

Of course men's derangement could also be linked to organic disturbance: blows to the head, brain fever, and war wounds. Only women, however, saw all their psychological functioning reduced to biological processes in general and reproduction in particular. In medical writings, women suffered not melancholy but *women's* melancholy. They did not fall prey to the "Elizabethan malady"—an affliction characterized by heightened sensibility and torpor brought on by too much civility and rich food; instead they suffered "feminine hysteria," brought on by repression of erotic desire. It was, in the end, female biology that predisposed women to insanity, particularly emotional instability owing to the ordeal of carrying a fetus and ultimately to the delivery itself.[22]

No one seems to have told the medical witnesses who appeared in insanity trials prior to McNaughtan, however, of the inevitable consequences of women's biology. Female defendants were in no way excluded from suffering (ordinary) melancholy, Byronic dejection, or the ravages of mordant wit. In fact, women's biology was not mentioned at all before the mid-nineteenth century with the exception of two cases of puerperal insanity, at which time the focus was on the strain of delivery rather than the hysteria generated by rampaging, if repressed, erotic desire. Medical testimony focused on the prisoner's mind—whether male or female—and the doubtful retention of reason. When medical witnesses invoked their professional experience, they usually prefaced their testimony with the expression "among my patients." One searches in vain for testimony beginning "among my *female* patients."[23]

The days of "equal employment" for women insanity defendants came rapidly to a close in the years following the abolition of capital statutes for property crimes women were likely to commit, such as shoplifting. Never deeply invested in sea piracy or commercial arson, it was the personal crime of murder—especially child murder—that constituted the majority of their criminal indictments ending in an insanity plea. Trials of child murder, even when no insanity was alleged, often broached questions of "knowing right from wrong" and criminal resolve, since the case was likely to feature pathetic, pitiable, unfortunate young women who killed their own infants when they were (literally) not themselves.

Just how pathetic they could appear is revealed in juries' decisions sometimes simply to acquit the defendant even when an insanity plea was not entered.[24] Juries reserved insanity acquittals for trials in which medical testimony framed the sudden killing of one's newly born infant or indeed young child as the regrettable effect of puerperal mania, a form of derangement familiar to the English courtroom since at least the sixteenth century. The sheer exhaustion and emotional upheaval of childbirth invoked by medical writers were apparently well accepted by jurors owing to folk beliefs that associated an unaccountable violent outburst with delivery and postnatal despondency.[25] Eighteenth- and nineteenth-century infanticide verdicts suggest lay willingness to consider such "unusual excitement through the nervous system," although acquittals were not automatic.

The specific reference to an "impulse to destroy the newborn child" was of most interest to the courtroom because the notion of a driving, internal force brought into question the defendant's capacity to choose: to act with criminal intent.[26] Given a victim so helpless and dearly loved, the inexplicable pairing of the assailant's murderous fury and overwhelming despair suggested that the delirium, hallucination, and depression associated with the physical effects of childbirth were also at work in child murder. Perhaps the ready acceptance of proffered impulses rooted in "inescapable biology" was also reinforced by the draconian punishments prescribed for a woman convicted of infanticide. An Act of 1624 [1623] mandated death for an unmarried woman who concealed the death of an infant if she failed to produce a witness to swear that the child was indeed stillborn. This punishment was altered in 1803, when a two-year penalty simply for concealing the child's birth was instituted.[27] Still, death remained as always a possible sanction for any child murderer, although these sentences all but disappeared in the nineteenth century.[28]

The willingness to accept the existence of extreme emotional stress was not limited to sympathetic jurors or expansively descriptive courtroom physicians. The Victorian era's most celebrated jurist, James Fitzjames Stephen, averred, "[W]omen in that condition do get the strongest sympathies of what amounts almost to temporary madness, and . . . often hardly know what they are about, and will do things which they have no settled or deliberate intention whatever of doing."[29] That a noted legal author and esteemed jurist should agree with medical witnesses and some juries, however, does not satisfy the historian's interest in puerperal insanity and other forms of derangement particular to women's reproduction: rather it invites further inquiry. Irregular menstruation, after all, did not "save" Mary Ann Hunt, although it must be acknowledged that she had committed what might be called gericide, not infanticide. Still, the uncharacteristic, inexplicable nature of violence committed by a normally "kind and humane creature," which would come to describe the women on trial for infanticide, was clearly in evidence. What was missing was a substantial effort to draw out the psychological consequences of suppressed menstruation. Beyond the rather tepid observation that "she would not have been aware of what she was doing," jurors were given little guidance to determine how the experience of irregular menstrual discharge produced either the impulse to crime or the inability to understand the nature of the offense these women were committing.

Although a review of the contemporary literature appears to reduce puerperal mania to a question of instinctual control and "blind impulse to destroy," medical testimony rarely accounted for women's impaired function at the level of impulse. Instead, the expert witness tried to link biological and behavioral phenomena associated with childbirth—delivery, nursing, pregnancy—and the properties of intellect essential to appreciate the legal significance of one's act. Thus unconsciousness, memory lapses, and delusion surface repeatedly in medical testimony. Functioning sometimes separately and sometimes together, they challenge the forensic assumption that the person is "continuous": that she remembers who she is, knows the difference between right and wrong, and is conscious of her acts.

Infanticide and "Inconsecutiveness"

I am eight years old, and live with my mother at 41, Flask Street, Hampstead—on a Wednesday, sometime ago, my mother came into the bedroom . . . took off my frock, and got a razor from the clock [?] and cut my arm across three times—it bled—she did not say anything—we had our dinner—we dine at 12 o'clock—she then did the same thing to my sister—I said, "Mother, are you sorry for what you have done?" She said "yes" and kissed us both, and said, "Now I am going to see Mr. Winter, and tell him"—he is a doctor . . . my mother has always been very kind indeed—she saw me in the hospital and I said, "Mother when I come home, you promise you will never do it again" and she said she did not think she had done it.[30]

The wounds young Sarah Harris suffered in this attack were not superficial. John Licette, House Surgeon at Middlesex Hospital, informed the court that one of Sarah's wounds had penetrated her arm bone, causing her to lose a good quantity of blood. "The principal wound was very near the principal artery running down the arm—if it had touched that, it would have been fatal without medical assistance and an amputation would have been rendered necessary." In hospital for a total of six weeks, the eight-year-old girl suffered wounds that would "permanently interfere with the muscles of her forearm." Mr. Winter, the surgeon immediately sought by the defendant, Susan Harris, informed the court of his six-year acquaintance with her.

MR. WINTER: I know that [the prisoner] had a miscarriage the Saturday before—I had seen her on the Wednesday and noticed irritability from the miscarriage, but I noticed nothing in particular about her mind . . . she was a very kind mother and very anxious—she was three months gone when she miscarried—sitting up so much with her [ailing] child would overtax her system very much—if she had symptoms of puerperal mania in her constitution, she would be more likely to give way after sitting up with a sick child night after night—I did not observe any symptoms of puerperal mania, but it sometimes comes on quite suddenly—it may affect people at a moment's notice, who have never been subject to it before—it makes them quite insane at a moment's notice, so as not to know what they are doing—it is a medical fact that the desire to kill may go off as suddenly as it comes on—a mother will sometimes attempt to destroy those nearest and dearest to her—the sight of the object itself is enough.

JUDGE: Do I understand you to say that a person is quite unconscious of what the act is?

WINTER: Yes, there was nothing the matter with the youngest child.

WILLIAM SMILES: I am surgeon of the House of Detention—the prisoner was admitted on remand, on this charge—she did not seem at all conscious of what she had done—she did not seem to know anything about it, and would not give any reason for it—I do not think she was capable of judging between right and wrong when she was admitted.[31]

Given the explicit mention of miscarriage, her habitual tenderness toward the child, and her daughter's opening observation that "she did not think she had done it," it would have been remarkable if Susan Harris had *not* been acquitted, yet there is no mention of mental derangement in the testimony—no delirium, no insensibility. The traditional language of insanity is employed to connect a failure to remember or to understand the nature of what was done, but it is the language of unconsciousness that one suspects was pivotal to the defendant's being found "not guilty being insane." In the case of puerperal mania, the court had an existing physical condition in which to house unconsciousness. For male defendants, grounding mental derangement in a standard organic condition was considerably more difficult.

There is a further element in the Harris trial that would characterize other attempts to link aberrant biological states with unconsciousness. Sometimes the explicit mention of conscious awareness was put in the form of a question from the bench, as seen above. Unlike Mr. Winter, however, not all witnesses were so eager to answer. Martha Brixley, who suffered "irregularities, or rather a suppression of constitutional functions," went to trial three years before Mary Ann Hunt for the murder of a neighbor's child. A local magistrate who happened to be visiting the unfortunate child's parents at the time of the crime was cross-examined by the defense attorney regarding the defendant's state of emotional distress. "Was her general manner and language that of a person who had become conscious of her act after it was done?" The magistrate answered, "That is a question I hardly dare answer."[32] Medical witnesses in infanticide trials were usually not so reticent. They spoke of a person variously "deprived of consciousness . . . like asleep," "not conscious" of having delivered the child, "perfectly unconscious" of what she was saying or doing. At times, the medical witness could elaborate on the use of the term, as in the trial of Martha Bacon for the murder of the neighbor's child. Described as "very ill after the birth of her son, at times under delusion [though] always manifest[ing] kindness and fondness for her children," the medical witness added his impression "that she was not conscious of the act having been committed, that is to say, to reflect upon the consequences. She appeared to be indifferent to everything."[33]

There was a particular form of "overridden" consciousness, however, that defense attorneys could employ when it was painfully clear that the accused knew exactly what she was doing. Hearing herself described as having "the peculiar look of puerperal mania," Adelaide Freeman faced an Old Bailey jury in 1869 for the murder of her daughter. The "vacant" defendant—whom neighbors described as "unconscious of her actions"—listened in court as surgeon Morrison explored the particular infirmity:

SURGEON MORRISON: [P]uerperal mania—a well recognized form of insanity with women about the period of their confinement—affects them where they are not able to give milk to a child, and [violence directed at "the nearest and dearest"] is the consequence of it—there is no fixed period at which it arrives at intensity—sometimes one, sometimes two weeks after confinement—there are two forms, the acute, wild raving and the other is the melancholy sort with which there are no delusions.

JUDGE: Tell us that again?

MORRISON: One is violent, with delusion, coming on usually within a day or two after confinement, and the other coming on after the fifteenth day, that is the melancholy, and is without delusions—they both lead to acts of violence—the second form is the melancholy type and is what the prisoner's symptoms indicated—the second form is a recognized form of insanity; there are no delusions, but it leads to acts of violence—I do not believe that persons who have that melancholy form have sufficient control over themselves to prevent them committing crime.

DEFENSE ATTORNEY: Are women in whose family there is a hereditary taint of insanity more likely than others to become affected in this terrible complaint?

MORRISON: They are—for the week before [the offense] the prisoner seemed wilder—she had a peculiar look, which is very difficult to give a definition of—it is not the look of a sane person—the appearance of her eyes was not so marked at the Police Court as I used to notice in her bedroom.

DEFENSE ATTORNEY: Is your opinion [reading from Dr. Taylor's work] that "In a person labouring under puerperal mania the killing of a child may be the result of an uncontrollable impulse seizing her at the time the act was done; but it may be done with a knowledge on the part of the mother that the act she is doing will cause death"? Knowing that the act of giving poison or cutting a child's throat would cause death, might she still be under the uncontrollable mania which would cause her to do it?

MORRISON: Yes.

JUDGE: You say that she would know the result of what she was doing?

MORRISON: Yes—sometimes persons have been known to kill other people that they should be hung themselves—[now, returning to author Taylor's argument], I believe that in this form of mania they would be conscious that they were doing wrong, but still not be able to prevent themselves from doing it.[34]

JUDGE: [of the next medical witness] Do you agree with Dr. Morrison, that she would know the probable result of what she was doing?

DR. HENRY LETHEBY: I think the depression, the melancholy, may be so great that, though she knew the result, still it would be an uncontrollable impulse—the mind may not be so disordered as to render the individual incapable of judging between right and wrong . . . yet the melancholy may be so great that she might commit the act—I think she would know that what she was doing was wrong, but carried to its greater extent [the depression] might prevent her knowing it was wrong.

PROSECUTOR GRIFFITHS: Would you accept a person suffering from puerperal mania could go to shop, converse rationally there, and buy poison?

LETHEBY: Yes.[35]

After prison surgeon John Gibson concurred with the opinions given by Mr. Morrison and Dr. Letheby, the defense attorney stated that he had witnesses "to prove the insanity of the prisoner's mother, grandmother, and great-grandmother." The jury, however, had had quite enough and expressed the unanimous opinion that "the prisoner was in such a mental condition as to be incapable of distinguishing right from wrong," thus acquitting her on the grounds of insanity. This seems a curious rationale, since the medical opinion had focused on uncontrollable behavior. The McNaughtan Rules may have mandated "knowing right from wrong" as the criterion for an insanity acquittal, but juries were free to employ a form of "volitional chaos" to arrive at their inference of cognitive impairment. In this case, the jury seemed to be linking the effects of puerperal mania to lay testimony describing the prisoner as "quite unconscious of what she was doing" and melancholy's ability to impair knowledge that the act was wrong.

Ultimately it is the failure of memory that surfaces prominently in a majority of these trials. Given the relatively few ways in which a defendant could deny involvement in a crime that so clearly points to her, it can hardly be surprising that persons accused of horrific deeds would claim to have had a "blackout." Women who killed their children, often in fits of puerperal mania, manifested a particularly heart-rending form of memory loss: searching frantically for the child they had killed. After slashing her son's throat with a razor, Mary Ann Payne threw herself from an upstairs window. She retained no recollection of having fallen out of the window and refused to believe her child was dead. "Where is Charley?" she asked beseechingly. As explained by the Newgate surgeon, "It is the fact that when women are pregnant, they are much more subject to depression . . . and they destroy the nearest and dearest to them." At Payne's trial, witnesses recounted the prisoner's "particular horror of razors" and her "fondness for her children." Someone, though, had wielded the razor and murdered her son; the prisoner's inability to place herself at the center of this attack was summed up by her continuing, pathetic lament, "Where is Charley?"[36]

"She had no memory," Esther Lack's sister-in-law testified, in defense of another mother who slashed her son's throat so violently that "his head was nearly separated from the body," and then killed her other children. When confronted with what she had done she said she did not know she had done it until she had kissed the baby. Afterwards she said, "I am sorry for it, but they had better be in heaven than knocking about the streets at the mercy of anybody." The fact that she later confessed to a policeman that she "knew" she had killed her children was put into context by a neighbor who stated that "she would often say strange things at times, and then forget entirely what she had said." Again, jurors heard of a "kind and affectionate mother." Again they heard of a ghastly attack accompanied by (caused by?) physical stress attendant to nursing.

DEFENSE ATTORNEY: Does not the fact of the cessation of giving the lacteal secretion to a child sometimes cause functional derangement?

EDWARD HIBBARD, MEMBER OF THE COLLEGE OF SURGEONS: Certainly it does, that functional derangement occasionally having a direct influence on the brain—the consequence is sometimes a mental derangement; as it would weaken the bodily constitution, so it would effect [*sic*] the nervous system.[37]

In each case of memory failure, the fatal or near-fatal assault on the child was described with reference to the mother's confinement before delivery, problems in nursing, or weakness following miscarriage. If medical men failed to clarify the precise connection between memory loss and physical strain, jurors were nonetheless confronted with mothers who either suddenly "came to" in the police station or gave the indelible impression that someone other than the "kind and affectionate" mother facing them had actually committed the unspeakable deed. In no crime in which memory loss was invoked did lay or medical witnesses raise the specter of an uncontrollable impulse. Like the earlier cases of suspended or lapsed consciousness, women with failed memories retained only a hypothetical relation to the perpetrators of the crime. They may have inhabited the same body, but the mother on trial was missing at the time of the killing.

A final mental element associated with puerperal mania—but not exclusive to it—was the ubiquitous forensic term delusion. That one could be possessed of a spirit or an impelling fear had long been a staple in medical and lay testimony at the Old Bailey. When puerperal mania or other elements of reproductive aberration combined with delusion, the prisoner was likely to suffer from "homicidal mania." Such testimony was not solely the preserve of alienists or surgeons at "lying-in" hospitals; prison surgeons could also supply the fateful connection. Testifying in 1856 at the trial of Sarah Price for the murder of her son, Peter, Newgate surgeon Gibson advised the jury: "I should say that she was not in a state to understand what she was doing—I am of the opinion that at the time this deed was done she was not in a state capable of distinguishing right from wrong—I should certainly consider that the absence of concealment of having done the deed was an indication of homicidal mania—[her condition revealed] many delusions concerning her state . . . that her milk had turned to water. I believe she had been suckling her child immediately before this [crime]; she had no milk then, nor any signs of any, but she thought her milk had turned to water . . . she told me there was a hole in the child's back into which she could place her fist, which I regarded as an impossibility and therefore as a delusion."[38] Believing she had no more milk to give, Sarah Payne strangled her young son, presumably to save him from a more protracted death of starvation. In the same year another mother came to trial, also suffering from homicidal mania, "under delusions" also "not conscious of what deed had been committed." She was afflicted with derangement soon after the delivery and, though normally manifesting kindness and fondness for her children, slit her daughter's throat.

Sometimes the suggestion that a delusion lay behind the crime was initially made at the prompting of an attorney. William Wood attended Emily Rider "in her confinement," seeing her again by chance several days before she killed her son.

WILLIAM WOOD: I found her in a very excited state, suffering from nervous fever—that would undoubtedly affect her mind.

DEFENSE ATTORNEY BALLANTYNE: You have not the least doubt that she committed this act under a delusion, and in a state of insanity?

PHYSICIAN WOOD: There is not the least doubt of it.

JUDGE: Would that be the ordinary course of the progress she had gone through, for her brain to be in so excited a state she would be entirely irresponsible for her acts?[39]

When the medical witness answered simply, "I should say decidedly so," the defense attorney could only have thought his presence in court superfluous.

Although it was not unheard of for medical witnesses to arrogate to themselves the right to address "ultimate issues" in their testimony—witness Mr. Rugg's contribution that a woman in Mary Ann Hunt's condition was not answerable for her acts—it is remarkable to read of the judge's authorizing Mr. Wood to do just that. Of course judges were never loath to comment on the direction a trial was taking, and to end a prosecution by directing the jury to bring in a particular verdict. For example, after a judge heard the following:

POLICE INSPECTOR SHILLINGFORD: I said "You have committed a very serious act," and she said, "I don't recollect anything at all about it. I did not
know anything till I saw [her daughter] with the blood on her nightdress,
and she said, 'You see what you have done' . . . I don't recollect anything
about it. I had a fall down stairs seven years ago, and often times since
that I have no recollection of what I do." After the remand she seemed
quite a different girl—she was well fed in the meantime and gave up the
suckling.[40]

he thereupon directed the jury to acquit the prisoner, stating that "it was
quite obvious she did not know what she was about." Whether due to
the fall or the termination of nursing, Sarah Child impressed the judge
as so pitiable that no culpability could attend her actions.

Afflicted with a range of physiological and emotional infirmities
owing to reproductive chaos, women described as "perfectly unconscious" or "lost in memory" presented the court with a variation in insanity unfamiliar to the Old Bailey. It was not just that there was no
logical reason for the crime—the common law had met that particular
form of "indifferent criminality" in the shape of moral insanity—it was
rather the frightening display of inexplicable violence visited on the person most cherished by the prisoners. The conventional medical explanation in print was to focus on uncontrollable impulse and weakened
will. But why, in pre-Freudian times, should one expect a murderous
impulse to be directed at the person most loved?[41] Why should exhaustion not lead to suicide, or to killing one's spouse? Although suicide and spouse killing were sometimes coupled with an attack on a
child, they were rare compared with the grisly assaults upon one's children alone. In any case, it was not impulse and weakened will that
served as the fulcrum for the testimony about puerperal mania but
rather haunting delusions, memory blackouts, and suspended consciousness. Taken separately and occasionally together, they presented
the jury with a prisoner whose relation to the actual perpetrator was
more apparent than real. Neither propelled into child murder by an uncontrollable impulse nor relinquishing their will to the force of an abstract passion, these women were aghast at their actions, regaining consciousness—and memory—as one mother put it, only upon kissing her
dead child's lips. In addition to asking "Where is Charley?" mothers
were likely to ask, "Who did this?"

Although puerperal mania was by far the most frequently invoked

medical condition, and women's obstructions the most common lay designation, a few trials for infanticide and child assault mentioned possible reasons for mental derangement that had nothing to do with gender, such as brain fever, nonspecific fits, stuporous states, delusion, and
melancholy, producing "lack of consciousness," "automatic behavior,"
and "like a person asleep" as the frequent resulting states. In the same
year as McNaughtan's trial, Sarah Dickenson slashed the throats of two
of her children, telling the police constable, "It is I that have done this
horrid deed." Her seeming awareness of the crime was immediately
questioned, however, by surgeon Joseph Arthur who had been called to
the crime scene, finding the two children and also the prisoner who had
endeavored to cut her own throat. As he advised the court:

> I cannot form a judgment as to whether she was in a state to be answer-
> able for anything she said at the time—when I arrived she was not in a
> state to give answers to questions, or to place any reliance on her re-
> marks—I do not think I would be right to attach any great weight to her
> answers—I have had enough experience to distinguish between real and
> imagined absence of mind—what I observed was absence or prostration
> of mind.

A second medical witness, William James, M.D., was asked whether as
a result of his treatment of the prisoner, he had concluded that at the
time she did the act, she was of sound or unsound mind. "Most decidedly of unsound mind," he replied.

Prosecutor Doane: What was the disease of the brain you found her recovering from?
Dr. James: Probably inflammation of the brain—the vessels of the brain
were surcharged with blood—it was determination of blood to the head:
my belief was that she had laboured under that disease, but that it was
subsiding—she described herself as all persons do who recover from insanity, as having passed a dream—insanity exhibits itself in a variety of
forms; sometimes in constitutional imbecility; sometimes from local
causes; sometimes from disorganization of the brain—and very frequently
from the press of blood on the brain—[referring now to the sensibility
she revealed soon after slashing her own throat]—a person laboring under
insanity arising from pressure on the brain, would be relieved extensively
and speedily by liberal blood letting—a person cutting her own throat
would be very much relieved—I have very frequently met with cases of

that sort . . . [then adding a gratuitous nod to the "ultimate issue"] I do not believe that at the time the prisoner did this act she was an accountable being, decidedly not.[42]

Although Dr. James was not the only medical witness to take it upon himself to pass on the quintessential concern of "accountability" or "responsibility," he was the only forensic medical witness to proffer such a state in a trial in which neither puerperal mania nor reproductive ills were alleged. "Irresponsible for her acts," "scarcely accountable," "not responsible" were phrases that came easier to alienists and surgeons "familiar with the diseases of women." Perhaps these specialist witnesses believed their pronouncements would resonate intuitively with the court and the jury for whom puerperal mania was hardly an esoteric, clinical discovery whose features had to be explained.

Perhaps, also, medical witnesses believed they had found a receptive public given the success of the plea of mental derangement in cases of child murder and grievous assault. In nine out of ten such cases, jurors voted either to acquit or to find the person unfit to plead. The sentences of convicted defendants ranged from six weeks to eighteen months imprisonment for assault, and two years in prison for a woman tried for murder but found guilty of "concealing birth." The generosity of spirit revealed in these acquittals incensed a host of contemporary social critics for whom infanticide symbolized "the foul current of life, running like a pestilential sewer beneath the smooth surface of society."[43]

Medical witnesses were particularly singled out for failing to "further the ends of justice by a conscientious interpretation of the facts submitted to them . . . [and not to] assist in the escape of the criminal."[44] This charge was leveled at the general practitioner who was growing noticeably doubtful that traditional "facts" about infant death should continue to inform his testimony. If his brethren specializing in mental medicine were becoming increasingly suspicious of a prisoner's police-station confession and apparent retention of consciousness at the moment of the crime, his reluctance to "assist" the court in punishing the prisoner was not hard to explain. He had at his fingertips a "mother-specific malady for a mother-specific crime"; such an elective affinity could hardly be kept out of courtroom testimony. But again, medical witnesses did not describe this malady in terms of an uncontrollable impulse or a defective will. They testified instead at the level of doubtful human agency, revealed in complete and utter memory lapses. A mother who killed could hardly believe her child was dead. How the bloodstains ended up on her clothes she was incapable of remembering, let alone understanding.

A final word for Mary Ann Hunt, whose victim and sentence were atypical but whose "obstructed" menstruation was not. The verdict of the Jury of Matrons did not end her case, but rather served as a cause célèbre for medical men who railed at the enduring use of untrained matrons. Fifteen years earlier, a similar verdict of "not pregnant" had to be set aside when the prisoner gave birth to a healthy baby four months later. Editors of the *London Medical Gazette* fumed, "We have yet to learn that the matrons of the Old Bailey are more skilled in the question of pregnancy and quickening than their co-juresses [in the earlier case] who, by a signal blunder, nearly consigned a living child to the untimely fate of its mother."[45] Whether the conscience of the editors had been stirred by the assault on their notions of justice or their professional pride—since the enduring use of this practice "would lead us to suppose that the art of midwifery had not advanced a single step since the reign of Edward"—it is difficult to say. One can easily say, however, that in the Hunt case, the Jury of Matrons verdict stimulated an active letter-writing campaign, including correspondence between a Deptford surgeon named Drury to the Home Secretary:

> Sir,
>
> Having carefully read the evidence as reported in the above case, tried at the last session of the central criminal court, I cannot allow the opportunity to pass without expressing my conviction, founded upon 30 years of experience, that the said Mary Ann Hunt must have been insane at the time of committing the awful act.
>
> It is well known to medical men that fits derange the proper functions of the brain. It is also well known to them that some women are mentally afflicted in the first stages of pregnancy. (This may not have been insanity's first appearance, [that her] brother was insane strengthens my position.)
>
> I have obtained the signature of medical acquaintances in support of this statement, and we earnestly beseech you to institute such further inquiry into the case as may appear to you necessary.[46]

On the back of this letter, a physician to the Royal Kent Dispensary had written, "as to her pathological state, I am of opinion that her case merits further investigation."

The next and last note in Hunt's file is a communication from the penal colony in New South Wales:

Arrival at Colony—	25/7/1850
Trial Date	28/2/1848
Original Sentence	Life (later commuted to 1–2 year's imprisonment, transportation for life)
Offense	Murder[47]

FOUR

THE PRINCESS AND THE CHERRY JUICE

✤

*B*RUTAL KILLING IN A LUNATIC ASYLUM—witnessed by a delusional patient who later offers courtroom testimony, accompanied by his ever-interrupting spirits—seems worthy of a script by Edgar Allan Poe, yet the manslaughter trial of Samuel Hill was anything but fiction. "I have 20,000 spirits," Richard Donelly informed the jury at the Old Bailey: "they are not all my own, I don't know whose they are—but I will inquire." As it happened, the other spirits came from the Queen, who was in the habit of making nightly visits to the asylum, and from Luther, Calvin, and "other controversial spirits" who also stopped by. These "creatures," Donelly told the court, continued to speak to him even as he was testifying. The inescapable question that surrounded his testimony seems to be, why was the court listening?

Richard Donelly was the key witness to the beating to death of a fellow asylum inmate, Moses Barnes. Along with several other lunatics, the two men were confined to the infirmary of Dr. Armstrong's private madhouse at Peckham. The men were supervised by keeper Samuel Hill, who slept in an adjoining room. Sometime before Christmas Eve 1850, Barnes had been thrown to the floor and struck repeatedly, the assailant fracturing five of his ribs and breaking his arm. As it was Hill's responsibility to dress the patients and to report any medical problems to the attending asylum physicians, his silence over the four days between the beating and the medical report meant that suspicion fell squarely on him. At the inquisition following the patient's death, the coroner refused to admit the testimony of the asylum patients, however. There was sound basis for the exclusion: English common law classed lunatics among persons whose testimony could not be received at court, owing either to a perceived lack of competence due to youth or derangement, or to lack of credibility because of a conflict of interest or deficient moral character."[1] The coroner's inquest resulted in a finding of "manslaughter against some person or persons to them unknown." Commenting on the coroner's exclusion of the inmate's testimony, contemporary medical writers averred that "no keeper could be held responsible for any act, no matter how brutal a nature, provided that act had been inflicted on a lunatic, and none but the lunatics were present when [it was] perpetrated."[2]

Whether because of the categorical nature of his preemptive exclusion of any and all testimony by asylum patients or of some feature particular to this asylum keeper, the coroner's finding did not rest well with the Commissioners in Lunacy, who enlisted the experienced Old Bailey prosecutor Bodkin to represent their interests.[3] Keeper Hill was eventually charged at Lambeth Police Court for the death of Moses Barnes. At the hearing, Bodkin asserted that the coroner's reading of the law excluding the testimony of lunatics was in error, and that "it would be his duty now to place in the witness box one of these poor men." Just which of the poor men he could select however, was a considerable challenge. The immediate witnesses to the event were three delusional patients who shared the responsibility for washing and dressing the similarly delusional deceased, Moses Barnes. Of the three, one was completely noncommunicative, one was of such weak mind that nothing coherent was likely to emerge from courtroom examination, and one was in constant communication with pesky, intrusive spirits. Richard Donelly's creatures, however, were of an unusual sort: they did not take over his being and crowd out all other facets of his psyche. They constituted instead a resident self that argued with him but did not force him out. Although it is always a hazardous undertaking to use a contemporary term for a historical phenomenon, the recently coined term *lucid possession* seems particularly apt for this nineteenth-century courtroom display.[4]

Prosecutor Bodkin intended to enlist Donelly's lucid qualities to bring Hill to trial, but he would first have to persuade the magistrate sitting at Lambeth police station that the keeper had been the assailant. According to the editor of the *London Medical Gazette*, "When [this] red-faced funny little Irishman mounted the witness-box . . . never, perhaps, did a witness give evidence with greater clearness and care than he did. 'The prisoner behaved a little more harshly than usual, and took hold of Barnes with both his hands by the upper part of the arms and threw him down suddenly on the ground. The fall was a hard one and a few minutes after the prisoner was gone Barnes called me to look at his shoulder, and he complained of being hurt. I felt the collar-bone and found that [it] was not broken. [The following day] the prisoner lifted up the arm and it slid down, as if powerless. . . . I observed [it] was swollen.'"[5] Under cross-examination, Donelly insisted that the keeper dressed Barnes daily, so there could be no way he would not have known of the injury or fail to hear the patient complain of pains in his chest. Donelly was not asked about the spirits, however, which also claimed to have witnessed the attack and were encouraging him to change his story in favor of the keeper's version. Had the opinionated spirits been asked any direct questions, it is doubtful that the magistrate would have commented that "he had never heard evidence given . . . with greater truth." Following the hearing, the keeper was committed to take his trial for manslaughter at the Old Bailey.

The continuing interest taken by the Commissioners in Lunacy was evident to all. Appearing on their behalf was a barrister, a solicitor, a lunacy commissioner, and a clerk to the Clerkenwell board of guardians, to whose union the deceased patient belonged. Opening the trial for the prosecution, Mr. Clarkson advised the court that the undisputed seriousness of the charge itself "was aggravated by the fact" that the victim had been placed in the prisoner's charge, to be cared for "with the utmost kindness and attention."[6] It was this consideration that elevated the trial to the "very greatest public importance," prompting the Commissioners in Lunacy to take an active role in prosecuting Hill. Clarkson also advised the jury that he would be compelled to call as a witness a patient who had been present at the time of the beating and who "under the sanction of his lordships, [he would] offer as a competent witness upon the present occasion."

Before calling Donelly to the stand, however, the prosecution enlisted the asylum's medical superintendent, Joseph Stuart Burton, to construct a particular view of the spirit world of the only witness capable of convicting the keeper. Burton had been at Armstrong's asylum for only two years before the fatal assault occurred. On 27 December, keeper Hill had informed him of the injury and, after examining Barnes, told Burton, "This must have been done some days ago." Hill reported that the victim had indeed complained of soreness, but as Barnes suffered from the delusion that he had bands inside his stomach, he had treated the newly supposed ills as nothing remarkable. Exactly how to receive the victim's account of the injury was problematic, as the medical witness advised the court, "Barnes was capable of giving a correct answer to a question, but his memory was affected: not a good deal— he was a lunatic in the ordinary sense of the term."[7]

Donelly, however, appeared to Dr. Burton as a credible potential witness. Although "never . . . free from that delusion . . . I believe Donelly to be quite capable of giving an account of any transaction that happened before his eyes." Of course, the Queen's visits—and Calvin and Luther's too—had also happened before his eyes, but this did not seem to diminish Donelly's worth as a believable witness. As superintendent Burton concluded, "[I]t is solely with reference to the delusion about the spirits that I attribute to him being a lunatic—when I have had a conversation with him on ordinary subjects I have found him perfectly rational, but for his delusion—I have seen nothing in his conduct or demeanor in answering questions otherwise than the demeanor of a sane man."[8] Although the defense attorney would soon have the opportunity to challenge this characterization of rationality, it bears noting that the prevailing legal opinion regarding lunacy and delusion had concluded that these two terms were practically "convertible."[9] Donelly had been committed to the madhouse *because* of his delusion, not because he was rational on all other subjects. To declare an asylum patient "perfectly rational but for his delusions" was tantamount to declaring a hospital patient perfectly healthy, but for his tuberculosis.

Dr. James Hill followed Burton to the witness box, and it was clear from his examination that the faculty most at issue was not Donelly's conversational prowess, but his memory. After referring to his nine years of professional experience with the insane, Dr. Hill was asked by the defense attorney: "[I]f a man is insane, is his memory necessarily affected?" The witness responded,

> Not always, not necessarily—it frequently is, but frequently is not—I have seen Dr. Haslar's [most likely John Haslam] work—I do not agree in all cases with his remark that "memory appears to be perfectly defective in cases of insanity"—certainly not . . . in certain cases of acute madness, the ideas in the mind of a madman succeed each other more rapidly than in the mind of a sane man, and in a more confused manner—it is quite possible for a man to entertain a delusion on one subject without its affect-

ing the mind generally on other subjects—in most cases where a delusion prevails and the man is mad, the rest of the mind is affected to some extent—I agree with Dr. Pritchard [Prichard] in his observation that, "In monomania the mind is unsound, but unsound in one part only"—there is no doubt, however, that all the mental faculties are more or less affected, but the affectation is more strongly manifested in some than others."[10]

Dr. Hill had been addressing the delusive imagination of both Barnes, the victim, and Donelly, the witness. Although Dr. Hill stated unequivocally that the victim had named the defendant as his assailant, the physician also advised the jury that Barnes's own "memory was impaired." Hoping to salvage the significance of the victim's declaration, the prosecutor asked Dr. Hill, "Speaking as a man of experience in these unhappy delusions, can you, in your judgment, trace any connection between the statements made by the deceased and the delusion under which he was labouring?" The doctor answered unequivocally: "None whatever."

Before concluding, Dr. Hill offered the jury a picture of the delusional person as only too aware of the inconvenient Other residing in his mind. Part of the reason it was difficult to examine the extent of delusions was the inmates' frequent "success in concealing their delusions from the medical man, particularly when they become aware that their delusions were the grounds of their detention." A "great deal of dissimulation could be effected" as patients endeavored to hide their delusional thoughts to gain release. It is common for a certain class of madman to exhibit a great deal of cunning, Dr. Hill continued, when they conceal their delusions "there has been an apparent and evident motive." No such motive for prevarication was suggested for Donelly; no dissimulation was even hinted at. Instead, the physician left the jury with the image of a trustworthy if distracted man. "I have always found Donelly perfectly rational, except in the subject of his particular delusion."[11]

With the medical testimony concluded, prosecutor Bodkin announced his intention to call Richard Donelly, the "lunatic patient" as a witness. Mr. Collier, attorney for the keeper, objected, asserting, "Enough appeared upon [your] lordship's notes to make it quite clear that he was not an admissible witness, as being a lunatic." Collier was referring here to various digests and legal commentary, but not to a specific case outcome; the judge immediately commented, "Unless the learned counsel could cite any case in which it was ruled that a lunatic of the character of this person was not a competent witness, the court should receive his testimony, and reserve the point for future consideration, if such a course should become necessary." The judge contended that the question had never in fact been decided in criminal court. Forced to acknowledge his inability to name any such case, the defense attorney adamantly asserted, "[I]t was contrary to every principle of English Law that a lunatic should be permitted to give evidence."[12] The judge answered that he would permit Donelly to be examined "upon the voir dire" with particular regard to the witness's understanding of what it meant to swear an oath.

DONELLY: I am fully aware that I have a spirit, and twenty thousand of them; they are not all mine; I must inquire—I can where I am; I know which are mine. Those ascend from my stomach to my head, and also those in my ears. . . . The flesh creates spirits by the palpitation of the nerves and the 'rheumatics'; all are now in my body and round my head, they speak to me incessantly—particularly at night.[13]

DEFENSE ATTORNEY COLLIER: Where do you expect your spirit will go when you are dead?

DONELLY: I cannot say; perhaps to heaven, or perhaps to purgatory.

JUDGE: Do you believe in purgatory?[14]

DONELLY: I do. I am a Roman-Catholic, and I have been brought up in the fear of purgatory from my infancy. [Then, being prompted to expand on this by prosecutor Bodkin], I know what it is to take an oath: my Catechism taught me from my infancy what it is lawful to swear; it is when God's honor, our own or one's neighbour's good, require it. My ability evades while I am speaking, for the spirit ascends to my head.[15]

PROSECUTOR BODKIN [realizing that Donelly is about to veer off course]: Do you appeal to anybody when you take an oath?

DONELLY: Certainly, I appeal to the Almighty, I believe that if a man takes a false oath he will go to hell for all eternity.[16]

At this point, defense attorney Collier tried to reexamine Donelly— one suspects, in the hope of returning to the subject of royal and religious spirits incessantly chatting to the witness—but the prosecutor objected, stating that the defense counsel was only interested in exciting the witness, not inquiring into the one salient issue: Donelly's understanding of the peril he assumed by lying under oath. Collier protested that all of his questioning had indeed sought to probe the witness's ability to understand a sacred oath. At this point, the judge stepped in and ruled that Donelly could indeed testify in the case of *Regina v. Samuel Hill.*[17]

DONELLY: I have been confined in Mr. Armstrong's infirmary four years and nearly four months this day week; I came backwards and forwards. I came out of it at my own pleasure when I thought myself fit for it. . . . I remember a little while before Christmas-day I had complained to the prisoner [that Barnes would not go to bed: the keeper] came to him and *catched* him, with the intention of putting him to bed, and threw him down rashly on the boarded floor, and they both fell down together— Barnes was hurt by the fall. . . . I did not pay much attention [to Barnes]— he was always complaining. . . . I recollect Attwood, another assistant-patient . . . Attwood was often irritated with [Barnes]—Attwood was a man of irritable temper, very easily vexed. . . . [Barnes] was particularly irritable with Attwood—I have known Attwood to be violent even with me—I have known him violent towards Barnes twice . . .

JUDGE: Can you say whether the fall was on Monday, Tuesday, or Wednesday or when it was that this business happened?

DONELLY: I am still in doubt whether it was Monday or Tuesday, but the creatures insist it was Tuesday night; and I think it was Monday—I am positive the prisoner dressed Barnes on the night after this took place, and on Christmas-day—I am sure it was not Attwood.

PROSECUTOR BODKIN [Trying to dispel the notion that the victim's wounds might have been inflicted by someone other than the prisoner]: Twice you say you saw Attwood push Barnes; on these occasions did he appear to hurt him at all?

DONELLY: There was no harm occurred from the [impression], but it threw him down—I do not know whether it did him bodily harm, but if he did it to me I would resent it and complain to the doctor about it.

JUDGE: Is what you told us what the spirits told you, or what you recollect without the spirits?

DONELLY: No, the spirits assist me in speaking of the date, I thought it was Monday, and they told me it was Christmas Eve, Tuesday, but I was an eyewitness, an ocular witness, to the fall on the ground.[18]

And this, as Bodkin addressed the court, was the case for the prosecution.

Electing to call no witnesses—or, indeed, to present any testimony in rebuttal at all—defense attorney Collier asked the jury to consider that the only evidence linking his client to the violent assault was given by Donelly, and to bear in mind the "danger that would result from convicting a person of so serious a charge as this, or indeed on any charge whatever, on the testimony of a person who was admitted to be a lunatic." The prosecution had argued "ingeniously" that Donelly was "perfectly rational" on every subject save that of his particular delusion, but how safe was it to rely upon the witness's mind, which had already been admitted as diseased? How far did Donelly's delusion extend; where in fact did sanity end and insanity begin? For all the display of apparent rationality, who was to say that the entire testimony had not been the work of his delusion?[19]

Collier was careful not to question the appropriateness of a criminal inquiry into the death of Barnes; nothing less could be expected of the Commissioners in Lunacy in these circumstances. Still, he argued that there was a variety of unexamined threads in the case. Consider the extent of the victim's injuries. Could one not easily imagine the violent, desperate struggles that ensued "between a number of madmen left together during the night without an attendant"? Was it likely that these horrific injuries should be "wantonly inflicted by the prisoner, who had always borne the character of a kind, humane man"? Although the jurors eventually voted to convict, this last argument had apparently fallen on receptive ears, for they recommended mercy for the prisoner "on account of his previous good character."

Had the jury voted to acquit, it is doubtful that the trial of a madhouse keeper, indicted for the manslaughter of a patient in his charge, would have occasioned much contemporary interest. Clearly, it was the admission of testimony by an adjudged lunatic and the subsequent conviction of the prisoner on the basis of such evidence that had caught the attention of both legal and medical practitioners. Indeed, one is able to reconstruct so much of this case because medical journals and legal commentary took particular interest in both the trial and the next stage of legal proceedings. As the judge informed the defense attorney when he took the unusual step of admitting the delusional Donelly to the witness box, the court would "reserve the point for further consideration, if such a course should become necessary." Immediately upon hearing the jury's recommendation for mercy, Mr. Justice Coleridge informed the court that sentencing would be postponed in order that the opinion of the judges of the Court of Crown Cases Reserved be delivered regarding the admissibility of the evidence of the witness Donelly.

Four months after the Old Bailey verdict, the matter of the lunatic witness was argued before the Court's five judges: Lord Campbell, Mr. Baron Alderson, Mr. Justice Coleridge, Mr. Baron Platt, and Mr. Justice Talford. Appearing for the crown were the original prosecuting attorneys, Clarkson and Bodkin, joined by Sir F. Thisiger. Mr. Collier was again appearing for the prisoner. His exposition of the issues laid before the trial court earned compliments for "the ability and learning he displayed."[20] The hearing began with the judge in the original trial, Mr. Justice Coleridge, laying out the salient events of trial testimony for his brethren. Paying particular attention to Dr. Hill's dispute with John Haslam's contention that the memory of a madman was necessarily impaired, he then affirmed James Cowles Prichard's notion that delusion consisted of a circumscribed belief, noting the difficulty of ascertaining, "without strict inquiry" the extent of a madman's delusions. He concluded his summary of the medical testimony by pointing out the circumscribed nature of the derangement. On all other subjects, the delusional are "perfectly rational." Donelly's testimony was also reviewed in minute detail, including his witness-box statement: "They speak to me incessantly—*they are speaking to me now.*" Coleridge next offered the court ample evidence of Donelly's professed understanding of the solemn character of giving one's word: "When I swear, I appeal to the Almighty—it is perjury, the breaking of a lawful oath . . . he that does it will go to hell for all eternity." Having satisfied himself that Donelly understood the proceedings, the judge had sworn the witness, who, in his opinion, "gave a perfectly correct and rational account of a transaction which he reported himself to have witnessed." Turning to the Crown Court judges, Mr. Justice Coleridge concluded that "the question for the Court is, whether this witness was competent."[21]

Defense attorney Collier began his argument by reminding the judges that Donelly, both at the time of the alleged assault and at the time he appeared at the Old Bailey, was *non compos mentis,* "in the legal, medical and ordinary sense of the term." The only reason he had been present at the scene of the supposed crime was that he had been committed to the asylum upon the examination and recommendation of two medical men who signed certificates attesting to his manifest lunacy. Had he been restored to reason, he would have been discharged. Even the prosecution's own medical witness declared him to be "in the strict sense of the term, a lunatic," captive to a delusion from which he was never free. Collier then invoked the authority of prominent medical author Francis Willis, who had described the essential characteristic of insanity to be "a confirmed belief in an assumed idea, upon which the patient is always acting . . . to the truth of which he would pertinaciously adhere, in opposition to the plainest evidence of its falsity."

Collier really did not require Willis's authority to convert Donelly's delusional spirits into the sine qua non of insanity's diagnostic symptoms. By the time Samuel Hill first heard the jury find him guilty of manslaughter, delusion had surfaced as the most frequently invoked forensic term employed by medical witnesses appearing in court to support an insanity plea. From the trial of James Hadfield (1800) to the trial of Hugh Pollard Willoughby (1854), medical witnesses returned time and again to the notion of a confined, sealed, often recondite well of mental distraction capable of impelling the unsuspecting sufferer into a brutal attack.[22]

Collier had difficulty employing the Willis quote—and relying on what was by then an established association of delusion with the insanity plea—because Donelly's delusion had produced no brutal attack. Donelly was not, after all, the defendant, although he was very much on trial. The defense attorney needed to reinforce the pathological nature of Donelly's nonviolent delusions by invoking the sort of legal authority that eluded him when Mr. Justice Coleridge asked at the outset of the trial for the name of a case that had specifically excluded consideration of the testimony of a lunatic. For the present purposes, Collier had such a case: *Dew v. Clark and Clark*. This celebrated 1826 decision, rendered by Sir John Nicholl, concerned the legal status of a will left by a father who had "conceived an irrational antipathy to his daughter, his only child, in her earliest infancy." Asking what were the "true criteria of insanity . . . where is it that mere eccentricity or extravagance ends and that this begins," Sir John Nicholl set down a standard that found its way into future legal arguments, among these Collier's in 1851: "The true criterion, the true test, of the absence or presence of insanity I take to be the absence or presence of what, used in a certain sense of it, is comprisable in a single term—namely, delusion. Wherever the patient once conceives something extravagant to exist which has still no existence whatever but in his own heated imagination; and wherever, at the same time having once so conceived, he is incapable of being, or at least of being permanently, reasoned out of that conception; such a person is said to be under a delusion . . . and the absence or presence of delusion, so understood, forms, in my judgment, the true and only test, or criterion, of absent or present insanity. In short, I look upon delusion, in this sense of it, and insanity to be almost, if not altogether, convertible terms."[23] In grounding his own opinion in medical authority, Nicholl expressly cited the writings of the eponymously named mad-doctor, John Battie, and the already mentioned Francis Willis.

Dr. Battie had played a central role in an oft-cited trial that had elevated delusion's importance to civil jurisprudence, a trial that Nicholl also considered germane to his own appraisal. A man named John Wood had sued noted Bethlem Medical Superintendent John Monro for Wood's allegedly false (i.e., unwarranted) imprisonment as a lunatic in a mad house at Hoxton. As recounted by the presiding judge, Lord Mansfield, Wood "underwent the most severe examination by the defendant's counsel without exposing his [delusion]." Indeed, Wood was a most impressive, by all appearances rational plaintiff, and Monro's prospects looked decidedly bleak until Dr. Battie approached the bench and suggested that Mansfield "ask [Wood] what was become of the *Princess* whom he had corresponded with in cherry juice." The cool, collected plaintiff responded that "there [is] nothing at all in that, because having been (as everybody knew) imprisoned in a high tower, and being debarred the use of ink, [he] had no other means of correspondence but by writing [his] letters in cherry-juice, and throwing them into the river which surrounded the tower, where the princess received them in a boat." Mansfield immediately released Dr. Monro, but, as the plaintiff had been carried through the city on the way to the madhouse, Wood brought a second suit for false imprisonment against the keeper in London. In words that would resonate with Dr. Burton's characterization of delusional lunatics in the trial featuring Donelly, "such is the extraordinary subtlety and cunning of madmen [Mansfield wrote] that when he was cross-examined on the trial in London . . . all the ingenuity of the bar and all the authority of the court could not make him say one syllable upon that topic which had put an end to the indictment before . . . but conscious that the delusion had occasioned his defeat at Westminster, he obstinately persisted in holding it back."[24]

The capacity to navigate self-consciously around delusional shoals and to present every appearance of rationality would have both medical and legal implications for the testimony of Richard Donelly. Medical witnesses who commented on the lunatic's capacity to dissimulate—to conceal his or her delusion—attested to the patients' acute awareness that somewhere in their functioning there existed some alien belief or entity that was capable of delaying their release. In Donelly's case, invading spirits embody these alien elements, and they had landed him in Dr. Armstrong's asylum. He could neither forget them nor expunge them; he could not even silence them. His account of their visits and their idiosyncratic memory of the date of the asylum attack begs their presence as mere beliefs. Delusions, after all, rarely have a memory all their own. And it is the question of memory that places the trial of the twenty thousand spirits not only at the midpoint of the century but also at the midpoint of medico-psychological thinking about amnesia.

Memory and Double Consciousness

Conceived for centuries as the logical way to account for inexplicable thoughts and actions, *possession* enjoyed a long tradition both in folk beliefs and educated circles. Whether it was Satan himself or nameless "imps of hell" that had led the invasion, afflicted persons found themselves either taken over completely—known as trance possession—or forced to suffer conscious awareness of a fate sealed and scorching: a lucid possession. This latter form reduced the tragically possessed to the role of passive onlooker, aware of the intruder's entry but powerless to change the lock. Although early modern Europe witnessed efforts to redefine demonic possession as delusion—and render it thus amenable to secular remedies and medical intervention—belief in possession continued into the eighteenth century (at least), capturing the interest of a new breed of healers, beginning with cleric Johann Joseph Gassner and the physician Franz Anton Mesmer. Persons believing themselves to be possessed by spirits and experiencing paralysis of various limbs or convulsive fits were encouraged into a state of deep relaxation and variously stroked, held, or "magnetized." The last technique involved placing magnets on or in various parts of the afflicted's body to bring the misappropriated life force into line with a universal magnetic field. In time, Mesmer disposed of the physical magnets, employing his own body's magnetic fluid as the curing agent, to be communicated to the patient's physical ills by passing over the affected body part with his own hands. Animal magnetism rather than material magnetism was the procedure Mesmer invented.[25]

As it turned out, possession not only provided the precipitating agent that brought the sufferer and the "magnetist" together, it also supplied the conceptual frame used to interpret the unfamiliar, foreign expressiveness revealed by the deeply relaxed patient. This "special life of its own" unleashed by the magnetist no longer appeared as an alien intrusion forcing the "host" aside in a territorial dispute. Instead it revealed the patient's "second condition," a personality often at marked distance from the conventional state of behavior. What had appeared to the uninitiated as possession was in fact a second self: periodically dominant, to be sure, but *of*—not imposed *upon*—the patient. Mesmer's pupil and eventual arch-competitor, the Marquis de Puységur, continued to investigate the possibility of a double or "alternate" consciousness, capable of being brought out by a magnetically induced trance.[26] Puységur's term, "artificial somnambulism," succinctly captured both the state of suspended consciousness that typified the curiously "disembodied" thought and behavior of the person in a trance and the fact that this state had been engineered. When English medical men wished to remove the fantastical—that is, the nonscientific fluid-based component of animal magnetism—they substituted the term "hypnotism."[27] Although forcefully denying any "mystical" communication between subject and operator, hypnotism obviously owed its method and theatrical result to the late-eighteenth, early-nineteenth-century enterprise known as "animal magnetism."

A host of medicolegal questions regarding consciousness and memory was engaged by artificial and natural somnambulism alike. As the state of a doubled consciousness posited the existence of unknown life, answers to the standard forensic question—"Did the prisoner know what he was up to?"—would confound judges, prosecutors, and medical witnesses. Surface impressions and articulate conversation were unreliable indicators of supposedly self-conscious behavior because such seemingly lucid moments were followed by the patient's suddenly "coming to" and expressing surprise—indeed, horror—at what had transpired. It was not the defendant's surprise but his amnesia that suggested to medical observers the possible existence of double consciousness and the likelihood that the unfortunate sufferer had not been conscious at the time of the crime. The defendant had no more knowledge of the affair than if it had been committed by another person. In effect, that was the substance of his plea.

An innovative rendering of the doubly conscious as a "succession of selves" carried further implications for the concept of amnesia. Only a unitary person can "forget"; losing the capacity to recall an event is the conventional way of defining amnesia. For obvious reasons, this condition is referred to as "event amnesia." But a person who is unconscious when his alternate self commits a crime does not suffer event amnesia upon awakening; the event, he hopes to argue, did not happen to *him* at all. States of double consciousness reveal a different failure of memory, associated instead with the emergence of a second self. "Identity amnesia" described the state of the person who "lacks connection with the subject who had the experience." As Adam Crabtree writes, "It is not as though someone forgets who he is or what he has done; there is instead a succession of 'someones' who may or may not have access to the memory of the others."[28] Mary Reynolds, the subject of the first nineteenth-century report of someone who went to sleep only to wake up as a different person, shared with other cases of double consciousness a failure to remember anything of the activities pursued or knowledge gained in the "doubled" state. Only in subsequent episodes of doubled personality or divided consciousness were they able to recall the events engaged in by *that* identity. Successive selves with individual memories were therefore the focus of "identity amnesia."

Not Competent, but Credible

For Richard Donelly's spirits to possess their own and, as it happened, contradictory version of events that had occurred "in front of his [their?] eyes" situates the trial of the asylum keeper at a critical moment in medico-psychological history. In one respect it looks to the past in depicting Donelly's spirits as possession; in another, it reveals how alien spirits have "kept pace" with changing medical thought. Had Donelly's spirits impelled him to fatally assault Moses Barnes, his defense attorney would have no doubt packaged the imaginary forces in the conventional garb of delusion and availed himself of the century's near elision of delusion with insanity.

But Donelly was not the accused, and the spirits posed an entirely different problem for medicolegal jurisprudence: the presence of an alternate self with its own train of memories and a peculiar state of "co-consciousness" with the host. Donelly was anything but unconscious when the spirits were active. Had he been missing or *displaced*, had he been subject to trance possession, he would have found himself bereft of memory. As it was, he typified the curious state of lucid possession regarding the activity of the intruders.[29] Persons so described are passive spectators; they do not have consciousness of their entire being because they can neither penetrate the mind of their delusive spirits nor drive them off the psychic stage. "They speak to me incessantly," Donelly informed the judge, "*they are speaking to me now*—they are never separate from me." When his spirits spoke, argued, and contradicted, Richard Donelly was, in Locke's own terms "beside himself."

And he was always beside himself. There is no lapse in delusion here: he did not "come to himself" only to return to possession at intervals. There was no "lucid interval," no period when he could be certain of the events surrounding the killing. Rather than successive selves—each with its own memory—there were "roommates" who witnessed the killing together and could not agree on the critical question before the jury: the date of the attack. This was, as the defense counsel advised the Court, "[a] fact material to the inquiry, because part of the evidence against the prisoner was, that several days had elapsed between the commission of the injuries and his communicating them to the medical officer of the asylum, during which it was assumed that he must have been cognizant of them, and would have reported them if he had not been the party who inflicted them."[30] Although it is not readily apparent why the one-day discrepancy between the witness and his spirits should prove so significant in the case against the prisoner, the attorney is clearly using the fact of the discrepancy—a dispute between a corporeal being and an immaterial, delusory entity—to drive home the point that this witness was a curious person to be offering evidence at all.

Citing a host of legal treatises—but not judicial rulings—defense attorney Collier closed his argument by maintaining that the common law had long included lunatics on the list of persons to be precluded from offering evidence at trial. That a Commission in Lunacy had been sustained against Richard Donelly there could be no doubt: his residence in the madhouse was evident proof. Collier further drew the jury's attention to the nature of the witness's distraction: "An insane delusion is a false premise concerning some matter of fact, which is constantly present to the mind and out of which it is impossible to reason the patient. Any such delusion shows the existence of disease, the extent of the delusion indicating its virulence." Regarding the contention that Donelly's delusion might be limited to his particular belief about spirits, the attorney argued that, though the body could be partially diseased because it was composed of parts, the mind was indivisible. To aver, as the prosecution was inclined to do, that the delusion was limited to a particular subject did not belie the fact that it was a delusion. Without

a full-scale examination, it was impossible to map the extent of the delusion.

It was also impossible to exclude judicial discretion in deciding the
criteria for evidence. Without taking issue with Collier's depiction of
Donelly's impeccable lunacy credentials, Mr. Baron Alderson inquired
of the attorney, "Is not the test for a lunatic's competency the same as
that of a child [also traditionally excluded from offering evidence]—
that is, whether or not he understands the nature of the oath?" Collier
conceded that a child could sometimes be admitted as a witness if he
"apprehend abstract ideas, such as that of right and wrong, the existence
of God . . . [and has a] memory sufficiently retentive to enable him to
know the truth . . . [and is] reasonably considered to be *compos mentis*."
But a lunatic, Collier maintained, "is confessedly *non compos*, on one
subject, if not more . . . his perceptions and imagination [are] false; he
therefore, on one subject at least, cannot know the truth." That Donelly
avowedly subscribed to religious sentiments counted for little: a lunatic
can "know the nature of an oath, and yet believe himself [to be] the
Pope." Hoping to sever the analogy drawn by the judge between children—who would in time reach the "age of discretion"—and the insane,
Collier concluded: "The test which applies to a sane intellect in the
course of development is not necessarily applicable to an adult intellect diseased, accordingly, it is not said that 'a lunatic shall be admissible who does not understand the nature of an oath,' but generally that
'a lunatic is inadmissible, except in a lucid interval, when he is (correctly
speaking) no lunatic.'"[31] Since there was no question that Donelly was
ever without his spirits, he could not be said to manifest lucid intervals.

In the end, the attorney's questioning of the lunatic's singular capacity to "understand" an oath—but not the illusory quality of his delusional beliefs—was a plea that the jury look beyond the witness's surface composure and the possibility that similar lucid intervals rendered
him a credible witness.[32] Of all the questions put to Donelly on the subject of purgatory and the pains of lying under oath, none touched upon
his delusion. Had the judge "protracted the discourse," had he asked the
asylum patient to put his name to the oath, the court might well have
discovered that Donelly fully intended to sign the document in cherry
juice.

As verdicts in individual trials are difficult to decipher in terms of
the effectiveness of a defense or the influence of an expert witness, so
the appellate decision handed down by the Court of Crown Cases Re-

served admits a variety of interpretations, especially in light of nine-teenth-century court reform. Collier's argument regarding the amor-phous spread of delusion was sound: without examination, who could say with confidence that all of Donelly's beliefs were not implicated? The attorney had also managed to challenge the court to consider the nature of memory. Could a witness who remembered the details of an assault be believed when he also remembered nightly visits from the Queen? Were these memories—like the memories claimed by the spir-its—kept in separate drawers? And what did it mean to remember what one had been taught in his catechism, if he could also believe he was the Pope? Does memory have no capacity to counsel, to question, to alert the mind to perceived gaps in consciousness?

That these arguments may have fallen on (judicial) deaf ears may have had more to do with the qualitatively shifting division of labor in the criminal courtroom than with the effectiveness of the defense. Di-minished in their capacity as examiner and cross-examiner in the court, relegated to legal issue "decider" rather "discoverer," and marginalized because the scrutiny of evidence was fast becoming the preserve of de-fense attorneys, judges were not likely to respond well to the assertion that common-law digests and ancient compendia should decide the ad-missibility of witnesses *tout court*.[33] Judge Campbell spoke to this de-velopment in unequivocal terms: "[W]henever a delusion of an insane character exists in any person who is called as a witness, it is for the judge to determine whether the person so called [has] a sufficient sense of religion in his mind, and sufficient understanding of the nature of an oath, for the jury to decide what amount of credit they will give to his testimony."[34] Concurring opinion was voiced by Baron Alderson and Justice Talford. Whatever Comyns' *Digest* and Buller's *Nisi Prius* may have set down as prescriptive principles for certain classes of witness, it was clear from the appellate decision that these judges were not in-clined to relinquish any more of their authority to determine who would enter the witness box.

It was also clear from their ruling that medical opinion was not without its uses; indeed, judges could appear at times surprisingly so-licitous of, and grateful to, expert witnesses. As Lord Campbell ex-plained, "[N]othing could be stronger than the language of the medical witnesses in this case to show that the lunatic might safely be admit-ted as a witness." Although medical witnesses had been appearing at the Old Bailey for almost a hundred years to assert professional insight about insanity as a medical condition, they had rarely been treated to such ringing endorsement from the bench. Indeed, it is safe to say that they had never heard anything even resembling this! Clearly, the judge had relied upon (or sought justification in) medical description of a thoroughly localizable derangement, allowing for a rendering of the mind that could house both delusion and trustworthy, coherent memory. Only with obvious difficulty could the judge state, "The proper test of insanity must always be: does the lunatic understand what he is saying and does he understand the obligations of an oath?" One feels compelled to ask: if the lunatic understands all that . . . why is he called a lunatic?

Why would the judges adopt such a tendentiously narrow conception of understanding? Clearly, it would have been next to impossible to convict the keeper of this or the killing of any asylum inmate if the only witnesses to the alleged attack were fellow patients. In the years following the assault in Dr. Armstrong's madhouse, similar prosecution would be brought against other attendants, and in one case, a medical superintendent, although none of these rested on the word of a lunatic witness.[35] That the judges in *Regina v. Samuel Hill* recognized the unusual nature of this prosecution and the need to protect future inmates when no sane witnesses were available is clear both from the judicial mention of this predicament and from the torturous logic revealed in the following statement, read to the keeper several court sessions after his conviction:

> You were convicted of a felony at a former Session of this Court, when a point was reserved for the opinion of the Court of Criminal Appeal, which was, whether one of the witnesses who was examined against you, and upon whose testimony, no doubt, the jury relied, was a competent witness. He was one of the unhappy patients in the Lunatic Asylum, in which you were a keeper, and it was suggested that a person in that condition was an incompetent witness. The court, however, after taking the matter into their careful consideration, were very clearly of the opinion that was not a question which went to competency, but to the credibility, of the witness, and that if the witness was in a fit state at the moment to give his evidence in an apparently correct and proper manner, his evidence was to be considered by the jury . . . [and they thought it perfectly safe] to act upon his testimony as to what he saw with his own eyes, and they convicted you of manslaughter with which you were charged.[36]

In adopting these peculiar distinctions between competence and credibility (the person in question was sufficiently incompetent to need confinement in a madhouse, yet, curiously, sufficiently credible to serve as star witness for the prosecution), the judges were also distinguishing one type of memory from another. "Recollections" of the Queen's visit were consigned to delusion; recollection of the assault was consigned to credible memory. The judges apparently conceived of memory as a faculty apart from and untainted by delusory beliefs. This is memory as "firewall": unbridgeable, stalwart, and, most important for the purposes of law, necessarily intact. A consistent consciousness linking thought to action is critical to the forensic construction of the person; critical too is the intuitive knowledge of the difference between right and wrong symbolized by the taking of an oath. One could forget one's name or one could forget a date. One could not forget the consequences of breaking an oath. To the evolving conception of double, then divided, consciousness featured in nineteenth-century medical literature, memory could be described first as a property of different states of consciousness and later as the possession of different states of personality. There was no overriding faculty of *über-memory* that rested intact, well above the fray of disputatious, psychic combatants. Although trance operators and hypnotists alike asserted that events experienced in disparate episodes of being became memories "unavailable" to the person missing, the Old Bailey was not about to admit that its star witness was a "divided being."

Although the court attempted to dismiss the witness's belief in possessing spirits as delusion, it was forced to recognize that this was a delusion with a difference: these beliefs had a memory all their own. Possession, the most familiar historical conceptual tool to account for uncharacteristic feelings and actions, was not replaced by double consciousness but rather metamorphosed into a state of consciousness that housed independently remembered experience. It would be this experience of forgotten, then repressed, and finally retrieved memory that would serve to unite the nineteenth-century amnesiac with the spirits of the twentieth century's long-forgotten childhood trauma.

FIVE

AN UNCONSCIOUS POISONING

❖

The individual first experiences faintness, depression, nausea and sickness, with an intense burning pain in the region of the stomach, increased by pressure. The pain in the abdomen becomes more and more severe, and there is vomiting of a brown, turbid matter, mixed with mucus and sometimes streaked with blood. . . . The vomiting is in general violent and incessant, and is excited by any liquid or solid taken into the stomach. There is a sense of constriction, with a feeling of burning heat in the throat, commonly accompanied by the most intense thirst. The respiration is painful from the tender state of the stomach. There is great restlessness, but before death, stupor sometimes intervenes, with paralysis, tetanic convulsions, or spasms in the muscles of the extremities.

ALFRED SWAINE TAYLOR,
"Arsenic. Symptoms of Acute Poisoning," 1865

S SAMUEL NELME SPRINKLED powdered sugar on a baked apple during his Friday night dinner, the last thing he could have suspected was that the white substance in the bowl was anything but confection. Alone among his family members, Nelme was in the habit of sweetening his fruit with liberal amounts of sugar, so anyone adding arsenic to the sugar bowl must have had him in mind. Immediately stricken with illness, Nelme lingered for several days while his wife and daughter looked on anxiously, powerless to interrupt his rapid slide into stupor. His grandson, William, also looked on, but the boy's attention was fixed on his grandfather's gold watch, gold eyeglass, and gold sovereigns. When he asked the family cook if she thought his grandfather "would die suddenly as his eyes looked queer," she interpreted the boy's question as expressing heartfelt concern. As it happened, William Newton Allnutt had been gauging the most propitious moment to pinch his grandfather's gold possessions, just as he had chosen well the opportunity to steal his grandfather's key to the bureau containing the arsenic, and to do some sprinkling of his own into the sugar bowl.

That such a deliberate and planned act could be carried out by a family member, let alone a twelve-year-old boy, ensured the attention Allnutt's crime received, both in the popular press and in medical commentary.[1] Rarely does one find a judge's summation reprinted word for word in a medical journal, or journal editors taking issue with testimony given by their medical brethren in a criminal trial. It was not only the means of murder and the tender age of the suspect that drew attention to the case of the poisoned sugar bowl, it was also the peculiar nature of Allnutt's defense. His attorneys would argue, and various physicians would testify, that there was a missing connection between the part of him that *knew* his act to be wrong and the part that *felt* it to be wrong. Unconscious to the monstrous evil he was committing, Allnutt had "not the moral sense of wrong distinguished from right." As his mother informed the court, the boy's episodes of lifelong misconduct always ended with her "remonstrations [and his avowal] that he did not feel he was doing wrong." How could the common law respond to a defendant whose conscience, not his intellect, had gone missing?

The defense of an insanity of deranged morals, not deranged reason, was hardly new to the Old Bailey in 1847 when William Newton Allnutt was indicted for the murder of his grandfather.[2] Seven years earlier, Edward Oxford's attorneys had employed a similar construction of perverted moral feelings to defend the actions of Queen Victoria's would-be assassin. Far from exhibiting the passion of a committed political partisan, Oxford, when asked why he had attempted to shoot the Queen, answered indifferently, "Oh, I might as well shoot at her as anybody else."[3] This patently cavalier response suggested the hallmark of a uniquely moral insanity: no motive, no hesitation, no "struggle of mind" and, manifestly, no remorse. Indeed, the very want of a reason for the act suggested a blind force that "neither reason nor sentiment determine." Although not all patients who suffered from moral insanity revealed Edward Oxford's apparently arbitrary choice of victim, standard to all was the illogical basis for the crime itself. With no long-standing enmity between assailant and offender and no logical motive to link actor to act, the question of whether the accused could be regarded as a voluntary agent in an apparently purposeless killing was an inescapable forensic element in a defense of moral insanity.

Moral insanity's "fellow travelers"—irresistible impulse, instinctive insanity, and what one medical writer called "homicidal orgasm"—further challenged the retention of human agency.[4] If any of these pathological forces could be rooted in obvious organic disturbance, the argument for "missing authorship" could be materially advanced. In the case of the juvenile poisoner, the defense did not lack for foreign organic agents burrowing into the boy's scalp (and conscience).[5] It would take both physical and metaphysical imagery, however, to convince a jury that such a methodical crime—indeed, methodical crimes, as this was the boy's second attempt to dispatch his grandfather—resulted from autonomous impulse, not a conscious intent.

Although an autopsy revealed grains of arsenic in the victim's liver, intestines, and brains, clearly pointing to poisoning as the cause of death, suspicion might not have fallen on twelve-year-old William had he not stolen his grandfather's possessions. Suspecting her son of the theft, Maria Louisa Allnutt confronted the boy, and later informed the court: "He said voices in his head whispered to him to do it. 'Do it, do it, you will not be found out,' that they talked to him in his head. I have great trouble with his health as well as his moral conduct; since his accident [a fall on the ice] he has walked in his sleep, and I have heard him halloo very loudly in his sleep, as if something had frightened him."[6] Mrs. Allnutt conveyed her son's confession to the police, and William was duly charged with theft. At his hearing at the Worship-Street police court, the victim of the robbery was identified as the widow of Samuel Nelme, regarding "whose mysterious death, by poison, a protracted investigation is still proceeding . . . and in the different stages of which the name of the prisoner has been more than once mentioned under circumstances of some suspicion." Although his grandmother and mother identified the recovered items as those reported stolen, "neither of them was in attendance, as they had not sufficiently recovered from the effects of the poison they had taken [stated in court as arsenic mixed up with loaf sugar. During his absence from the dinner table, mother and daughter had apparently decided to sample from Samuel Nelme's dessert bowl]." Although the court was likely to release the prisoner on bail, Mrs. Allnutt's solicitor advised the court

that "both the family and friends of the boy were averse to his libera-
tion at present, for reasons which it was obviously unadvisable then to
state, and would prefer his being detained in safe custody until the
whole matter had been finally disposed of."[7] Although the "whole matter" was never made explicit, the boy's light fingers and the fact that he
was the only family member with arsenic-free intestines was rapidly el-
evating him to the status of chief suspect in the murder case.

In its account of the police court's decision to retain the boy in custody, the *Times of London* concluded with the note, "The Reverend Mr.
Goodchild was understood to suggest the same course." Mr. Goodchild
would not prove to be the only member of the clergy to play a pivotal
role in the eventual outcome of the boy's trial. While he was in prison
awaiting trial for stealing his grandfather's gold possessions, William
met with the Reverend John Davis, chaplain to Newgate. After one of
his Sunday sermons, Davis notified the boy "that the Coroner's warrant
was lodged against him for willful murder" and added general instructions with regard to his religious exercises. The outcome of this interview was a letter William wrote to his mother and read to the jury at
his murder trial:

> My dearest Mother . . . I know I have sinned against God, and I deserve
> to be cast into hell; but what is my only comfort is the Bible, for our Lord
> says, "if ye repent I will forgive you." . . . Mr. Davis preached a beautiful
> sermon on Sunday; he took it from Proverbs xvi. If I had only attended
> to what you were teaching me I should not have come into such a place,
> but Satan had got so much power over me. . . . I now confess that I have
> done what I am accused of. How I got the poison was this: on the 20th
> of October Grandfather went to his desk for the key to the wine cellar
> to get some wine up and to look over his accounts, and whilst he was gone
> I took the poison out, and emptied some of it into another piece of paper,
> and put the other back; and then after dinner I put it in the sugar basin;
> and why I did it was I had made grandfather angry with something I had
> done and he knocked me down in the passage . . . and he said next time
> I did it, he would almost kill me; but in future I will say the truth and
> nothing but the truth. [I]f I am transported I know it will be the death of
> me therefore I hope they will pardon me. With kindest love to you and
> all at home, believe me, ever your affectionate son, W.N.A.[8]

It was the precise nature of Reverend Davis's instructions regarding
confession that served as the basis for his cross-examination. "The boy

in this letter attributes to you to say, that if he did not confess, God would not forgive him." Reverend Davis replied, "No doubt. I told him that unless he confessed his sin to God he could not expect forgiveness from God—I said confessed his sin *to God*" (emphasis in the original). The defense attorney asks again, "Taking the greatest possible care that he should not imagine any other confession?" Reverend Davis replied, "No other allusion was made—I did not tell him I was sure he had done it . . . his mother's name was not mentioned in the interview—what he stated is the imagination of his own brain altogether . . . he has been guilty of telling a vast variety of falsehoods; they have been denials of his guilt, which he afterwards confessed."[9]

Shortly before Reverend Davis testified, the judge had queried Henry Letheby, a physician and lecturer in chemistry (and by now a somewhat frequent medical witness at the Old Bailey), appearing in court to testify about the presence of arsenic in the victim's body and the medical implications of the prisoner's reported sleepwalking episodes. Asked, "Are you able to say whether walking in the sleep is indicative of a disordered mind?" Dr. Letheby responded, "Yes, of a disordered state of the brain—fancying sounds in the head may be indicative of unsoundness of the brain—calling out in the sleep may be caused by a disordered stomach—it is possible that a violent blow across the nose, quite at the top, such as has been described, might cause such mischief to the brain, or give rise to an alteration in its formation—a fall on the ice might do so, I cannot say it would—ringworm is a species of scrofula [Allnutt's scrofula had been mentioned by his mother], scrofula very often disorders the brain."[10]

Testimony such as this, delivered not by a mad-doctor or asylum superintendent but by the prosecution's own medical expert, could not go unchallenged. As soon as Reverend Davis finished reading Allnutt's letter to the court, the prosecution called prison surgeon Gilbert Mc-Murdo to the stand. Any courtroom spectator could have predicted Mc-Murdo's finding and perhaps even his formulaic phrasing: "I have seen him almost daily . . . with a view to ascertaining his state of mind—I have not observed anything about him which induces me to doubt his being of unsound mind—the evidence to-day does not alter my opinion of his sanity." Although McMurdo could sometimes expect pointed questioning in cross-examination, only in the trial of William Newton Allnutt was his expertise in divining insanity thrown into sharp relief.

DEFENSE ATTORNEY BALLANTYNE: You have not, I believe, particularly studied matters of this sort?

MR. McMURDO: I have been obliged to do it, in connection with the prison, but not besides that—it has been made a branch of itself for many years—there are many distinctions in the forms which insanity takes, not at all apparent to ordinary observers—I have heard . . . that the boy was suffering from scrofula—I do not agree with the other gentleman examined, that scrofula is very liable to affect the brain, not to that extent—I differ with him—I have not seen any madness result from it . . . it is not within my experience that scrofula driven inwardly is liable to produce a certain character of insanity—I have reasoned with him and talked with him—I have found his reasoning correct—there has latterly been a great distinction made between what is called a disease of the mind and moral insanity.

BALLANTYNE: Am I right in supposing that almost in every case of insanity the moral faculties are the first to be implicated in the disorder? I am putting the question from Dr. Winslow's book, which I conclude is one of high authority.

McMURDO: I have read it, it is not of very great authority, but I should be sorry to detract from it—I should consider that in an infant the mind is rather a matter of feeling than of understanding—they understand from others that a thing is right or wrong and do not reason upon it—I consider Dr. Conolly a person of very high authority—my opinion is that the prisoner shows no indications of insanity whatever—I was asked my opinion whether [Allnutt] was sane at the time of the commission of the act—I do not give my opinion on that subject now, but only spoke of the time I saw the prisoner.

JUDGE: Did the boy appear to you to be a person capable of distinguishing between right and wrong?

McMURDO: Yes—I have no reason to say that at some former time he was unable to do so, as I have taken special pains to come to a right judgment—it is impossible to say he was not insane at some former period, but there was no indication of it at present.[11]

The prosecution closed its case with the prisoner's letter confessing the poisoning to his mother (providing a rationale for murder), and the court's most familiar medical witness's denial that the boy's medical condition had mental consequences. Defense attorney Ballantyne could not have regarded his client's prospects as overwhelmingly positive.

Taking full advantage of his opportunity to address the jury before presenting the defense, Ballantyne immediately sought to limit the damage caused by his young client's letter. In no way implying that the Reverend Davis had "exceeded his duty," he suggested that it was "exceedingly probable that a child like the prisoner might have misunderstood the effect of the reverend's observations, and [that they] might have induced him to make such a statement in the hope of escaping [eternal] punishment." He was not denying that Allnutt had poisoned the sugar bowl—indeed, he was not denying that the boy probably understood that his grandfather would die. He would argue, nonetheless, that the boy should not be held accountable, and would provide witnesses of his own who "would induce the jury to return a verdict to that effect."

Edward Henry Payne, medical man and uncle to the young defendant, informed the court of the family's florid history of mental disturbance, replete with epileptic attacks, "disease of the brain," and mysterious paralysis. Payne's familiarity with the prisoner's mental state began with attending young William for ringworm. "[A] disease of an irritable, painful and excitable character, it was very obstinate—the irritation of ringworm might have the effect of disturbing an already excited and disturbed mind—he was suffering from scrofula—the nature of the scrofula is calculated to affect the mind—I think he is partially insane, that partial insanity, when he was suffering from it, would prevent his distinguishing right from wrong." The medical witness was careful not to leave the impression that the morally outrageous act itself suggested insanity: "I do not actually say that a boy who would murder his own grandfather must be insane." Instead he drew the court's attention to the possibility that the voices pressing William on constituted a delusion, and that a consequent impulse lay behind the horrific deed. "[H]e is a scrofulous boy . . . the brain was certainly in a diseased state—as a medical man, I have no hesitation in saying so." After calling the jury's attention to the boy's sleepwalking and calling out in his sleep, Judge Baron Rolfe asked, "Had it occurred to you to think him insane before last Saturday?" Payne replied, "Yes, and I have expressed it before, before I knew I should be called."[12]

A second medical witness, surgeon Edward Croucher, testified about a head injury Allnutt had suffered as an eighteen-month-old infant. "The wound was of a character calculated to affect the brain . . . such an injury might produce epilepsy and derangement, but sometimes it does not show itself for years—by derangement I mean insanity." Like

Payne, Croucher supplied the defense with an organic basis for the boy's supposed derangement, but little else. That the defendant knew he had poisoned his grandfather and even feared God's punishment suggested to the medical witness that an excitable, irritable, scrofulous boy had carried out a crime he knew to be wrong. What the defense counsel needed was medical testimony that would dispute the assumption that knowledge of wrongdoing necessarily implied appreciating why the act was wrong. This pivotal element in Allnutt's defense appears to have entered courtroom testimony only at the prompting of the prosecutor, who asked Dr. Duesbury, a third medical witness, to clarify his statement that "he did not believe [Allnutt] to have been in a sane state of mind at the time [his bouts with sleepwalking] had occurred."

PROSECUTOR: Do you mean that you consider him permanently insane, or liable to occasional derangement?

DR. DUESBURY: My opinion is that it is the early stage of insanity, implicating the moral sentiments, the sense of right and wrong, and not as yet having reached the intellect in any marked degree or interfering with his judgment of right or wrong . . .

PROSECUTOR: What do you mean by a marked degree, has it gone to a length to injure the intellect, so as not to know he was poisoning a person when he did it?

DUESBURY: He might know it as a principle of hearsay, but not as a controlling principle of his mind—I think he would understand that he was poisoning his grandfather, if explained to him, but at the time the sense of right or wrong was not acting with sufficient power to control him— I mean a morbid state of the moral feeling, of the sense of right and wrong—I think he knew what the act was that he was doing, but that he did not feel it as being wrong—I am speaking of moral feeling.

PROSECUTOR: You would consider a pickpocket had not got much moral feeling, but do you consider when he did this that he did not know that poisoning his grandfather was a wrong act?

DUESBURY: I am not prepared to answer; I think he has not the moral sense of wrong distinguished from right, or right distinguished from wrong, to give him a moral sense of feeling; that it was an irresistible impulse on his part—I draw that conclusion from his having perpetrated this act without hesitation, or struggle of mind, or remorse, or compunction and without any sensible object, and also another circumstance which I have heard [not specified] leads me to believe his conscience is diseased, that he could not feel it as an influential agent to distinguish right and wrong, although his intellect leads him to understand what others tell him.[13]

Why would it take an explanation for Allnutt to understand that he had poisoned his grandfather? What else could he have thought he was doing? How did a "diseased" conscience fail to restrain him, to exert any "power to control him"? And ultimately, what did "irresistible impulse" introduce to the defense? Were these impulses in reality his at all, any more than the actions he had undertaken when sleepwalking?

"It would be absurd to deny the possibility that such impulses may occur," wrote James Fitzjames Stephen in 1863, referring to the sudden impulse to kill, an instantaneous, uncontrollable "impulsive insanity."[14] The groundwork for autonomous, homicidal instincts dated, in mental medicine, to the school of clinical practice credited to Philippe Pinel and his energetic acolytes Jean-Etienne-Dominique Esquirol and Etienne-Jean Georget. In professing a form of insanity that featured no intellectual delirium or delusion—*manie sans délire*—Pinel and his circle described a state of "clear-thinking" insanity. Those so afflicted lamented their state of powerlessness during an attack: "Je ne puis m'en empêcher, c'est plus fort que moi" [I cannot help myself; it is stronger than me]. In time, Esquirol and Georget would articulate further states of an emotional but not a cognitive derangement, including *monomanie* and *lésion de la volonté*.[15] Homicidal mania (or monomania) was familiar to the jury members of Allnutt's day because it described the state of distraction associated with pregnant and newly delivered women accused of the murder of their infant.[16] The familiar elements of no motive, no concealment, and an inability to resist the impulse to destroy drew puerperal and homicidal mania into close proximity. Indeed, Stephen had once isolated the ravages of puerperal mania as the strongest case for irresistible impulse.

The problem with positing a purely autonomous impulsive insanity in Allnutt's case was both general and specific. Among the signs that pointed to irresistible impulse, Dr. Duesbury asserted, was an act "with no sensible object[ive]." It was clear from the boy's letter, however, that the prisoner had been forcibly struck by his grandfather, who had threatened to "almost kill" him should the boy continue his mischief. Jurors also learned that the victim had survived an earlier bout of arsenic poisoning, suggesting that the boy was making rather a habit of not resisting these homicidal impulses. Even without the prior attempt, there were formidable difficulties in ascribing Allnutt's act to impulse. To acknowledge the probable existence of murderous impulses was not necessarily to accede to the claim that they were irresistible. Judge and jurist alike pointed out that there was no clear test to distinguish an irresistible from an unresisted impulse. Even medical writers thought that it was impossible in many cases to provide evidence of "suspension of will." Still, the jurors' acceptance of murderous impulses fueled not by revenge or self-defense but by autonomous physical force, as in a case of puerperal mania, suggests a potential popular willingness to entertain the possibility of killing unaccompanied by conscious choice.

The final medical witness to testify on Allnutt's behalf was the redoubtable John Conolly, superintendent of Hanwell Lunatic Asylum, who had "for some years applied [his] mind exclusively to these matters." With regard to the boy's sleepwalking and his scrofula, "[T]he opinion I have formed is, that he is imperfectly organized and, taking the word 'mind' in the sense in which it is used by all writers, I should say he is of unsound mind . . . his brain is either diseased, or in that excitable state in which disease is most probable to ensue . . . the future character of his insanity would be more in the derangement of his conduct than in the confusion of his intellect—that is conjecture."[17]

Without invoking the contentious issue of "irresistible impulse," the noted asylum superintendent returned to the issue of the split between conduct and intellect, between the William Newton Allnutt who knew what he was doing and the William Newton Allnutt who knew it to be wrong. As the case for the defense closed, the jury was left with the image of a boy whose own instinctual awareness that murder was morally reprehensible simply could not be assumed. It was a very peculiar sort of understanding the medical witnesses had alleged: one that could rarely if ever expose a person to culpability and hence punishment.[18]

Defense attorney Ballantyne did not have to wait for the jury's verdict to learn the likely fate of moral insanity as a creditable defense for his client. Judge Baron Rolfe began his detailed, exhaustive, and impassioned summation, advising the jury that the importance of the present case transcended the consequences to this particular prisoner. If juries did not put an end to defenses of this sort, the consequences would be "disastrous for the rest of society." Judge Rolfe's rejection of Allnutt's defense engaged the substance of the medical testimony as well as the jury's responsibility to treat professional opinion as only one piece of evidence. His words do not merely revisit the territory dispute between medicine and law; the judge singled out lawyers as well for their capacity to confuse jurors. "The forensic subtlety of our lawyers and the metaphysical dexterity of our modern philosophers, have combined to complicate the discussion and [to] leave the uninitiated in hopeless perplexity."[19] The largest measure of his disfavor, however, was reserved for the medical witness who certified the defendant's self-proclaimed impulse to be "uncontrollable." It is precisely such impulses that the law was designed to control.

Reserving for a moment his comments on moral insanity and monomania, Judge Rolfe advised the jurors on how they might consider the medical testimony. His subtle phrasing at the beginning of his instructions reminds one of Ballantyne's comments regarding the prison Reverend, whom he did not mean to suggest "in any way . . . had exceeded his duty," though that was of course exactly what he was suggesting. As the *Times of London* reported, Judge Rolfe pointedly did not "for a moment desire to disparage the evidence of scientific men, but he must tell the jury that all they were required to do was to listen attentively to such evidence. . . . They were not bound to pay a slavish obedience to it, but might reject it if they felt it did not accord with their own common sense and experience."[20] To underscore his reminder of the proper division of courtroom labor, Rolfe urged the jury to scan such evidence "with very great jealousy and suspicion." The term *jealousy* was wisely chosen: it was the jury's prerogative to deliver the verdict, not the medical witness's. The judge's use of *experience* in the above quote was also not haphazard. Alone among courtroom witnesses, men of expertise and unique experience were permitted to give opinions, not simply report facts. By urging jurors not to abandon their own good sense and everyday experience in considering the medical man's testimony, the judge was reminding the layman that practical reason—not medicalism—must inform their deliberations. That jurors might find themselves perplexed after a trial such as this did not escape the judge, who again faulted first the attorney and then the medical man.

[T]he juryman's attention is diverted from [points of law] by elaborate, mock-scientific examinations on delusion, illusion, hallucination and morbid imagination; and the replies are dissected with metaphysical subtlety, till the witness is as much at a loss to understand himself as counsel or jury can be to arrive at his meaning. . . . We doubt whether even the most practiced logician would appear to advantage in such an academy of science as the groves of Newgate. Still, our medical brethren are not free from blame: there has been too much disposition to envelop the subject of insanity in a murky atmosphere of its own—to assume that the mind in its pure essence, is susceptible of disease which the body does not share, much less occasion.[21]

Beyond his efforts to circumscribe the medical testimony, Rolfe's charge to the jury is remarkable for the legal—and by implication, moral—critique to which he subjected the concept of monomania in particular and moral insanity in general. That the passions may be perverted and endowed with force beyond a person's seeming control is no divine misfortune or natural affliction. Monomania is indeed distinguishable from other forms of insanity when traced to its "probable source: an habitual self-indulgence of a weak or a criminal disposition . . . moral insanity is only the self delusion of hardened conscience." By "indulging habitually in a moody, resentful disposition," in tastes "cruel and perverted"—which of course describes Allnutt's childhood temperament, as relayed to the court by his mother—is it a mystery one ends up "absorbed by his delusion?" This thoroughly Victorian rendering of delusion—that the afflicted were in fact largely responsible for their affliction because of the willful indulgence of false beliefs—permitted the judge to deny categorically any significant qualification of responsibility. "What does criminality imply but that passion [nurtured by the individual] has got the mastery of reason—that the importunity of temptation is too clamorous to allow the voice of reason to be heard. What is this but the subjugation of reason to vice?"[22]

Taking only fifteen minutes to reach a guilty verdict, Allnutt's jurors "earnestly recommended the prisoner to mercy on account of his tender age." Whether the trial had finally taken its toll on him, or whether he was genuinely surprised that the medical witnesses were ignored, William Newton Allnutt became "dreadfully agitated" and had to be supported by one of the bailiffs. Following a short interval, the judge prepared to don the black cap of death, but paused to advise the prisoner that he "rejoiced" at the jury's verdict, for Allnutt was clearly "guilty of the horrible crime laid to his charge." But he wanted Allnutt to understand why he rejoiced at the jury's painful decision: "[T]he jury had not shrunk from the discharge of a duty which men of weaker minds might have recoiled from . . . [t]he jury had treated the defense of insanity . . . as trifling with their judgment—they felt that [Allnutt] knew but too well that the act he committed was one that would send his grandfather, to whom he owed his existence, to the grave."[23] The judge placed ultimate emphasis on the *knowing* faculty, both in this short extract and in his rationale throughout. He clearly acknowledged the exculpatory significance of obliterated reason: the state of perfect or total insanity. A person in such a state "is placed out of the pale of society . . . because he is no longer *man*, though he still wears the human form. [H]is affliction is only curable by miracle, and the same Almighty Power which first gave, and then redeemed his intelligence." As for the variation of so-called derangement known as moral insanity, the judge had only scorn and a warning. "This was a defense which was frequently made and which was too often successful, and [I] rejoiced that the jury had thrown to the winds the idle sophistry by which the defense was sought to be made out on the present occasion." As for the jury's recommendation that Allnutt's life should be spared, Rolfe agreed to couple this request with his own, owing to the boy's lack of experience and youthful years. This recommendation would be "laid at the foot of the Throne, where alone the power of mercy existed." Were his life to be spared, the prisoner must expect "to pass the whole of the remainder of it in ignominy and disgrace."[24]

One cannot help thinking that the disgrace Allnutt merited in the judge's eyes stemmed not only from the coldly calculated murder of his grandfather but also from the attempt to lure the jury to "swerve from the strict path of duty." Beyond "idle sophistry," moral insanity tampered with this judge's bedrock conception of the Almighty's role, not only as the source of intelligence, but in man's "consciousness of right and wrong." "Practically and personally, [Adam] had no knowledge of good and evil: but he had a conception given to him (for unless it was bestowed, he had no means of acquiring it) that a certain act was wrong because it was forbidden, and yet it rested with himself to refrain, [i.e.,] to invest his reason with freedom of action."[25] For Judge Rolfe, consciousness of right and wrong was simply "intuitive," an innate capacity to distinguish good from evil that had been bestowed by the Almighty along with the faculty of reason. Law could not function without a beginning assumption that consciousness binds a person to his acts (Locke), and fundamental to that consciousness was an intuitive capacity to know right from wrong. A defense of insanity threatened none of this. The delirious, the profoundly confused, the seriously deluded had lost their reason, or at least the ability to reason from correct premises. The capacity to distinguish right from wrong was one casualty among many.

But moral insanity, irresistible impulse, and homicidal monomania struck at the core of the law's construction of the person: the forensic entity responsible for his action. Allnutt's presence in the courtroom brandishing a "captivating defense" raised the specter of persons oblivious to the moral nature of their transgression—pitiable rather than punishable. The judge would have none of this and equated "moral insanity" with moral depravity, the latter "not only consistent with legal responsibility, but such as legal responsibility is expressly formulated to restrain." It was inevitably the suppression of instincts—for revenge, for lust, for destruction—that the law was designed to serve. Passion gets the better of Reason *for* a reason: the person's willful indulgence of these passions.

Although it would be tempting to cast the court's forceful rejection of Allnutt's defense and the testimony of his supporting witnesses as a predictable clash between the law and medicine, each striving mightily to be the rightful caretakers of the wayward youth, the divergence in medical opinion regarding scrofula's necessary effects on "consciousness of right and wrong" suggests considerable variation within medical circles as well. Apparently outraged that the court ignored his explanation, Dr. Duesbury published an expansive account of Allnutt's debility in the *London Medical Gazette* emphasizing his phrenological symptoms and sleepwalking episodes, the purposelessness of his thefts, and his complete disregard for the peril in which he placed himself. Indeed, the boy appeared at the inquest "humming a tune to himself, and looking out of the door or the window with the utmost unconcern." His seemingly blasé attitude to the serious charge he faced mirrored Oxford's breezy dismissal of the implications of shooting at the Queen. This blatant disregard for the very real precariousness of one's well being was thought to be the hallmark of moral insanity. The editors of the *Gazette* were unimpressed, however, prefacing Duesbury's letter with the brief comment, "We can find nothing in the reports of the case to alter our opinion that the young criminal was very properly convicted."[26]

"If That Is the Question, It Can Surely Be Answered"

Three years after Allnutt's conviction, moral insanity and "irresistible impulse" returned to the Old Bailey and again evoked heated comments from a judge. But this time the judge's impatience with the nature of medical inference would surface during the cross-examination of the éminence grise of asylum superintendency. A policeman had approached defendant James Huggins when he was found lurking at the scene of a probable case of arson. The young man politely declined to answer the officer's questions on the grounds that he himself was likely a suspect. Huggins revealed a street-wise knowledge of his rights and an acute awareness of the limit of the policeman's rights as well. He pointed out that without a summons or a warrant from the Lord Mayor, he could not be taken into custody. Such surface equanimity, the jury was to learn, belied the suspected arsonist's lifelong history of violent outbursts, threatened suicides, and intemperate attacks on his wife. Although his actions were bizarre and certainly inexplicable, there was little in his psychological background that would have cast doubt on his capacity to distinguish right from wrong.

All this would change with John Conolly's return to the witness box. Informing the court of interviews he had conducted with Huggins while in prison (at the behest of Huggins's family) he stated, "I am, as a physician, of [the] opinion that his mind is not perfectly sound, that his judgment is impaired." The defense counsel next asked Conolly a carefully crafted question. Suppose that a husband had suddenly turned on his wife of many years and ill-used her in the cruelest way; "to what, in the absence of an explanation, would you refer such a change?" The superintendent of Hanwell asylum answered directly, "It is one of the most frequent of symptoms of insanity. . . . I should not consider a man quite sound that beat his wife, under any circumstances, not a *gentleman*." Prosecuting attorney Mr. Ballantyne cross-examined Conolly with the following result:

PROSECUTOR BALLANTYNE: You do not consider, for a moment, that this man has not understood right from wrong?

MR. CONOLLY: I feel this to be so important, this question is so often asked, and medical men think so much depends upon it, that, perhaps you will permit me to say . . . [that] we medical men do not consider that a question of distinction at all—I should question the power of the mind in the state in which the prisoner's has been to appreciate right from wrong.

BALLANTYNE: You can perfectly understand my question, because, as you say, it is one so often put to you; do you mean that at the time he was beating his wife . . . he could not distinguish right from wrong?

CONOLLY: I am perfectly aware that is the question.

JUDGE: If that is the question, it can surely be answered.

CONOLLY: I do not think it can absolutely be answered. I think it can only be answered in the manner in which I have answered it.

BALLANTYNE: You can give me your opinion, and I must trouble you for it . . . could he distinguish right from wrong?

CONOLLY: Well, sir, I do not understand rightly that question—if you mean positively, absolutely, on every subject, I cannot answer you—I could not say he was unable to distinguish right from wrong, but I say his power of appreciating it is impaired, his power of reasoning accurately is impaired, the power of controlling or resisting a train of thought tending to criminal actions [is impaired].

JUDGE: How do you apply that?

MR. CONOLLY: I think in many morbid states of mind, the patient is in that condition that ideas will present themselves in his mind having a tendency to crime, while he has not an equal and constant power of resisting.[27]

A historian of forensic psychiatry could be forgiven if at this point his or her interest shifted from the mind of the defendant to the mind of the medical witness. Did Conolly purposely invite the prosecutor's increasingly testy query by refusing to be drawn? Did he enter the witness box with the intention of confronting, finally, the narrowness of the law's construction of "knowing"? One can say with certainty that this would not be the first time cross-examination would generate such a forceful avowal of professional expertise.[28]

Conolly's rejection of the significance of "knowing" divorced from "appreciating" is reinforced by the testimony of Sir Alexander Morison, physician to Bethlem Hospital, prolific author, and a witness at McNaughtan's trial. Asked by the judge whether he believed Huggins to be incapable of distinguishing right from wrong, Morison responded:

DR. MORISON: I am not here to decide the question of responsibility in an insane person, and therefore I cannot go to the length of answering what lawyers frequently ask, is he capable of distinguishing between right and wrong. I mean to say his brain is in a diseased state, but I cannot define the degree of responsibility and consciousness which he possesses.

DEFENSE COUNSEL: I will take it in that way; we understand from Dr. Conolly that many persons have not the power of resisting ideas that may lead in a criminal direction?

MORISON: Yes—I put the circumstances I have heard under the class of irrational conduct—there is a disease which you may call a morbid state
of the feelings—some persons call it moral insanity . . . others [call it]
madness without delusion . . . and others lesion of the will. I do not admit
the definition of knowing right from wrong . . . he was not equally sensible of the distinction as a sane person would be . . .

PROSECUTION COUNSEL: Suppose you were to take into consideration a
deliberate preparation for eighteen months to commit an offense, the
commission of the offense, and then an avoidance of answering questions
from fear he should get into difficulty, by saying that being a suspected
person he would not answer any; would that be indicative of a sane or unsound mind—that is, of a person knowing right from wrong?

MORISON: His saying he would not answer questions is not anything at all,
it very often happens that in committing a crime, an insane person is quite
sensible he is doing wrong—I mean to say that on [the day of the crime]
his brain was disordered in such a degree as to take away his perfect
knowledge of right or wrong—I am not aware he knew the distinction
between right and wrong at the time he did it; I will undertake to say
on my oath he did not—I will undertake to say that he was in a diseased
state when he did it, that his power of preventing crime was impaired
and that he did not possess that degree of consciousness and responsibility.[29]

A witness who began his testimony carefully sidestepping the question of "responsibility and consciousness," Morison—like Conolly—
found that cross-examination elicited ever more professionally self-
conscious testimony. The language of the medical man had begun to
diverge from the laypersons' earlier in the century, as specialists in mental medicine increasingly spoke in terms of delusion and specific organic
disturbance as the signposts and origins of insanity. Now, with publications behind them and many patients in front of them, medical men
specializing in the treatment of the mad extended their distinction from
lay conceptions of derangement by proffering a form of derangement
that reified not only the existence of separate faculties of knowing and
feeling (or appreciating) but also the possibility of a *split* between them.
Just as Allnutt had failed to "feel" that murder was wrong, Huggins
could appear to "know" both the law and the very real peril in which
he stood without possessing a consciousness of why he should be pun-
ished at all.

The indicted arsonist was eventually convicted and sentenced to death. Although Judge Wightman expressed his agreement with the jury's finding, there is no evidence that he took satisfaction in the verdict in his comments after sentencing.[30] He acknowledged Baron Rolfe's concern that a defense of moral insanity carried dangers to society beyond any particular trial, but his tone was measured and judicious. Arson was a capital offense, but in this case there was no loss of life. Allnutt's premeditated murder of a family member—on the second try, at that—was so atrocious that any attempt to argue nonresponsibility owing to a split between sense and sensibility was likely to provoke a rhetorical judicial flourish. But jurors were not so predictably disposed to reject such a defense. Ten years after the Huggins decision, another trial at the Old Bailey combined murder, possession, and irresistible impulse, but ended in acquittal.

Battle's Vermin Killer

On first reading, one might be tempted to classify Ann Vyse's murder of her two young children as yet another tragic case of puerperal mania.[31] That this kind and devoted mother, exhausted from nursing her newborn infant and overcome with grief following the death of another child, killed her "nearest and dearest" would not appear to distinguish her from other women of the era who had been indicted for infanticide and child murder. What sets this case apart is that Alice and Annie Vyse were not impulsively smothered, drowned, or decapitated. Instead, they dined on roast beef and rice pudding, the latter laced with prussic acid.

Pleading, "I am so afraid of [the rats] getting at my baby," Ann Vyse eventually succeeded in convincing a chemist to sell her a quantity of Battle's Vermin Killer, a highly toxic poison that required unusually careful handling. Returning home, she waited until the cook had prepared the children's dinner and then secretly stirred in several grains of the lethal powder. After both her children had died, she laid them out carefully, fully dressed, on their bed, took up a razor and slashed her own throat. Discovered in her room shortly after, Ann Vyse claimed to be mad, to be better off dead, and insisted that her children were already in heaven.

It was the careful placement of the children—the near artistic rendering of the scene—that struck Edwin Payne, a physician called to attend Mrs. Vyse's wounds: "[O]ne child was on one side of the bed, and the other on the other, and the impression on my mind was that they had been placed after death, and had not died there—supposing she had poisoned them and then laid them out, I should consider it to be a morbid condition, or morbid dwelling on a deed—I mean to convey that a person who did it was not in her right senses." Dr. Payne "supposed" the prisoner to be pregnant, to have ceased menstruating—"always a critical period"—and stated that such conditions "very seriously affect the brain." He could not speak to the matter of her composure after the killing, although he surmised that her own loss of blood would have relieved any extreme excitement. These sentiments could hardly have been welcomed by the prosecuting attorney, prompting him to say to the witness, "I am anxious to have a little further explanation about what you said about a morbid dwelling on a deed." The state's medical witness proceeded to further the defense claim that this was the work of a person substantially unhinged. "I should consider the deed accomplished to furnish such a repulsive spectacle that a sane person could scarcely behold it—a sane person would rush away from a deed such as this—I should consider it a morbid dwelling on a deed, to place the children in bed after they were poisoned; an unhealthy condition of mind—I have not met with instances in which persons have killed others, they have then laid out their bodies." Dr. Payne's observations were reinforced by surgeon William Savory, who was called by the Crown to comment on the amount of strychnine found in the children but also commented on the odd placement of the victims: "Put perfectly in order as if a person, after killing another, laid out the body without any apparent motive of concealment. I should regard it as a strange state of mind."[32]

It is hard to imagine how much more effective the medical witnesses called by the defense could be in drawing the jurors' attention to the disturbed mental state that created the macabre scene in the children's bedroom. Further, Dr. Payne's mention of suppressed menstruation and its "serious effect on the brain" was a standard and well-accepted basis for acquittal in cases of child murder. The problem facing the defense counsel, however, was that traditionally at the Old Bailey, the successful application of "women's problems" to inexplicable maternal violence occurred in episodes of spontaneous, impulsive fury. Tossing one's children impulsively into the Thames does not, on its face, resemble lying to a druggist, waiting until the cook folds in all her ingredients before adding some of one's own, and lingering in the next room while the rat poison did its work. How, then, to cast such purposeful resolve as a nonthinking, impulsive act?

An array of witnesses, including shop clerks, domestic servants, and distant family members of the accused, attested to the sometimes comical, always unexpected antics of the defendant. Subject to "sudden irrational impulses," she was nevertheless described as unusually "quiet and ladylike." The death of her young child from diphtheria—a tragedy she believed she could have averted—had preyed on her mind and disposed her to a brooding melancholy. Owing to the defendant's pregnancy, Dr. Augustus Merritt testified that she was in a state of mania suffering from "irregularity of impulse." Cross-examined by the prosecutor and pressed to give an example of this "irregularity," Dr. Merritt replied, "She would rush away in the middle of a conversation, leave me in the most abrupt manner and come back and be perfectly unconscious of her want of good taste and decorum—there were sudden expressions of excitability, not of anger." The mention of anger was not accidental. Under cross-examination, Dr. Merritt had been asked whether he could attribute the prisoner's seemingly manic behavior to "some anger or motive." He said he could not, instead citing the family's hereditary insanity, the "deterioration of [Vyse's] general health from anxiety and fatigue," and, finally, her irregularity of impulses.[33]

The concluding medical witness, Dr. Forbes Winslow, turned his attention to the subject of inexplicable impulse.

DR. WINSLOW: There is a form of insanity termed "paroxysmal madness" recognized by all writers . . . that very frequently takes a suicidal form, and very frequently the homicidal, connected with acts of violence, either on the patient himself or others—the patient would undoubtedly be incapable of distinguishing right from wrong, he is apparently sane and tranquil, the insanity coming on in paroxysms from some exciting cause, and the patient often committing some serious overt act, either on himself or others—such a state is not inconsistent with the general management of the affairs of life.

PROSECUTOR CHAMBERS: These paroxysmal attacks are very nearly allied sometimes to fits for ordinary passion, are they not?

WINSLOW: They may be so—taking the paroxysm by itself, it may be difficult to distinguish a burst of passion from a burst of insanity.

This time the defense attorney stepped in to ask for clarification, lest his witness aid the prosecutor's case.

MR. BALLANTYNE: But for the purpose of coming to a conclusion, would you look at the preceding acts and the health of the family?

DR. WINSLOW: Yes: and if I found no good ground for passion I should come to the conclusion that the mind was itself off its balance, and that there was insanity of the kind I describe.[34]

Describing the case as "undoubtedly most extraordinary and melancholy," Judge Wightman informed the jury that it had to consider, "in the first place, the extraordinary fact that the prisoner had destroyed the lives of her two children, to whom it was proved she was most devotedly attached, and that this had been done, without the slightest motive." The only question remaining, "undoubtedly one of the most difficult that could be decided in a court of justice," was one of the prisoner's state of mind.[35] Difficult it may have been, but not time consuming. The jury took only four minutes to acquit Ann Vyse on the grounds of insanity.

There is a curious postscript to this trial. Two days after the verdict, Dr. Charles Hood, medical witness for the defense, and the first to introduce the concept of "paroxysm" in describing the defendant's condition, believed it necessary to write to the *Times of London* about the verdict, lest the "morally and socially dangerous term, 'impulsive mania,'" might be misunderstood, and perhaps too readily appropriated. "I believe that Mrs Vyse is suffering from cerebral disease [which she had described as 'a perspiring of the brain'], which rendered her at the time an irresponsible agent. The public may take alarm at the admission of such a disease as impulsive mania, which is so difficult to distinguish from passion; but they may remember that cerebral disease ought to be first established and irresponsibility acknowledged and then the sudden impulse or the skillfully conceived attack will be looked upon as the effect of insanity, not the disease itself."[36]

With "skillfully conceived attack" put on the same footing as "sudden impulse," Hood's own dexterous rationale aimed to minimize the obviously premeditated character of the prisoner's act. His further criterion—that the "attack" followed organic disturbance—also spoke to legal concerns that unchecked passion was indistinguishable from uncontrollable impulse. Of course, Allnutt also presented the court with an array of organic assaults: head injuries, facial scars, and ringworm burrowing into his scalp. His crime and Mrs. Vyse's were methodically planned, with no effort taken to avoid detection after administering the poison. Mrs. Vyse of course was a sympathetic character: a loving, devoted mother driven to distraction by maternal duties. And her defense could draw liberally upon commonly accepted folk—and medical—beliefs regarding exhaustion and sudden, violent outbursts. But nowhere in the judge's summation does one discern the slightest anxiety that medicine might have overstepped its bounds in equating passion with blind impulse, or that society would be put in peril by the admission of "impulsive mania" to the court.

What provoked judicial outbursts was not professionally adventurous medical testimony reclassifying unruly passion as impulsive mania, or the fact that such a dangerous defense could threaten the purpose of law: to *restrain* destructive impulses. Clearly, it was the particular configuration of victim, offender, and crime narrative that rendered the judge (and apparently the jury) either solicitous of the prisoner's torment or contemptuous of an attempt to escape justice. Even the method of dispatching the victims did not satisfy the law's vital interest in whether the prisoner knew the nature and consequences of the act. On its face, the most transparent of intentions—the fact of poisoning—in no way guaranteed a conviction for murder. In fact, it guaranteed nothing.

Poisoning Judicial Temperament

Although missing from the judge's instructions to the jury in the trial of Ann Vyse, the contemptuous dismissal of scientific evidence the court unleashed in the Allnutt trial surfaced again in the murder trial of William Dove.[37] Almost ten years after Allnutt's conviction, an English court was again faced with the poisoning of a family member, a defense of moral insanity, and a medical claim that though the prisoner knew he was killing his wife, he was unable to appreciate that he was doing wrong. Caleb Williams, a York physician and the principle medical witness for the defense, testified that owing to the disordered state of Dove's moral faculties he had been "deprived of his free agency . . . render[ing him] irresponsible for his acts." Williams's assertion that the continued existence of any propensity or desire may become a disease, "and he has no power over it . . . this is moral insanity," prompted the judge to ask, "If a man nourishes any passion until it becomes uncontrollable, that is a moral insanity?" "It is," replied the physician, "and he would be irresponsible, if he is insane."

Whether Justice Baron Bramwell was familiar with Baron Rolfe's contemptuous rendering of medical testimony uttered in the Allnutt trial is anyone's guess, but it is certain that the two judges would have shared a disdain for expert opinion that departed so conspicuously from "practical reason." Judge Rolfe had considered the existence of an "evil propensity" as the willing indulgence of a pernicious habit, not as grounds for exculpation. "What does criminality imply," he had asked the Allnutt jury, "but that passion has got the mastery of reason—that the importunity of temptation is too clamorous to allow the voice of reason to be heard?" Judge Bramwell's seemingly temperate questioning of Caleb Williams regarding passion's relation to moral responsibility was a prelude to his dismissal of the doctor's notions of reason and disease as "monstrous." At the end of the trial, the judge summarily dismissed the opinions of all medical witnesses, indicating that "the jury were as competent to form a correct opinion on matters of this kind as anybody else." When the defense attorney objected that certain witnesses called by the prosecution did not, in fact, merit the status of experts in madness, the judge let loose a memorable screed: "Experts in madness! Mad-doctors! Gentlemen, I will read you the evidence of these medical witnesses—these 'experts in madness.' And if you can make sane evidence out of what they say, do so; but I confess it's more that I can do. Of course I do not say you don't understand it, but I say 'place what value upon it you think it worth.'"[38] As reported in the *Leeds Mercury*, the judge "frankly told them that he would rather take his own opinion upon the facts than the evidence of the three medical gentlemen, [preferring to] exercise his own opinion than be led by the theories of gentlemen who held opinions that were extreme in their profession." The jury took only twenty minutes to find Dove guilty.

The "Experts in madness! Mad-doctors!" exclamation found its way into the era's medical and legal tracts, as well as recent historical analyses of the evolution of forensic psychiatric testimony. The judge's pique at medicine's professional claims to unique knowledge is matched only by Dr. Williams's outraged professional sensibilities when confronted with the judge's dismissiveness and contempt. But it must be stressed that Bramwell's vituperative attack on the expert knowledge delivered by medical witnesses in no way typified the opinion prevailing in the nineteenth-century English courtroom, at least not London's central criminal court. With rare exceptions, Baron Bramwell's sentiments expressed in Dove's trial regarding the use of medical testimony were unique in tone and substance. There was certainly close questioning of medical, and other witnesses, and there were sometimes comments made about the larger damage that might attend the admission of a questionable defense, as in the Allnutt trial. But there was certainly no blanket suspicion greeting medical witnesses, who were, after all, just as likely to be called by the prosecution as the defense.

It would be wise to remember, however, the specific courtroom elements for both Dove and Allnutt. These were purposeful, planned murders, each involving multiple administrations of the poison. The utter callousness of watching a family member die slowly, by degrees, could not have been lost on the jury. The two murderers also claim that something was "missing": the necessary intuition that the act itself was irretrievably monstrous. Neither judge nor jury would permit any dilution of the law's bedrock assumption that murder had to be recognized inherently as morally abhorrent. Courtroom reaction to various defense arguments did not suggest total dismissiveness toward various states of suspended consciousness. In fact, quite the opposite was true. One's self could be missing; one's memory could be missing. One could claim unconsciousness or an inability at the time to recognize a weapon in one's hand. The court would even entertain testimony that spoke to impulse—physiologically driven—that could render the prisoner unconscious even as she stealthily procured and deliberately administered poison to young children.

What the court would not accept was an inability to recognize that the act was wrong in itself. A nation of citizens each with his or her own moral compass could not sustain a standard of moral responsibility. Indeed, the Victorian court's continuing effort to "raise the bar" of reasonableness aimed to accomplish just the reverse: engineering a nation of Englishmen scaling almost Olympian levels of prudence. Certainly people were both sense and sensibility, with cognitive as well as affective resources that could sometimes diverge. But sense, however defined, could not lawfully separate from sensibility: knowing an act to be wrong meant appreciating why it was wrong. Anything less invited a corrosive moral relativism that the criminal law was envisioned to punish, certainly not to sanction.

⚔ SIX ⚒

CRIMES OF AN AUTOMATON

✛

$\mathcal{D}$ O YOU THINK," DEFENSE ATTORNEY Ribton asked of Henry Bullock, house surgeon to St. Mary's Hospital, "that the prisoner's conduct might be the effect of some terrible dream?" Nursemaid Sarah Minchin's conduct consisted of rising from her bed, entering the room of her young charge, and attempting to slash his throat with a large carving knife—all while in the throes of a sleepwalking episode. Indicted for felonious wounding, she sat at the Old Bailey and listened as her attorney read from Alfred Swaine Taylor's *Medical Jurisprudence*, employing the following account to support a defense of somnambulism: "Two persons had been hunting during the day, and slept together at night; one of them was renewing the chase in his dream, and, imagining himself to be present at the death of the stag, cried out, 'I'll kill him! I'll kill him!' [T]he other one, awakened by the noise, got out of bed, and by the light of the moon beheld the sleeper give several deadly stabs with a knife on the part of the bed which his companion had just quitted."[1]

There is every reason to suspect that the tale of the hunter's narrow escape was familiar to jurors in Sarah Minchin's trial. Often recounted in mid-nineteenth-century folklore as well as in medical and legal literature, this story had taken its place alongside other descriptions of sleepwalking and suspended dream states that ended in an "unconscious killing." Thus one reads of a man, frightened by a phantom in a dream, who desperately seized a hatchet and attacked the specter, only to discover upon awakening that he had killed his wife. Charged with murder, he was eventually pronounced not guilty on the grounds that he was not at the time conscious of his actions. There is also the familiar tale

129

of a peddler who was suddenly awakened while sleeping on the high-way "by a man seizing him by the shoulders and shaking him roughly." The peddler, who had been in the habit of walking the roads with a "sword-stick," drew his sword and stabbed the man who had awakened him. Despite the defense attorney's ardent plea that "he could not have been conscious in his half-waking state of terror"—a defense supported by medical witnesses—the peddler was found guilty of manslaughter.[2] Perhaps the most celebrated Old Bailey trial that employed a sleep-walking defense in a case of homicide—and extreme cruelty to ani-mals—was the seventeenth-century prosecution of Colonel Cheyney Culpeper for the shooting of a guardsman on patrol—and also his horse. Culpeper produced almost fifty character witnesses who attested to his status as a "famous sleeper," providing the court with a host of re-markable feats he had accomplished while in this state. The jury first returned a verdict of manslaughter, "but were sent out again, and con-sidering that he might be distempered to do such a rash action found it special" (that is, a reduced verdict of manslaughter because of his de-fense). Culpeper's Home Office file reveals a letter from the Palace granting him a pardon.[3]

Standard in each of these sleepwalking episodes was the complete lack of animus between the two parties. Indeed, in cases where the sleeper was suddenly shaken awake, the victim was completely unknown to his assailant. The absence of a reason for the assault buttressed the attorney's claim that the offense was unconscious: "the result of a 'half-waking' state." And it was just such a state that Sarah Minchin was said to manifest when, dressed only in her nightgown, she wandered into the room of young Frederick Smith. As a border in her house testified: "I heard [the victim] calling out, 'Oh Sarah! Oh Sarah!' I got out of the bed, ran into the boy's room, and saw the prisoner on the bed with the little boy underneath the clothes, she had a large carving knife in her hand, and she struck at the boy's neck with it, and he caught it with his hands. The moment the prisoner found that somebody had inter-fered, she fell on the bed apparently insensible."[4]

Confronted with her deed by the boy's father, Sarah Minchin made no reply, nor did she speak to the policeman who carried her on his shoulder to the police station. The house surgeon called to attend the boy saw the defendant two days after the assault. It was while the sur-geon was giving his testimony on the boy's wounds that the defense at-torney tried to lay the groundwork for a defense based on sleepwalking.

DEFENSE ATTORNEY RIBTON: Suppose a person had had some alarming dream, had started from the bed under the influence of that dream, do you think that the condition of the prisoner could be accounted for in that way?

SURGEON BULLOCK: Hardly—I have read the *Medical Jurisprudence,* of Mr. Taylor.

RIBTON: [Reading the tale of the two hunters] Do you think that the prisoner's conduct might be the effect of some terrible dream?

BULLOCK: I should think it would be exceedingly improbable that a person would commit a manual act in that way—I have had no experience of somnambulism. I have read of cases similar to that which you have quoted . . . and they are doubtful; I should not be disposed to believe them, unless the evidence was exceedingly good in their favor—I think it quite possible that the prisoner might have done the act in a state of phrenzy—when she was not in her right mind—I should hardly think that a state of phrenzy could be produced by any horrible dream she might have had; but taking all the facts into my mind, her starting from [the] bed and running into the room, I would not undertake to say that it is not possible.

Pressed by the attorney to clarify his term, "a state of phrenzy," Mr. Bullock grew irritated and characterized it as "a state of temporary insanity," protesting that he could go no further because Minchin had not been under his care. "I merely went to see the boy—I cannot account for this act in any way." The defense attorney, however, was not ready to dismiss the surgeon:

RIBTON: If a girl of the age of the prisoner, about seventeen, was suffering from a disordered state of menstruation, would that be liable to affect her head?

BULLOCK: No; there is a disease called nymphomania, but that would not be likely to do it—persons often have pains in the head, caused by a disordered state, or a temporary suppression of the menses, but never to be mad, or out of their heads through it—I do not know that it frequently makes them delirious.[5]

The last witness called was the defendant's mother, who attested to her daughter's dreams, her screaming out in her sleep, and her suffering "a great deal from her monthly periods being irregular, which I believe has had an effect upon her mind."

In his address to the court, the defense attorney urged the jury to consider the probability that the act had been committed "while under the influence of some frightful dream and that she was not aware of what she was doing." He then referred ambiguously to "the condition of the prisoner [that] precluded him from obtaining the evidence of eminent medical men upon the subject," calling attention to other cases in which extraordinary acts had been committed in a state of somnambulism. Just what "the condition" was that kept the attorney from calling medical witnesses he did not say, though one presumes he was referring to her state of menstrual distress. After a short deliberation, the jury found Sarah Minchin guilty only of the minor offense of unlawful wounding, prompting the judge to limit her sentence to three months in confinement.[6]

There is of course no way of knowing whether eminent medical men would have helped the defense attorney secure an acquittal, although the jury's willingness to downgrade Sarah Minchin's offense to a crime much less serious than attempted murder reveals some appreciation for her extraordinary state of being. When seen against the backdrop of the era's other cases of "lethal sleepwalking," her (partial) conviction stands out as the exception. Successful defenses were recorded in cases where a defendant killed or attempted to kill her own children, although child murder was hardly a stranger to the Old Bailey and in no way guaranteed an acquittal. Somnambulism introduced a new element to such "inexplicable" deeds: the possibility that purposeful action could be devoid of conscious choice and, hence, of intention.

"Unconscious Criminality"

Seeing only those objects already present in his imagination, the sleepwalker experiences "a suspension more or less complete of external feeling."[7] Although he is unable to compare ideas, to reason, to direct thought and action to an "appropriate" end, the night wanderer is curiously able to maneuver his way around furniture, to reach over one person to stab another, and to appear so nimble as to "emulate the feat of an acrobat." The reason for this selective perception is that the sleepwalker is pursuing objects to which his mind had been directed in waking moments, giving the appearance of engaging in purposeful behavior. His actions are impelled by habits since his senses appear to be inactive. As the prolific writer and noted medical man Henry Maudsley explained, "There is a purpose and there is a coordination of acts for its accomplishment but consciousness is still asleep, and memory retains no record of the transaction."[8]

Common to forms of suspended consciousness that intrigued nineteenth-century medical writers were mental impressions received in the "deliriant period" that completely vanished from memory, and "retain[ed] no record of the [mental] transaction." But as witnessed in similar periods of suspended consciousness, the somnambulist episode symbolized more than just behavior undertaken in a state of sleep, it was "a new life." A sleepwalker appeared "as a person might be supposed to do *who had two souls.*"[9] The failure of memory suggested not mere amnesia, but an unknown self, capable of a level of self-management and self-direction unknown to the waking person. The question confronting the nineteenth-century courtroom, however, was the sleeper's culpability, not her mobility.

The failure to remain a constant person suggested an inability to know what one was up to, let alone an awareness that any specific act was wrong. Without a fundamental knowledge of the nature and consequences of one's act, there could be no intentional choice to do evil. When he wrote that will and intention were required to make an act criminal, James Fitzjames Stephen singled out somnambulist acts as voluntary and yet not accompanied by intention. "Hence, if a man killed another in his sleep, there would be no crime, because there would be no intention and therefore no action."[10] The question for the jury was whether the crime revealed purposeful will and malicious intent.

Some medical writers answered this question by arguing that the crime was very much the accused's action because he was responsible for his own conscience, even in sleep. If the conscience is directed toward crime when fully awake—if one indulges aggressive thoughts "during waking hours"—the fact that such thoughts find fatal expression in sleep is neither surprising nor exculpatory.[11] As ever, the proposed medical condition carried no automatic legal consequence, because every crime occurs within a particular social circumstance; it was the meaning of the crime that the jury had to determine in order to reconstruct the defendant's intent. The tale of the hunters is exemplary for that purpose. On its surface, it seems like a very lucky escape from a perfectly innocent and "blameless" dreamer. But suppose, wondered William Best, the original teller of the tale, that "a blow given in this way had proved fatal, and the two men had been shown to have quarreled previously to retiring to rest?" Medical author Taylor continued Best's focus on the preexisting relationship between offender and victim, following this tale with an account of a trial for assault in which a defense of sleepwalking had been offered. "It was proved, however, that the prisoner had shown malicious feeling against the [victim], and that she had wished him dead . . . [and besides] . . . the knife bore the appearance of having been recently sharpened."[12] In another trial, a dreamer had proven rather too dexterous: "reach[ing] over someone to inflict the wound." The mere mention of a bizarre mental phenomenon in expert testimony therefore, conveyed no automatic legal significance; it was the social relationship between dreamer and victim that set the dream-induced action into context. Further, jurors may well have concluded that there was something a bit formulaic, a bit too convenient, about sleepwalking. It invited comparison with "temporary insanity," another proffered medical condition that was also both intuitively credible and legally suspect.

Once a jury is informed of preexisting animus between the accused and his victim, therefore, the "purposelessness" of the sleepwalker's behavior begins to resemble intentional, not unconscious behavior. When no prior enmity existed, however, when no relation at all linked victim and offender, how could perfectly unconscious criminality be explained? There was only one meaning the law would entertain with regard to purposeful, yet unconscious behavior: the activity of reflexes. The automatic act of breathing had long served to exemplify neuromuscular action that required no awareness of the person for its performance. Walking, W. E. B. Carpenter argued, was "so automatic that it may be done in sleep." He wrote of soldiers fatigued beyond all measure who continued to walk, although technically asleep.[13] The medico-physiological literature also introduces the example of the centipede which, though decapitated, "goes steadily forward."[14] In humans, these movements are set in motion not by conscious plan or motivated pursuit but by reflexes that direct the automaton to walk. Such acts were the expression of ideas with which the mind was possessed; the person who has the ideas is curiously missing at the time of the action.[15]

Medical authority Alfred Swaine Taylor explicitly considered the fit of sleepwalking to a criminal defense. If violence was indeed perpetrated unconsciously during sleep, it was to be assumed that malice and intention, the chief ingredients of criminal culpability, were lost. Although sound in principle, Taylor recognized that even this unequivocal pronouncement could not be taken as a predictor of jury verdicts. It was impossible to lay down general rules: "the circumstances attending each case will sufficiently explain how far the act of murder or suicide had been committed during a state of somnambulism, or under an illusion continuing from a state of sleep."[16]

Even with the allowance for circumstances that could vary with each alleged offense, there remained one standard hurdle: How to determine that the accused had been actually asleep. The court could hardly repeat the centipede procedure and remove the defendant's head to see if forward motion was still possible. A clinical history of sleepwalking might be of probative value (as in Culpeper), or perhaps the murder of one's own children in a stuporous, confused state would argue for unthinking criminality. But even with individuals who had documented previous sleepwalking episodes, it was clear to medical writers—and doubtless to courtroom personnel as well—that felons could take advantage of half-conscious states or could purposefully fall asleep near an enemy to effect the desired result: a homicidal sleepwalking episode. Taylor particularly warned it was "difficult to suppose that an individual should not recover from his delusion, before he could perpetrate an attack like murder."[17] It would, therefore, take evidence of something more than a tragic, regretful assault to invoke the image of persons not conscious of what they did, not the "masters" of their action.

"Save My Children!"

In January of 1859, the Marylebone Police Court heard Sergeant Simmons give the following frightening account of dream-induced violence:

At half-past 1 o'clock this morning, while on duty in East street, Manchester Square, I heard a female voice exclaim, "Oh my children! Save my children!" I went to house No. 71, whence the cries proceeded . . . and while making [my] way to the first floor front room I heard the smashing of glass. I knocked at the door, which I found was fastened, and said, "Open it; the police are here." The prisoner, who was in her nightdress, kept exclaiming, "Save my children!" and at length, after stumbling over something, let me and my brother officer in. When we entered we found the room in darkness, and it was only by aid of our lanterns that we could distinguish anything in the room. On the bed there was a child five years old, and another three years of age by her side. Everything in the place was in great confusion. The prisoner told me that she had been dreaming that her little boy had said the house was on fire, and [she had thrown her son through the glass window] with a view of preventing her children from being burnt to death. I have no doubt that if I and the other constable had not gone to the room, all three of the children would have been flung out into the street . . . the window had not been thrown up. The child was thrust through a pane of glass, the fragments of which fell into the street.[18]

Owing to her excited state, the policeman explained, Esther Griggs was not taken into custody. He understood from the surgeon that "it was a species of nightmare, which the prisoner was laboring under when the act was committed."

Esther Griggs returned to the Police Court twice more in the weeks following, as the court awaited news of her son's fragile hold on life. Eventually he recovered, and the grand jury empaneled to consider an indictment for assault with intent to murder refused to find a true bill, in effect rendering judgment on the ultimate question of Griggs' guilt or innocence, which was of course the sole province of the petit jury. This arrogation of responsibility had implications not only for the prisoner but also for future medicolegal historians.[19] As Nigel Walker notes, it was only the sharp eye of medical authors Bucknill and Tuke, spotting the tale of Esther Griggs in the popular broadsheets, that preserved this remarkable tale of sleepwalking and crime for future scholarship.[20] One reason, then, that it might be difficult to find defenses of sleepwalking in criminal trials may well be that the grand jury self-consciously acted as gatekeeper to the trial court, as in this instance, refusing to let the case go forward when jurors were convinced that the accused was too pitiable to be prosecuted. Evidence that other juries assumed this prerogative has been noted in proceedings regarding probable unconsciousness due to epilepsy, to be discussed shortly.

The readiness of grand jury members to acquit by refusing to indict affords the medicolegal historian some insight into the likely willingness of nineteenth-century jurors to conclude that sleep-induced mania could cancel criminal culpability. But circumventing the trial court also meant precluding the testimony of medical men regarding the mental and behavioral features of somnambulism, vital historical elements for reconstructing how various states of unconsciousness were explored in court. Alexander Morison and Henry Maudsley, two noted medical authors on insanity in general and sleepwalking in particular, testified throughout the post-McNaughtan years, though never in a trial that centered on somnambulism.[21] That experience would belong to the medical witnesses who appeared at the trial of Simon Fraser for the brutal slaying of his son.

Awakened when she heard her husband "roaring inarticulately like an animal," Mrs. Fraser was horrified to see that the object he was smashing against the wall was their young son. Her husband had dreamt of a wild beast attacking the boy, and had bolted out of bed to chase the animal around the bedroom, throwing tables and chairs at the beast.[22] He eventually laid hold of it and threw it against the walls of the room. Simon Fraser had a history of bizarre behavior that was amply documented by his father—once the victim of a similar sleep-induced assault—and other family members who had been "saved" when not drowning or pulled from imaginary fires. The defendant retained no memory of these acts, which invoked the question of whether it was indeed Fraser who had behaved so rashly.

Responding to the testimony of family members about the accused's inexplicable antics, the foreman of the jury announced that there was little reason to proceed with the case, "as the jury believed the prisoner was not responsible for his actions."[23] Lord-Justice Clark interposed, however, that they ought to hear the testimony of the medical witnesses. Dr. Yellowlees, physician superintendent of the Glasgow Royal Asylum was the first to appear, describing the prisoner's somnambulism as "a state of unhealthy action of the brain producing a morbid activity during sleep of varied intensity, sometimes developing delusions and violence. A person in such a state was quite unconscious of what he was doing." Under cross-examination, the superintendent acknowledged that he had no personal familiarity with cases of somnambulism and could discover no known forms of insanity "about" the prisoner. Pressed by the judge to expand his comments regarding the somnambulist's lack of conscious awareness, Dr. Yellowlees commented, "A man in that condition was unconscious of what he was doing, and was not responsible."[24]

Two more medical witnesses appeared who affirmed that Fraser was unconscious of the act, but, curiously, not bereft of sensation. Dr. Alexander Robertson averred that Fraser "actually did see. His senses were awake. He saw or felt the child, and mistook it for something else." Apparently the sleepwalker "sees" only those items that are alive in his imagination. By the time visual (or auditory) sensation is relayed to the mind, the dream has converted the associated image to its own use. But the status of sleepwalking in the classification of delusory pathologies was uncertain. As Robertson informed the court: "It was not a known form of insanity in medical science." Following Robertson to the stand was a Dr. Clousten of the Royal Asylum, Morningside, who also "could not detect any symptoms of insanity about him." On the contrary, he testified, he had been impressed with Fraser's "fair judgment" and affection for his wife. Asked if he "felt the death of his child [Fraser answered] that he did, but that as his wife was much put about, he had concealed his own feelings for her sake." Dr. Clousten completed his testimony by saying he "did not consider a man in such a condition as responsible."[25]

Lord-Justice Clark closed his address to the jury as follows:

> I suppose, gentlemen, you have not the slightest doubt that the prisoner at the time was totally unconscious of the act he was doing. There is not the slightest doubt that he was laboring under one of those delusions, which occur in a state of somnambulism—he was under the impression that some animal had got into the bed. I see no reason to doubt, and I do not suppose you, gentlemen, have any doubt, that the account as given is correct. It is a matter of some consequence to the prisoner whether he is found responsible or not, because you are aware that his future must to a great extent depend upon the verdict you shall return. The question whether a state of somnambulism such as this is to be considered a state of insanity or not is a matter with which I think you should not have to trouble yourselves. It is a question on which medical authority is not agreed. But what I would suggest is, that you should return a verdict such as this—that the Jury find the [prisoner] killed his child, but that he was in a state in which he was unconscious of the act which he was committing by reason of the condition of somnambulism, and that he was not responsible.[26]

This was a directed verdict, certainly, although hardly a novel feature in British courts. In insanity trials in particular, juries could hear the instruction, "then you will acquit to be sure, gentlemen," or "it is unnecessary to go further." Indeed, McNaughtan's verdict was a "directed acquittal." In Fraser's trial, jury members heard for the first time that they might (or should) find a sleepwalking defendant not responsible on the grounds of unconsciousness. And, as reported in the case report, "the jury returned a verdict accordingly."

According to Nigel Walker, the precise status of Fraser's verdict in British jurisprudence is unclear. Following the jury's finding, the Solicitor General suggested that the case be adjourned for two days, in order to determine what sort of disposition should be arranged for the accused. After "giving an undertaking" that he would henceforth sleep in a room occupied by no one else, Fraser was dismissed from the stand. This dismissal, however, was not an acquittal. Rather, note is made that the "Counsel for the Crown refrained from moving for sentence," and the Court "deserted the diet simpliciter [i.e., released him summarily]."[27] Walker is certainly right in drawing an analogy here to the special verdict in inanity cases allowed to English juries in the nineteenth century. In fact, the disposition of prisoners acquitted on grounds of insanity remained a fluid matter until 1800, when Parliament mandated indefinite detention for prisoners acquitted "by reason of insanity."[28] Fraser's verdict and innovative disposition drew somnambulism into the orbit of defenses and verdicts based on abnormal mental states, although medical witnesses at his trial went to considerable lengths to distance sleepwalking—an affliction sane persons could manifest—from diagnosable insanity.

The judge also lent his considerable weight to keeping somnambulism and insanity completely separate: as medical opinion was divided, he asked jurors not to "trouble" themselves with the differences. Instead he drew their attention to the possibility of finding the accused not responsible solely on the basis of the alleged state of unconsciousness. For the first time a British jury received an instruction embracing the notion that the indictable crime was in effect not the prisoner's at all. Fraser was little more than an automaton put into action by a compelling, insistent dream. Acquittal following judicial directives along such lines was not new. What distinguished the Fraser case was an instruction of this kind in the trial of a purportedly sane prisoner. No physical or mental disease preceded the fatal assault. No memory linked the antics of the sleepwalker with regular, responsible behavior. And no continuous consciousness united the two personas presented to the jury. If the sleepwalker and the prisoner really did constitute a person "with two souls," how could the court, in Locke's terms, "imprison one twin for the actions of the other"?

The Unconscious and *Vertigé épileptique*

In an article published in the *Journal of Medical Science*, Dr. Yellowlees examined Fraser's condition, trying to distinguish "normal" dreaming from the impelling and determined state that resulted in the brutal death of Fraser's son. The prisoner's dream seizures—which Yellowlees called "somnomania"—resembled attacks of nocturnal epilepsy, "in which the nervous explosion assumes a mental instead of physical form."[29] It was the unusual timing of their emergence during sleep that distinguished the somnambulist's "seizures," and yet the same degree of unconscious behavior linked the two states of "not being oneself." This medical witness was not alone in drawing attention to the similarity between sleepwalking and epileptic seizures. Writing forty years before the Fraser trial, noted author James Cowles Prichard singled out for comment the category of "ecstatic somnambulism: the most severe affection . . . most frequently connected with other disorders of the brain. In females it is often conjoined with catalepsy and hysteria, and in males with epilepsy."[30]

The association of somnambulism, epilepsy, and unconscious behavior had entered the Old Bailey two years before the Fraser decision, in 1876. This time, it would not be a judge's instructions and the consequent directed verdict that would signal the acceptance of unconsciousness as constituting a successful courtroom defense. Instead, it would be the jury's sole initiative to return a verdict of "not guilty on the ground of unconsciousness." The trial of Elizabeth Carr for the maiming of her infant daughter—an assault that proved fatal in time—was not the first occasion for a jury to consider the possible influence of epilepsy on (criminal) behavior. Since the late eighteenth century, "fits" played a prominent role in the testimony of neighbors, lovers, and coworkers who appeared in court to describe the behavioral pandemonium of the putative insane. These attacks, when given a specific term, were often described as "apoplexy," but the lay witness's frequent mention of froth and drooling suggests that jurors were hearing of characteristics that more conformed to a folk notion of epileptic seizure. In the years following McNaughtan, one in ten Old Bailey trials that turned on the accused's mental state featured some formula of fit, foam, or fainting (see Appendix table A.2). Epilepsy was mentioned by name in half of these trials, in prosecutions ranging from arson to assault, from forgery to infanticide.[31] The association often made between epilepsy and convulsive seizure activity did not preclude a criminal defense that tied wandering fits to criminal activity as obviously calculated as forgery.[32] Of course, presenting a criminal defense and convincing a jury of its merits was a different matter. Even in cases of impulsive criminality, epilepsy did not afford the defendant with persuasive grounds for arguing nonresponsibility. With the exception of an 1862 trial for attempted suicide that ended in an acquittal on the grounds of insanity, not one defendant between 1843 and 1876 who invoked epilepsy as a possible exculpatory condition escaped conviction.[33]

On first consideration, the implications of epileptic seizure for the jury's inference of nonresponsibility would seem manifestly obvious. Stephen himself provided a legal interpretation of the significance of seizures when he singled out convulsive fits in a discussion of the two elements required to make an action criminal: will and intention. "[A] man in a convulsive fit strikes another and kills him. He has committed no crime, because he has done no act. He has been acted upon. His muscles do not contract in consequence of an act of the will . . . he neither willed nor intended the act . . . the case would be the same as if a third person had pushed against the person hurt and so done the mischief."[34] Contemporary medical opinion joined the noted jurist in depicting convulsive epilepsy as instinctive, blind madness: the individual cannot be held responsible in any degree for acts perpetrated by him during the perfectly automatic, though short-lived, delirium. Did the prisoner act "with intention, will and malice [Stephen asked]; Was it his act?"[35] Nineteenth-century medical authors invoked Paolo Zacchia's long standing belief that a "plea" of epilepsy should be valid within three days of an attack—either before or after the seizure—although opinion was divided regarding whether such a general rule was practicable.[36] Certainly a person could not be held responsible for actions committed in the midst of a seizure, but these wildly manic episodes lasted a matter of minutes. It was the necessary consequence of these seizures on subsequent mental functioning that medical men debated. For some clinicians, the mere existence of epilepsy in the patient's biography should preclude a finding of guilt. For others, such a doctrine would spread the notion of irresponsibility to the point that their courtroom testimony would eventually become meaningless at best, and risible at worst.

For all of epilepsy's popular association with unconscious seizure, the courtroom's inquiry into the legal implications of vertiginous spinning resembled the negotiation of other, standard states of abnormal functioning. Isolating and naming a disease did not end courtroom inquiry; it rather invited further questions that probed the link between the crime and the purported impairment. A person with epilepsy, after all, could also be a jealous person. Was it the convulsion that struck the victim or the spurned lover? What degree of moral accountability did an epileptic person retain, for all his conspicuous, uncontrolled "froth-ing"? Was his "loss of free will" a result of suspended consciousness or of willfully indulged emotions? These questions, one should add, were asked by medical writers, not by a suspicious legal community.[37] One sees no medical crusade—either in print or in the witness box—to re-place culpability with convulsion, or to draw epilepsy and insanity into an ever-tightening circle. Indeed, a great number of authors vocally dis-puted a necessary connection between the two.

In the second half of the nineteenth century, however, there was a noticeable shift in medical writing and courtroom testimony that mir-rored an earlier development in forensic psychiatric testimony. As long as madness was a matter of plainly visible behavioral excess and verbal pandemonium, medical witnesses were rarely thought to be a critical presence in the courtroom. If neighbors testified that someone was in the habit of dancing naked in the street while holding burning candles, one hardly needed a Fellow of the Royal College of Physicians to di-agnose delirium. As nineteenth-century madness moved inside, and a hidden, recondite delusion replaced legible, unambiguous distraction, specialists in mental medicine were called by enterprising defense at-torneys to question the observations of lay witnesses who informed the jury of the prisoner's customarily calm demeanor and rationality.[38] While one can certainly argue that unmasking the misguided surface impressions of the lay person was pivotal to medicine's claim to expert knowledge regarding the nature of mental derangement, the appearance in court of medical specialists was instigated by the legal, not the med-ical, profession. Such expert testimony might not only reveal the neigh-bor's limited knowledge, but the general practitioner's claims based on a limited, passing familiarity with the distracted, not on insight gained by asylum superintendency.

Just as medical writing on the hidden character of delusion antici-pated its association with the mad-doctors' increasingly frequent ap-pearance in court by several years, a refinement in medical writing re-garding epilepsy would find expression in the 1876 trial of Elizabeth Carr. From antiquity to the early modern era, epilepsy had unambigu-ously been defined in terms of spasmodic and convulsive seizures.[39] Such episodes might involve fainting, writhing on the floor, or foam-ing at the mouth, and they were always accompanied by unconscious-ness. In the first quarter of the nineteenth century, medical writers turned their attention to epileptic attacks that were neither convulsive nor violent, but that nonetheless left the patient unconscious to what was transpiring. In these fits of absence, or "vertigo," apparent calm and a demonstrated capacity to answer questions belied the actual state of unconsciousness. When recovered "to himself," the patient professed no memory of the conversation or the activity that had passed. Medical writers referred to such an interval of calm and apparent return to reason as *un vertige*.[40] That a patient spoke "in an odd voice" came as little surprise; was it, in fact, the patient who was actually speaking?

When periods of absence were in evidence, the temptation for acquaintances of the accused—and the magistrates—to infer a return to normal functioning was obvious and, according to medical writers, a perceptual trap. The French clinician Falret explained, "[P]atients appear to be conscious of what is passing around. They speak and act in such a manner as to inspire doubt as to the real nature of attacks—and to attach to what is said and done . . . a character of moral liberty to which they possess no title."[41] Falret among others spoke of this medical condition as *vertigé épileptique,* and though English writers would refer to states of dizziness or light-headedness as vertigo, the French term was used to depict a very particular type of absence. Often between two episodes of manic convulsion or immediately following a single seizure, the individual returned to a moment of apparent calm that appeared to be true recovery. Sudden, completely unmotivated actions sometimes erupt in the midst of a conversation. "A girl of 16 suddenly lost all consciousness of her acts, and dropped or more frequently threw away at a distance anything she was holding . . . the attack scarcely lasted half a minute, and as it passed off she called out, 'It is over.'"[42]

Not all episodes of absence or "disappearance" were characterized by violence. Trousseau wrote of a violinist subject to "epileptic vertigo" who, while playing the violin, "goes on playing during the attack, although he is perfectly unconscious of everything around him; and neither hears nor sees those he is accompanying, still he plays in time. It would seem as if his will were powerful enough to direct the movements of his hands for a given, though very short time; as if these movements were guided by memory, just as his mind became afflicted."[43] When Trousseau ended the story with "this condition of absence is somewhat analogous to somnambulism," he forged yet another link between *vertigé épileptique* and automatic behavior. Both the sleepwalker and the "automatic" violinist revealed the enduring influence of habit on subsequent behavior (hence the reason for the court's interest in preexisting enmity in cases of murder while sleepwalking). As an example of "unconscious behavior," Carpenter wrote, "I set my automaton to walk to a certain place and direct my thoughts to something altogether different."[44] This image of an automaton "set in motion" could therefore describe both consciously willed and unconsciously performed behavior. In both cases, the behavior is "automatic": something (someone?) has taken over and performs the deed. *Vertigé épileptique* introduced a wrinkle into medicolegal writing: the epileptic person's unconscious behavior could take place without convulsions. "Every physician who has studied epileptic vertigo particularly must have seen cases of individuals speaking and answering questions during the attack (perhaps in an odd voice) but still answering questions *to the point*. The paroxysm once over, they have no recollection of what has just passed."[45] That the automaton's voice might not resemble its "owner's" further underscored the discontinuity in being when the afflicted was unconscious. In medical writing, the diagnosis of *vertigé épileptique* clearly gained a footing by the 1860s and 1870s; its legal consequence had yet to be tested at the Old Bailey.

In a Vertiginous Spin

"What shall I do? I have cut my baby's hand off!" cried Elizabeth Carr moments after walking into the kitchen to slice a piece of bread and slicing off her daughter's hand instead.[46] Described in court as "a kind and affectionate mother" who unfortunately did "all sorts of ridiculous things" as she moved about her room in a habitual state of unconsciousness, Carr was initially put on trial for "feloniously cutting and wounding" her daughter. Tragically, the infant would eventually die of massive blood loss, resulting in a coroner's jury and a likely indictment for murder. "I hope you will not think I was in a clear conscious state when I did it" was her only defense, given before the magistrate and read to the Old Bailey jury.

Dr. Edward Merrion, physician to the Hospital for Diseases of the Nervous System, and with "a great many of these cases . . . under [his] notice," was the sole medical witness to appear in Elizabeth Carr's defense.

I have made notes of 600 to 700 cases—the prisoner came under my observation as an out-patient in July, 1871. [I]t is very unusual for these acts to be performed during epileptic fits, but it is a recognized form of epileptiform disease. They are purely automatic acts, the patient is perfectly unconscious . . . the fit comes on with a perfectly quiescent condition. [T]his poor woman . . . after she has been in such [a] quiescent state a few minutes, she gets up and will occupy herself in household work, putting things away, perhaps, but she does not know it herself—I have not a doubt but that she was absolutely unconscious of what she was doing—I have not a doubt but that [the daughter's injury] was a purely automatic act—she had the child in her hand and was going to cut a piece of bread and butter . . . it would not take much force to cut off the hand of so young a child if the knife was applied at the wrist—this is not convulsive epilepsy, we have no name for it in English, but the French call it *vertigé épileptique*— the complaint is not characteristic of insanity in the slightest way, the patient may be perfectly sane and fall into that condition, there is neither homicidal or [*sic*] suicidal tendency, but any act which is begun before the fit may be continued . . . it is not looked upon by the profession as insanity in any form.

Asked a series of questions touching on the possible medical connection of epilepsy to insanity, the physician affirmed, "[E]pilepsy has nothing to do with insanity . . . I do not consider that the patient is in the slightest degree insane." In answer to a question by the judge to clarify his use of the term "automatic," Dr. Merrion concluded his testimony with the following: "I should say that an automatic act and an unconscious act are identically the same; if I might illustrate it, I would give the instance of a simple experiment: you cut off a centipede's head and put the body on the table and the centipede will go on walking automatically, although it will run against anything."[47]

The jury had the option, of course, of a simple conviction or acquittal, although neither outcome seemed likely, given the extraordinary circumstances surrounding the child's wounding. There was no question that the mother had wielded the knife, but there seemed little justification to acquit on the grounds of insanity after the medical witness had forcefully denied that the prisoner was mad. Rather than turning to the judge for advice—an option exercised by earlier juries facing ambiguous states of intention—the jury in the trial of Elizabeth Carr elected a singular solution: "Not Guilty on the ground of unconsciousness." Given the novel wording of the verdict, there was no clear guideline regarding how to dispose of the defendant. An insanity acquittal would probably have resulted in Carr's commitment to Broadmoor; an outright acquittal would have meant her immediate release. The judge announced his intention to make a special report to the Home Secretary, but in the meantime he "considered that the verdict amounted to one of not guilty on the ground of insanity . . . ordering the prisoner to be detained during Her Majesty's Pleasure."

The judge presumably intended to keep Elizabeth Carr confined pending the coroner's jury's consideration of an indictment for murder, as her infant eventually succumbed to her frightful wound. In a move strangely reminiscent of the decision taken by the grand jury in the matter of the woman who threw her child through the plate-glass window—refusing to return a true bill owing to the probable existence of sleepwalking—the coroner's jury refused to implicate Elizabeth Carr "in any way as being the cause of death."[48] One wonders again how many other grand juries or coroner's juries might have "narrowed the field" of legal history by refusing to return a verdict that would have initiated criminal court proceedings. One can say with certainty, however, that by 1876, non-insane automatism had entered into jury deliberations. It would take only five months for *vertigé épileptique* to appear again in a criminal defense at the Old Bailey.

"The Memory Is Blank . . . The Brain Stands Still"

Shortly after sitting down with his friend John Collins and warmly greeting Collins's wife, Frederick Treadaway pulled out a revolver and shot his friend once above the eye, then turned the gun on Elizabeth Collins, whom he subsequently beat savagely. She later testified: "I opened my mouth to cry murder, and he put his hand in my mouth so I could not speak, and with the other hand he took me by the neck and threw me down outside the outer door, and then he beat my head several times—I struggled hard for life as he knelt upon me—I put my hand to the floor to try to get up. . . . I put my hand in a pool of blood."[49]

Abandoning the bleeding woman in the alleyway, Treadaway suddenly "returned to himself" and was carried off by a constable to the police station, where he protested that all these events were a "blank." With a family history abounding with mad or suicidal relations and well-documented episodes of absence, Treadaway seemed the next likely defendant to fashion a defense of *vertigé épileptique*.

The prisoner's father provided the court with a most vivid example of "disappearance." Father and son were out for a walk on a Saturday afternoon when the boy suddenly "staggered." Asked what was the matter, the son mumbled something indistinctly and fainted. Frederick's father, George Treadaway, told the Old Bailey jury, "I dragged him into a doorway, and rubbed his back and opened his hands and rubbed them, and kept speaking to him, but he was not conscious—he seemed to be quite unconscious of what I was doing, he could not speak to me—this lasted altogether, I think, as nearly as possible twenty minutes—he trembled very much, and shook violently and turned deadly pale, and then afterwards seemed gradually to recover."[50] The jury did not have to take the father's description on faith. The day before his father appeared in court, the prisoner had fainted dead away in the courtroom and had to be removed from the dock. Prison surgeon John Gibson advised the court, "He is clearly insensible for the time being, I do not think he will be likely sufficiently to recover today to enable him to go on with the trial." Gibson added that the fits were "more of an hysterical character than epileptic," and added, "I have not seen any symptoms of this kind before."[51]

When the trial resumed the following day the jury heard that a probable suicidal intention had prompted the purchase of the gun that Treadaway used to shoot his friend. Financially pressed and facing uncertain job prospects, the melancholic Treadaway had visited John Collins, apparently planning to take his own life soon after, as he had given instructions for the disposition of his personal effects. No reason for the assaults was discernible, from either Mrs. Collins or the prisoner's family. This would not be a trial that would turn on motive or intent however, for the thrust of the medical testimony was that these crimes were not the prisoner's at all.

Dr. Hughes Bennett, a member of the College of Physicians and a frequent witness to the differences between epileptic fits and epileptic vertigo, informed the court of his familiarity with patients whose seemingly purposeless behavior was attended with "unconsciousness" and a complete loss of memory.

> At the time of the attack of vertigo the patient is unconscious . . . during the time of an attack of epileptic vertigo, the person can perform acts of which he is unconscious, and speak, but not rationally: he may speak apparently rationally . . . there are a good many writers upon this subject, eminent medical men; among the English are Doctors Maudslay [Maudsley], Jackson, Russell and Reynolds and among the French there are Trousseau, Fabret [most likely Falret] and Esquirol . . . it is after an acquaintance with the writing of these authors that I have given the last answer.

[O]n the morning of the 15th he had a very severe headache, [and while] sitting with Mr. Collins, he was seized with a violent shooting pain in the head, with giddiness, and with the sensation of a black cloud coming over his senses, and from that moment his mind was blank until he found himself in the street.

After referring to the episode of the "dark cloud" crowding out the prisoner's senses, the judge read aloud the father's account of his son's episode of "absence" while walking with him. Dr. Bennett acknowledged that some of the symptoms were "quite consistent with epileptic vertigo," but added that symptoms can belong to a host of affections; without witnessing the fit firsthand, he was uncomfortable giving an opinion.[52] Electing not to force the doctor to choose between epileptic vertigo and other, less dramatic conditions, the attorney asked the doctor if he "was able to form an opinion as to what the state of the prisoner was at that time." This time, it was the judge who expressed his discomfort with such an opinion-begging question: "This was the form of question often put and objected to, and it was really not a question of medical science, but was the question which the Jury alone could properly decide."[53]

Following Dr. Bennett on the stand was Rhys Williams, a member of the Royal College of Physicians of Edinburgh. Affirming that the medical profession recognized epileptic vertigo as a disease, Dr. Williams continued, "Some years ago I saw a gentleman who simply suffered from headache occasionally; at the time I had no suspicion of epilepsy. One morning suddenly whilst at breakfast he made a violent attack on his wife; when I saw him shortly afterwards he could give no account of it, nor any reason for so doing." As the witness informed the jury, the act of persons afflicted with epileptic vertigo is "automatic, that is the state they are in . . . they act as mere machines, and when they recover they are utterly unconscious of anything that has happened."[54] The final medical witness, Joseph Peake Richards, medical superintendent of Hanwell Lunatic Asylum, agreed with the two previous physicians that persons in a state of epileptic vertigo are not only unconscious during their crime but are also disbelieving when confronted with a description of the offending behavior. He informed the Treadaway jury of his experience with one particular patient:

On one occasion she was talking very agreeably and sensibly, and suddenly I saw that her mind seemed to get vacant . . . she did not look at me in the face, and suddenly hit out at me, and as soon as that was done she went on talking in the same agreeable strain—I said to her, "Why did you hit me?" she said, "I don't think I hit you, I don't remember anything about it at all."

Summing up his characterization of epileptic vertigo, Dr. Richards underscored the perfect unconscious fit that accompanies the paroxysm: "The memory is a blank, the brain stands still, and muscular action goes on."[55]

The three medical witnesses had spoken at length and in detail regarding the characteristics of epileptic vertigo and had spoken indirectly to how the disease "recognized by the medical profession" accounted for the circumstances of the prisoner's alleged crime. It is impossible to say whether there might have been a different outcome if the image of a "mere machine" or automatic action had been the last words the jurors took into their deliberation. As it was, Judge Lash permitted the prosecution to call two medical witnesses in rebuttal, not a novel circumstance but not a conventional one either. Prison surgeons Smiles and Gibson of the house of detention at Clerkenwell and of Newgate, respectively, denied having heard of epileptic attacks occurring previous to the prisoner's appearance before the Old Bailey, and attributed the courtroom fit to hysteria.

DEFENSE ATTORNEY BEASLEY: You say there was hysteria mixed up with the attack yesterday; do I understand you to contradict point blank the statement of Dr. Williams and Dr. Bennett?

PRISON SURGEON SMILES: On the contrary, I merely mention what I saw from that part of the Court, I cannot go so far as that.

JUDGE: From what you saw of him whilst under your supervision, had you any suspicion of epilepsy in any form?

SMILES: Not the least in the world; not the slightest.

Newgate surgeon Gibson next referred to the possibility that a genuine state of unconsciousness accompanied Treadaway's courthouse fit. He described efforts to bring the prisoner around:

Some snuff was blown up his nose, that had no effect—I tested him with the same snuff this morning, and it had a very ready effect—I think the graver symptoms were probably of an epileptic nature—in a person with a tendency to epilepsy, I think a prolonged trial and strong emotion would certainly produce such an attack.[56]

Although compelled to concede that the fit was genuine, the two prison surgeons endeavored to focus the juror's attention on epilepsy as a cataleptic convulsion: yes, unconsciousness could be the result, but no mention was made of inexplicable violent acts committed for no reason at all, and upon friends who had precipitated no resentment or animus. By the end of the trial, few courtroom observers—least of all the jurors—could doubt the prisoner's status as an epileptic. The issue was the state of his consciousness during the assault and whether the law could accommodate a sane unconscious.

In summing up the case, the judge reminded the jury:

> Every man was presumed to be sane and to possess sufficient reason to distinguish right from wrong. It must be clearly proved that at the time of committing the act the prisoner was not sensible of the quality of the offence . . . of which he was charged . . . in other words, did he labor under such an affliction of Providence that he was for the moment deprived of consciousness to such an extent that he was a mere automaton from an attack of epileptic vertigo. If he did not know what he was doing, the jury might acquit him and find him guilty [sic] on the ground of insanity. [Precluding its ability to convict on a lesser charge, he informed the jury] there was nothing in the case which reduced it to the crime of manslaughter.[57]

Following the murder conviction, the judge assumed the black cap and passed sentence. Affirming that he "entirely concurred" with the jury's decision, Justice Lash dismissed the argument that any weight should be given to the lack of motive for the killing or the contention that the killing was meant to be a suicide. The only act before the court was clearly a willful one, and he could "exhort [Treadaway] to prepare for the fate which awaited him." The *Times of London* report concluded: "The convict, who is a very young man in the prime of life and of prepossessing appearance and manners, was removed from the bar."[58]

As mentioned at the beginning of this volume, one interprets the significance of a verdict with enormous respect for the myriad factors that might have influenced the jury. Even if verdicts could be read as persuasive evidence that medical testimony did indeed influence an individual jury, the significance of any one verdict is far surpassed by evidence of a judge's willingness to incorporate novel medical ideas in the formal instructions given to subsequent juries in considering a possible acquittal. Judicial instructions are not as equivocal as verdicts and offer important insight into the growing utility of specialist knowledge to the law's consideration of culpability. One can supplement judicial case summations with the trial narratives themselves, which offer similar clues to the reception of medical testimony in the tenor of the courtroom debate, evident in questions asked of the judge, of the various attorneys, and, in some trials, of the jury members themselves.

The suggestion that sleepwalking lay behind Sarah Minchin's crime was not laughed out of court or contemptuously dismissed by a prosecutor. Ironically, perhaps, the one courtroom participant reluctant to consider its possible role was the medical witness. The judge in the Fraser trial not only considered the possibility that the defendant really thought he was bashing a phantom beast, he directed the jury to acquit on the grounds of unconsciousness, as the Carr jury did, with no prompting from the judge. And in the trial of Frederick Treadaway, none of the medical witnesses proffering *vertigé épileptique* faced hostile cross-examination that attempted to reduce the new forensic psychiatric term to ridicule. More significantly, their diagnosis was cited by the judge in his instructions as possible grounds for acquittal.

Given the elements shared by sleepwalkers and defendants afflicted with *vertigé épileptique,* and those who claimed periods of absence, W. A. F. Browne's observation regarding the effects of epilepsy are particularly haunting. "There is a portion of each epileptic's moral life during which he has not lived—of which he has no record nor experience such as other men have. [I]n this transitory stupor of the *petit mal,* no conscious thought is present . . . the individual ceases to be, morally."[59] Although it is conventional for the nonepileptic and the epileptic alike to claim that during their uncharacteristic episodes they were not "themselves," the patient with epileptic vertigo and the person who emerged from a sleepwalking trance were more than simply not themselves: they were in fact *missing.* During periods of perfect unconsciousness, some alchemy of motor skills and forward motion resulted in inexplicable, unintended action. In the clinic, the physician had to account for seemingly purposeful behavior unattended by consciousness. In the courtroom, the same ambiguities remained but the question of doubtful agency was forced to conform to legal criteria for assessing culpability: *knowing* right from wrong, *knowing* the nature of one's act. Juries confronted with the most dramatic examples of suspended consciousness did not acquit on the grounds of insanity but found the defendants either guilty or not guilty on the ground of unconsciousness.

Faced with medical testimony that forcefully denied the notion that *vertigé épileptique* had anything to do with insanity, jurors refused to resort to the traditional categories of mental derangement. One can only wonder at the questions they debated. What did an automaton know? Was it, in Stephen's words, *his* act? Although the sleepwalker is doubtless the most dramatic example of a "missing" defendant, she shared with the epileptic, the defendant described as "quite absent," the alternating examiner and ranter, and the patient possessed with thousands of spirits a common feature: a fatal lapse in consciousness and memory. In some part of a life "not lived," inexplicable criminality resulted in an Old Bailey trial at which the defendant had no more answers than the jury.

CONCLUSION

$\mathcal{I}$N HIS REMARKABLY INSIGHTFUL STUDY of the origins and evolution of Multiple Personality Disorder, Ian Hacking encourages his readers to look beyond the supposed psychopathology of the patient, to inquire instead into the perceptual tools of the diagnostician: "I am not concerned with what [the multiple personality] 're-ally had.' I am concerned with what was said about him, how he was treated, and how the discourse and the symptom language of multiple personality came into being."[1] Hacking's preferred focus reminds one of social scientists who, ever since Max Weber, have sought to answer a similar question about social action: what meaning do we give to social behavior? What are the social resources—the definitions, motives, and *symptom language*—available for interpreting the behavior of others as well as ourselves? For the historian of evolutionary changes in diagnostic imagery, a further question suggests itself: When interpretive language shifts—when explanatory terms divert down an unfamiliar path—what can one infer about the changing preoccupations and emerging anxieties bedeviling contemporary culture?

Until the time of Daniel McNaughtan's trial (1843), jurors, witnesses, and judges at the Old Bailey possessed relatively few conceptual tools with which to "make sense" of a defendant's action. They could of course find the action intentional and deem the person culpable. They could interpret the behavior as accidental and find the prisoner responsible for a lesser crime, or even not culpable for any crime. Or they might consider the crime to be the result of some compelling force brought on by the defendant's personal or economic distress and then find the whole affair pitiable and perhaps not punishable. The jury's function was not to infer the defendant's motive, although it would be the unusual juror who did not ask the "why" question, if only to himself. Instead, the nineteenth-century juror's attempt to interpret the behavior of the accused followed a narrower path: What must the defendant have thought he was doing; what did he *intend* to do? Contemplating the psychological reason for the act might help in gauging the prisoner's intention—what he meant to do—but divining the *reason* for the crime was not, specifically, the jury's business.

That jurors could not discern a motive for an alleged crime should not, judges cautioned, preclude a guilty verdict once they had concluded that the accused understood that he had a weapon in his hand and appreciated the consequence of using it. Actions freely chosen, with or without an intelligible motive, were intentional, purposeful, and culpable. In those trials when jurors concluded that the accused had not understood the wrongfulness of his actions—the mortal consequence of his action and the legal harm to which he was exposing himself—the only meaning the jury could give to the action was to consider it as an act of madness. Insanity, to the contemporary jury and to today's historian of courtroom behavior, provided the meaning for seemingly opaque human behavior.

Clearly not all madness was insanity. During the years that witnessed the introduction and rapid rise of medical testimony bearing on mental derangement—1760 to 1843—juries at the Old Bailey heard witnesses, and often defendants themselves, describe a host of mental states believed to cloud the prisoner's capacity to understand the nature of his actions. Thus insensibility, delirium, being "out of one's wits," paroxysms of mania, and ultimately delusion figured prominently, not only in medical testimony, but also in neighborly impressions reported by the defendant's lovers, coworkers, and acquaintances. A juror's task was to assess the likely impact of these extraordinary mental states on the prisoner's capacity to choose to do wrong: to act with intent. Insanity was thus a legal, not a medical, designation. Jurors might accept a medical witness's characterization of the defendant as delirious or delusional and still not consider the mental state to have been sufficiently distracting to preclude responsibility. Defendants acquitted on the grounds of insanity were therefore those whose madness rose to the legal criterion of nonresponsibility.

In the years following McNaughtan, a further state of extraordinary being entered the testimony of medical witnesses. Although at first it resembled certain elements of diagnosable madness, this novel condition eventually departed from the language of mental symptoms altogether. Often with no history of mental distress, and certainly with no time spent in an asylum, a set of defendants in the Victorian courtroom could nonetheless be described as "not responsible," "not answerable," although "not looked upon as insane in any form." Witnesses characterized these prisoners simply as "quite unconscious of the act."

To be sure, states of gauzy consciousness and absence were not unknown to the Old Bailey; lay witnesses in the early nineteenth century had invoked images of the prisoner's wandering mind and obliviousness to the act when describing what it was that first prompted the inference of madness.[2] But it is only after McNaughtan that one finds medical witnesses citing the vagaries of consciousness, and specifically the condition of unconsciousness, in testimony that sidestepped a diagnosis of madness. The migration of symptoms and images from lay to medical language is yet further evidence that psychiatry—in this instance, forensic psychiatry—was very much "shaped from below." Witnesses framing their testimony in terms of *medical* opinion and the professional "gaze" first borrowed and then codified folk beliefs and common cultural understanding about variations in consciousness to assert the presence of non-insane mental episodes in court.

But to situate (eventual) medical conceptions in what were originally lay perceptions still begs the question of how the language of lapsed consciousness came into being, and why, particularly, in the mid-nineteenth century. One might argue, for example, that after McNaughtan, prisoners really did "have" something new, that the language of delusion that had served possessed defendants earlier in the century failed to address the condition of persons now on trial who seemed to manifest spirits that really did constitute a second self. For medical witnesses to focus on unconsciousness and automatic actions would therefore (merely) reflect new medical insights and a more precise description of the malady.

The difficulty with such a historical approach to understanding how contemporaries made sense of aberrant behavior is that, as Hacking points out, one must assume the existence of an essential pathology out there (or *in* there) that was interpreted by successive generations of classifiers.[3] Little attempt is made to examine how prevailing cultural images and linguistic convention shape the expression of mental torment and perhaps even the experience of torment itself. Whatever the "essence" of mental distraction may be, the language used to interpret and subjectively to name it is historically contingent and responsive to the distinct social setting—the court, the clinic—that gave it meaning.

Nineteenth-century London experienced few displays as trenchant—and as mystifying—as those supplied by the mesmerist, the hypnotist, and the animal magnetist, engaging not only the public's imagination but likely that of the mentally distracted as well. One defendant at the Old Bailey explicitly described his torment with reference to the popular craze: "[He] said that a mesmerist was downstairs below him who was trying to throw him out the window by force, trying experiments, and that there were wires from the room below to his room, that he was cutting those wires, and while he was cutting them he was interrupted, and that he was sorry he had shot the policeman."[4] As the language of delusion and insensibility had enabled the distracted of an earlier generation to name the dis-ease they experienced, the world of mesmerism, of hypnotism "beheading" the will, of the possibility that someone else had committed the crime, offered the defendant a way to comprehend what had happened in the period that was "simply a blank to me."[5] The historical progression of diagnostic categories does not reveal the history of successive attempts to penetrate the true essence of madness so much as the evolution of cultural meanings that make the mental distress knowable—to both the observer and the afflicted.

Certainly the medical observer's inference was not a passive exercise in "reading the patient": his role in asylum superintendence and the emerging consumer market in private medical consulting engaged issues of professional identity that rendered diagnosis a many-sided thing. The Old Bailey, after all, functioned not only as London's premier legal forum, but also as theatre, replete with audience, stage, and compelling—not to say deadly—scripts. Just as the defense attorney's skill in securing an acquittal functioned to ensure future clients, the medical witness's (successful) claim to medical insight and understanding might establish both his voice and reputation. In this regard, one might be tempted to explain the emergence of an innovative medical concept as a professional gambit. Eager to assert and maintain their cognitive territory in the courtroom, medical witnesses found in the varying states of consciousness a conceptually attractive language to counter the restrictive criteria imposed by the McNaughtan Rules, and by so doing ensured their role in the professional division of labor in the courtroom.

This argument assumes, however, that forensic psychiatric witnesses wanted to testify in criminal trials—a debatable assumption then as now.[6] Certainly some witnesses were driven by self-conscious professional ambition, although a great many medical men were simply responding to court subpoenas or a city administrator's summons. That their testimony sometimes revealed ambitious claims to unique professional insight is doubtless true, but one could more easily argue that the attorney's questions revealed considerably more of their own professional ambition, attempting to employ the medical gaze to effect an acquittal. What appears today as adventurous medical testimony may well have been coaxed, even pulled, out, the better to win an acquittal.

These observations are not made to suggest that medical witnesses were disinterested courtroom participants; certainly the frequency with which a Conolly or a Winslow appeared in the London courtroom belied the notion that all mad-doctors were dragged into court kicking and screaming. It is to argue, instead, that even as late as the beginning of the last quarter of the nineteenth century, one does not discern the voice of a professionally conscious forensic psychiatric witness. Professional consciousness, when it appeared, was forged in the cut and thrust of cross-examination; the Old Bailey papers suggest that territorial or cognitive designs did not initiate courtroom participation. Although *lapsed memory* and *unconsciousness* may have emerged as terms of preference for medical witnesses in this period, one simply cannot draw a line between budding professional designs and the creation of a new medical term to employ in medical testimony.[7] The courtroom was not the clinic; medical witnesses were appearing in "borrowed robes."

It is, in the end, the social setting of the courtroom one must return to in searching for the historical conditions that framed the new symptom language of the nineteenth-century trial. Although medical science doubtless enjoys considerable cultural authority, individual trial judges decide if scientific opinion is credible and relevant to the court's purpose. This was no less true in the mid-nineteenth century than it is today. Indeed, the authority of the medical claims to knowledge in the Victorian courtroom was a decidedly negotiable commodity, and nowhere more so than in matters of mental medicine. Any modification in the content of forensic psychiatric testimony, therefore—any adoption of a particular professional language embracing new terms of preference— must be placed within the context of changes first experienced in the

courtroom setting itself. And there were few changes more fundamental to the mid-Victorian criminal trial than the pronounced alteration
in the courtroom division of labor. A marked change in what was said
about the accused—the emergence of a shift in allowing for purposeful, yet unconscious, behavior—could hardly have occurred independently of initiatives undertaken to reform the criminal law in general and
the substance of criminal evidence in particular.

The Long-Deferred Spotlight on Evidence

Sociologist Robert Merton often examined the effects of social
change in terms of manifest and latent functions, the latter promising
considerably more far-reaching and often unanticipated consequences
for social organization.[8] Criminal law reform early in the nineteenth
century affords a vivid example. The avowed purpose of the consolidation of the unwieldy number of capital statutes known as the Bloody
Code in the 1830s into a list of fifteen serious crimes was to bolster the
deterrent value of punishment by ensuring juror compliance in predictable and proportionate sentencing.[9] Prior to this reform, criminal
trials focused primarily on the question of the accused's character, or on
a particular circumstance surrounding the crime that might allow the
jury to find the accused guilty of a noncapital crime and thus to evade
the draconian criminal sentencing provisions. Thus the jury's determination to "downvalue" the worth of goods stolen or to find a killing accidental—and thus not murder—produced guilty verdicts and attendant sentences more in keeping with community notions of the relative
seriousness of different types of criminality.[10] Jury mitigation and in-
dependence were the source of continuing ire on the part of both judges
and legislators who bristled at this early modern form of "jury nullifi-
cation."

In an effort to effect greater regularity in predictive punishment, and
thus to influence directly the psychology of the criminal "gamester," re-
formers such as Samuel Romilly argued for the consolidation of capital statutes and the introduction of lesser punishments, both envisioned
to encourage the jurors' willingness to convict.[11] If the manifest function of criminal code consolidation was to increase the number of convictions and hence to bolster the deterrent value of punishment, the latent function appears to have been an extensive reconsideration of the
essential nature of criminal guilt itself. With the constant threat of execution eliminated and the consequent feverish search for any and all

possible mitigating factors removed from what had heretofore all been "hanging crimes," jurors were increasingly free to ponder the nature of criminal evidence itself: the standard of "reasonableness" to apply to the accused's reaction to a set of circumstances, the credibility of witnesses, the appropriate weight to give the testimony of specialist witnesses.

Old Bailey juries before the 1830 consolidation of capital statutes had certainly grown accustomed to medical witnesses giving expert evidence; insanity was in fact one of the "partial verdicts" delivered by jurors actively avoiding convictions that would lead to a hanging. Mental derangement, economic need, or youthful immaturity functioned primarily, though, as "character issues," rendering the accused pitiable and therefore less deserving of Parliament's "just desserts." Beginning in the late 1700s and gaining increasing attention by the 1830s, one finds evidentiary issues raised both in court and by legal writers that addressed long-deferred questions regarding the prisoner's actual guilt: restrictions on hearsay testimony, refinements in the privilege against self-incrimination, raising the standard of guilt to beyond a reasonable doubt.[12] Although one might have assumed that such safeguards had long been fundamental to the common law, John Langbein cautions that as late as the mid-1700s, "decisive steps had yet to be taken in the Anglo-American law of evidence."[13] The delay in fashioning rational and procedural rules regarding evidence could be laid at the feet of an omnipotent judiciary that ruled on all questions of admissibility, credibility, and examination of witnesses. Theoretically acting as "counsel for the prisoner," Old Bailey judges throughout the mid-eighteenth century questioned and cross-examined witnesses, discovered errors in the indictment, and generally "guided" the jury in interpreting courtroom testimony.[14]

Criminal evidence only became a proper subject of inquiry, therefore, when the defense attorney replaced the judge, serving not as the theoretical counsel for the prisoner but as a full advocate. His role throughout the eighteenth century had been substantively constrained; he could neither address the jury nor mount a recognizable criminal defense.[15] Devising a defense strategy required having access to the depositions taken by prosecution witnesses, and until 1836, these were unavailable to him. It is therefore with the Trial for Felonies Act of 1836—commonly referred to as the Prisoner's Counsel Act—that the courtroom division of labor altered qualitatively, subjecting criminal procedure and courtroom evidence to persistent scrutiny by the defense bar. Finally afforded access to pretrial testimony, able to address the jury prior to witnesses being called—to "prepare" the lay juror for the opinion of the expert—and eventually given the right to address the jury after the expert testified, defense attorneys sought to "nourish growth in the law of evidence." The standard of proof of culpability—guilty beyond a reasonable doubt—had been articulated late in the 1700s but became a continuing theme in legal writings only in the mid-nineteenth century.

Even before the Prisoner's Counsel Act, defense attorneys appearing in insanity trials had been employing the specter of mental derangement as part of a defense strategy. It was, after all, an attorney who introduced delusion into courtroom testimony in 1800, inaugurating the qualification of "total insanity" in English jurisprudence.[16] Throughout the first half of the nineteenth century, defense attorneys continued to craft carefully worded questions that elicited from medical witnesses the most forensically friendly opinions. One need not suggest that wily barristers simply manipulated forensic psychiatric witnesses. The point is, rather, that whatever professional interests led medical witnesses to claim madness as ultimately a *medical* concern, the active solicitation of their opinion functioned first and foremost to expand the evidentiary reach of professionally based opinion that spoke to a criminal defense: the defendant's inability to exercise self-control.

The Paradox of Insanity Reform

Given the Victorian era's well documented preoccupation with impulse control, restraint of instinctual appetites, and anxiety over the disintegrating political and social hierarchies, one might well have predicted rough sailing for the defense counsel's continuing attempt to expand the array of exculpatory mental conditions, especially if he planned to ground his defense on provocation or willful inebriation.[17] Nineteenth-century Victorians revealed a growing revulsion at the thought of interpersonal violence and a willingness to use the criminal court to articulate and enforce a rigorous standard of morality and civility applicable to the population of industrializing Britain. Martin Wiener has recently argued that, by restricting the scope of criminal defenses based on provocation and drunkenness, judges compelled jurors to raise the bar for reasonableness to create an "objective" standard for the "reasonable man."[18] This construction was not a contemporary description but a normative prescription: how the self-governing, self-controlled

Englishman ought to behave. The common law considered man a rational being; retaliation against an assailant could be justified only by blows struck, and even then, the battery must be immediate, with no time for the passions to cool. It would take quite a lot for a reasonable Victorian man to lose self-control.[19]

It is striking, therefore, that as defenses based on provocation or alcohol-related violence met determined judicial efforts to restrict their acceptance (and juries obliged by returning convictions for murder) insanity defenses became more frequent in the Victorian courtroom—and increasingly successful.[20] No doubt one could look to an increasingly energetic defense counsel and a growing acceptance of expert evidence, apparent from the beginning of the century. But Wiener contends that insanity served in a unique way to introduce mitigating circumstances when standard courtroom defenses were no longer available.[21] Of course, the easily provoked, the easily inebriated, and the easily deranged were not ordinarily interchangeable as "types," although the Old Bailey certainly knew drunken wife-beating defendants who claimed (convenient) blackouts. But the jury was much more likely to meet prisoners who claimed the intervention of devilish, not alcoholic, spirits propelling them into murderous violence.

The increasing incidence of insanity pleas in the Victorian courtroom does not then suggest the reworking of provocation and alcohol into a defense of temporary insanity—a construction rarely heard at the Old Bailey, and more rarely still, successful. Instead, one finds in courtroom testimony a profusion of defenses resting on claims to lapsed or gauzy consciousness that had nothing to do with incitement by a third party or John Barleycorn. At times related to epileptic fits, at times associated with convulsions, these conditions sometimes left the prisoner "lost" and at other times "as if in a dream." The missing defendant had wandered into a space where he could no longer be characterized as a consistently present person, let alone a reasonable person.

Medical testimony and courtroom questioning that introduced variable states of consciousness into criminal evidence no longer needed to ascribe the incriminating behavior to the act of a madman; aberrant behavior could now be described as the work of an unknown person. When defense attorneys encouraged witnesses to speculate on the moment when the defendant might have "returned to consciousness," when judges asked if a defendant deprived of consciousness was like a man "in a sleep" or whether the witness had been struck by the defendant or by her fit, the range of mental states thought to inform evidentiary proof of intentional conduct had expanded considerably. In part, one could attribute this broadening to the ambitious defense attorney, reaching beyond the symptom language of insanity to introduce into evidence non-insane yet nonresponsible states of being. But one also hears the unmistakable voice of the judge, willing to question and at times actively entertain categories of lapsed consciousness new to the court, even to the point of instructing the jury to consider consciousness expressly in their deliberations.[22]

Whether this judicial solicitude stemmed from a desire to compensate for restrictions placed on the doubtfully provoked or the indulgent tippler is difficult to say. What one can say, however, is that early-nineteenth-century reforms in criminal law and criminal procedure—manifest in the dramatic reduction in capital statutes, the introduction of full defense advocacy, the setting of ever higher standards of "reasonableness"—functioned to expand the court's inquiry into the essential mental element requisite for culpability. One had to be conscious to be "reasonable." One had to remember cultural norms to be culpable. One had to maintain a continuous sense of self to be answerable. Courtroom narratives reveal that evidence bearing on the defendant's intention expanded to accommodate a range of debilitating mental states that were not themselves convertible to insanity but nonetheless were legally relevant. That it was the lay witness who first introduced the symptom language of unconsciousness into the court underscores the broad resonance these new interpretations of behavior enjoyed in the surrounding culture.

But again, medical witnesses did not spearhead this change. To repeat an earlier assertion, the history of forensic psychiatry is the history of law. Before one examines medical writing and legal commentary of this period to infer the dynamics of the change in the apparent designs of the profession, one would do well to ask how the courtroom dynamics themselves were changing. Examples from the present work reveal that the assertion of professionally conscious statements in court emerge only during cross-examination, suggesting the extent to which the court itself framed medical assertions to expert knowledge. It was the space opened by the receding control of the judge that freed up territory for the attorney to explore the nuances of intentional behavior: consistent consciousness, retention of memory, purposeful action. Space was also opened up—ironically, according to Wiener—by Victorian efforts to instill greater resources of self-control that perhaps inadvertently expanded the territory for mental waywardness.

The migration of medical conceptions of doubling and double consciousness from the clinic to the courtroom was not an inevitable odyssey, although it would be unusual for the courtroom not to reflect surrounding cultural concerns. The arrival of *vertigé épileptique*, unconsciousness, and sleepwalking could only have found traction, though, in a courtroom that was prepared to contemplate gradations in consciousness. Still, variations in awareness were not mere additions to insanity's arsenal; something new was in the offing. Once transported into court and expanded by medical witness and defense attorney alike, states of suspended consciousness would prove to have lasting significance for the common law's conception of the person as a unified entity.

The Disintegrating Unity of the Person

Medieval England bequeathed to subsequent legal thought a dramatically new conception of the person. Where liability had traditionally rested with the simple doing of a crime—the *actus rea*—the first codification of legal thought after the Norman Conquest placed intent at the center of criminal responsibility. The emergence of the person as a being with an identifiable inner self was not merely an innovation in legal thought. It was, Lawrence Rosen has argued, part of the mid-eleventh through the twelfth centuries fundamental shift, apparent also in religion and literature: from a conception of persons as the fulfillers of obligations and aristocratic conventions to individuals conceived as sentient beings with an inner world of feelings, experiences, and intentions. The capacity to discover a "sense of the moral" in law, religion, and literature defined the medieval approach to the individual as a being capable of self-knowledge and self-definition. It follows logically that this era would witness the first qualification of absolute or strict liability for one's actions based on compromised intention due to extreme mental distraction, immature years, or compelled action.[23]

The inner element most critical to the needs of law—and to a rational and effective judicial system—was the property of self-consciousness: the necessary moral and physical link between one's self and one's act. The needs of justice insist that man is continuous, that a consistent consciousness binds him to his present and past actions.[24] States of "identity amnesia," periods when someone was not only not himself but someone else, sleepwalking episodes, and moments of absence or *vertige* challenged the essential fairness of punishment meted out for intentionally committed acts. In those moments when the accused revealed a physical being and a conscious person no longer one, juries were forced to negotiate the responsibility of a person who was in two places at once: at home asleep *and* out committing a murder. Clearly, justice requires a unitary person because responsibility can belong only to one person per body: the common law cannot apportion blame among a series of successive selves. Above all, culpability cannot be assigned to the passive self, dominated by a counter, and active, self, rendering the person on trial no more than a mere bystander.[25]

The "requirements of justice," in Mary Douglas's sense, were challenged by the newly arrived offender of the mid-1800s: the disappearing Hugh Pollard Willoughby, the morally discontinuous juvenile poisoner, the "absent" killer of her own child. What each of their trials shared was a defendant whose presence and, in some cases, whose antics challenged the law's conception of a consistent, conscious self. Although sleepwalkers doubtless offered the most dramatic challenge to the notion that a person is always "herself," defendants after McNaughtan illustrated an array of unknown selves: "kind and gentle" mothers who killed their children, good and constant persons who shot their friends, witnesses giving testimony interrupted by spirits that possessed their own memory. It may have been a generic notion of mental distraction that served as the rubric for courtroom inquiry, but trials that turned on the possibility of lapsed consciousness strike us today as unique events, given the jury's evolving practice of withholding insanity acquittals and voting either to convict or acquit altogether, or even to acquit on the grounds of unconsciousness. When witnesses averred that Mary Ann Hunt was "absent," Elizabeth Carr was "unconscious," and Frederick Treadaway's killing was the work of an automaton, they were asking the jury to consider responsibility, not only as a moral assumption, but as a unique psychological state.

Were the defendant's fingerprints truly on the weapon? Was the court looking at persons bereft of continuous consciousness—unable to understand the nature and consequence of "their" actions—who shared the jury's bewilderment that anyone could have done such a horrid thing? That the defendant was the person suspected was simply too fantastic to believe. When asked to promise that she would not repeat the attack on her injured daughter, an Old Bailey defendant had replied, "I do not believe I did it." If the jurors believed her to be telling the truth, they were faced with the question: Who precisely had attacked the young girl?

Imagining the Unconscious

Historical studies of nineteenth-century medical psychology often contend that the notion of the unconscious revealed in mesmeric trance and suggested in sleepwalking episodes was not the seething cauldron of repressed desires that would surface in Freud's account of psychic process later in the century. The earlier descriptions of dull and doltish servant girls waking from profound sleep only to find themselves gaily chatting away and almost histrionically animated revealed stark polarities in temperament, not psychoneurotic repression. Still, one might have thought that the frequency with which observers of double consciousness noted the "far greater achievement in the second state" and the mirthful, totally unexpected intellectual liveliness might have generated some interest in how these lively, engaged spirits had become split off from the dullard's conventional composure. Instead, contemporary speculation regarding these pronounced swings in personality centered restrictively on memory and consciousness as the defining elements of personhood. In moments of suspended consciousness, "personal identity is altered, for the individual is separated into two distinct beings."[26]

A generation of medical psychologists and practitioners spanning Dewar, Dwight, Mitchill, and Browne therefore, was consumed with the defining characteristics of personal identity: "amongst the most fundamental principles of mind is the conviction . . . that a man continues to be always himself."[27] When their patients became "two creatures," however, it was not the sharp demarcation in temperament (or intellectual curiosity) that suggested a second self. Failed or periodic-specific memory was the criterion of greatest significance. With no recollection of the knowledge acquired in the second state, and memory active only during subsequent "attacks," the doubly conscious could be succinctly described "as unconscious of her *double* character as two distinct persons are of their respective separate natures," in Mitchill's words.[28] To fail to remember an event may of course betoken nothing more than a simple act of forgetting, but to fail to recall oneself *at* that event called into question whether the two personalities belonged to the same person.[29] A substantial alteration in memory thus suggested a "change in the mental identity of the individual, a change in the principle about which memories cluster." That principle, in the eyes of the chroniclers of double consciousness or "divided personality," was the Lockean notion of personal identity: "the consciousness of existing continuously."

But does consciousness itself truly exist continuously? Certainly one experiences consciousness when aware that a change is taking place "within": when hearing a sound, smelling an odor, remembering a name. Between the sensory impression and the mental representation of the idea that names the external stimulus, however, there are innumerable intervening linkages, countless associations that one cannot capture in one's consciousness because of the speed and minute connectors linking these ties. These innumerable links must be stored somewhere, and the highly debated venue for this "left luggage" in mid-nineteenth-century Britain was the unconscious. To be sure, medical psychologists eager to keep the subject matter of the mind's phenomena accessible and knowable evidenced no initial desire to propose the existence of un-conscious mental states. Authors who argued for "unconscious cerebra-tion"—the mental process that linked sensory experience, or a train of thoughts constructing a memory—were roundly criticized for limiting, a priori, the scope of functioning that medical psychology could claim to explain. Still, when William Hamilton pondered whether there were "mental activities and passivities of which we are unconscious, but which manifest their existence by effects of which we are conscious," he con-cluded that "what we are conscious of is constructed out of what we are not conscious of."[30] One simply cannot be conscious of the myriad links connecting one thought to another, as in the fraction of a second it takes for each drop of water in the ocean to hit a pebble. What we hear is the wave against the shore. And when we remember an associ-ation between idea A and idea F, all the intervening associations reside stored away in the unconscious.

"Unconscious cerebration" was not only apparent in the innumer-able connections required to link ideas to sensory experiences. It was clear to Hamilton that performing habitual actions—engaging in purely automatic behavior—provided ample opportunity to observe action similarly unattended by consciousness. The mind housed a reserve of knowledge and experience that it was "wholly unconscious of possess-ing in its ordinary state, but which [is] revealed to consciousness in cer-tain extraordinary exaltations." Hamilton termed this situation *mental latency*.[31] Thus states of febrile delirium, madness, and catalepsy allowed the distracted to excavate arcane knowledge acquired in early life but heretofore exiled to some remote region in the unconscious. The "records of wit and cunning [displayed by] madmen revealed pronounced talents for music, poetry, and drawing." Sleep *talkers* might speak in the dialect of their youth, "possessed, as it appeared, by a very learned devil." Thus illiterate young woman spoke "incessantly" in Latin, Greek, and Hebrew, "in very pompous tones and with most distinct enunciation." Sleep *walkers*, revealing similar "reserves" of consciousness, migrated to a state with their mental faculties "usually in a higher degree of power than in the natural," again speaking languages "wholly forgotten." The somnambulist with no musical training will sing "with correctness and with full enjoyment," but not, on awakening, with memory. Consciousness, Hamilton wrote, "is thus cut in two."[32]

Habitual, automatic action divorced from consciousness (for example, piano players carrying on a conversation while executing an intricately fingered passage); evidence of skills and knowledge far removed from conscious retrieval but in florid display when transported by an "exalted" mental state; and the clear demonstration that activities could be performed seemingly effortlessly while asleep argued persuasively that there were indeed vibrant mental states beyond one's conscious grasp. But one need not comb the case histories of double consciousness and *dédoublement de la personnalité* for clues to how medical observers made sense of wildly disparate temperaments and deeply secreted knowledge suddenly brought to the fore. There was the remarkable contemporary evidence of unconscious criminality, conspicuously reported in the *Old Bailey Sessions Papers*, to suggest that there was more to the unconscious than attenuated sensory perception and the concatenation of memory links. There was something altogether more dramatic: the haunting specter of repressed anger and hidden resolve that would find its expression in the actions of prisoners described in court as "quite unconscious of having committed a wrong act."

Unconsciousness at the Old Bailey

The questions asked of medical witnesses at the Old Bailey and the testimony given by these medical men reveal a shift in the depiction of the unconsciousness from a matter of states of awareness to a mental region that housed the truly unknown features of the prisoner's affect. At the most basic level, consciousness served as a synonym for simply being awake, for being aware that one was physically present. "I fainted away" (and only became conscious afterwards); "I do not think he was altogether conscious of what he was doing"; "he was not at all conscious."[33] One could also fail to be conscious of things, as in "I was unconscious of using the knife." Tried for infanticide after "over-laying" (rolling over in her sleep and unknowingly smothering the infant), a woman could be described as "not conscious of her delivery."[34] And finally, one could be described as unconscious of the moral context of physical activity, "incapable of consciousness of the wickedness of the act," or the implications of one's behavior: "she was not conscious of what had been committed; that is to say to reflect on the consequences."[35] Finally, medical testimony could frame the question of consciousness in ways that were reminiscent of moral insanity: indifference. Following author Henry Maudsley's testimony that a defendant was "nearly unconscious of what he is doing," physician George Fielding Blandford added, "he regretted that the whole occurrence had happened, but he seemed indifferent to it as regards any special feeling of remorse; he did not burst into tears or anything of that sort, very far from it; there was a degree of one might almost say cheerfulness about the way in which he talked of it.[36] Like the other observations expressed above, unconsciousness signified that a train of thought had become, in the language of the medical psychologists, "dissevered": an inability to complete the mental connections linking action to consequence, weapon to injury, "conscious" deed to moral wrong. Although this missing connection had long characterized the mad, owing to their profound confusion, "inconsecutive consciousness" could now describe the mind of the sane.

Over time, these individual, periodic lapses in consciousness gave way to the frightening display of automatic behavior: "what he did was in a state of unconsciousness, having no malice whatever for the child."[37] No malice, no memory, and no consciousness: the London courtroom was finally presented with no *one* person at all. As reports of double consciousness, divided personality, and *dédoublement* circulated among London's professional elite—and as demonstrations of magnetic sleep, hypnotism, and folk tales of somnambulism circulated in the London populace—courtroom tales of missing persons were readily recognized by a culture already fascinated with, and horrified by, the existence of this unregulated and uncontrolled universe of functioning. From moments of simple absence to periods of identity amnesia, from accounts of delusory belief and compulsion to far-flung episodes of automatism and *vertige épileptique,* the centuries-long forensic conception of the person as a unitary being was nearing fatal rupture.

Delirium, insensibility, and even delusion had left Locke's conception of the person intact; insanity could well account for the unaccountable by picturing the afflicted as confused, emotionally explosive, or simply bewildered. Locke's "continuously conscious self," however—the "non-negotiable link between the person and his living body"—could hardly absorb displays of identity amnesia, lucid possession, and automatism.[38] Where was the unitary person here? Under what principle of equity could one be called to answer at the Last Judgment—or indeed at the Old Bailey's interim judgment—if another person had in fact committed the crime?

The only conceptual tool afforded by the contemporary medical literature to account for behavior unattended by thought was one of reflexes: the "ideo-motor principle of action" of Carpenter, for example, which spoke to the possibility that an idea could act directly on motor processes, bypassing the mental processes of reflection and volition. Hypnotism also illustrated that "unthinking" actions could be produced by the elemental properties of command and behavior. What the courtroom offered, however, was evidence of automatic behavior engineered neither by the hypnotist nor the mesmeric operator.

Emerging in the mid-nineteenth-century courtroom narrative was the specter of "ideo-motor" reflex in which the idea could only have originated in the unconscious. The prisoner described as having killed the child "in a state of unconsciousness, having no malice whatever for the child," introduced into cultural inquiry a new wrinkle in the unconscious: an unknown force that very much harbored malice. Old Bailey juries were confronted for the first time with unconscious acts that were anything but random, directionless activity. Indeed, given the conspicuous relation between victim and offender, the moment chosen for the assault and the means employed to effect the result, the "idea" element in the ideo-motor reflex transported the unconscious crime into someone's intentional activity. Reflexes, after all, only pull back the trigger; the crime itself represented some person's intention.

The Emergent Multiple Personality

Broad-ranging academic subjects have enthusiastically proposed explanations for the causes of crime. Psychology, economics, and history have, to name but a few, dabbled from time to time with explanations for criminal behavior. Few disciplines are as attractive in this respect as biology, however, with the tempting prospect of unraveling the complexities of dangerous behavior by assigning them to the workings of neurological substrates. Usually what is aimed for, and enthusiastically claimed, is a localization of aggression somewhere in the brain, fatefully equating aggression with criminality.

Before appropriating ideo-motor reflexes to explain violently aggressive behavior, however, one would be well advised to remember that criminal assault almost always has a specific target, most often a weapon, an opportunity for commission, and a certain requisite technique. Criminality is no more the simple expression of a failure of instinctual control than is the behavior of British soccer fans or the on-field activity of the leading yard-gainer for the National Football League. Indeed, each of these groups may share the same biological drive for aggression, but this only begs the question of why one particular outlet is chosen and not the others. Criminal behavior is *intentional* action; it is socially—not physiologically—defined. Jurors at the Old Bailey heard of mothers poisoning, decapitating, or maiming their children; of a man in a period of epileptic vertigo shooting a friend; of an absent young woman strangling an aged roommate; of a disappearing/reappearing defendant shooting his would-be homosexual seducer. The victims were not accidentally bumped into, carelessly tossed out of a window, or thoughtlessly impaled on a stick. The Old Bailey victims were meaningful to the accused, the weapons were purposely procured and employed, and the right moment to act was *chosen*. Finally, the crimes themselves were usually not remembered; little if any continuous consciousness linked the perpetrator to the deed. The image of mental functioning one derives from the *OBSP* is of something more than a lapse in consciousness.

Indeed, one glimpses the unconscious as a somewhat more dynamic resource than the filing cabinet where links between units of sensory impressions are stored. One derives, in fact, the haunting suspicion that the "doubled" self and the hidden, divided personality revealed by the hypnotist and animal magnetizer have made their way out of the parlor and have forcefully entered the criminal courtroom.

It would take a century, however, before the "crimes of the unconscious" would generate a comprehensive debate in American jurisprudence between forensic psychiatry and law regarding the status of the "alter" in matters of criminal responsibility. Doubled personality had "hit the headlines" in 1876, as a "wave of multiplicity swept over France" in the years 1874 to 1886.[39] Its impact on medical psychology and by extension on the courtroom, is difficult to trace, Hacking explains, because "multiplicity" over time became associated with hysteria, fragmented into anxiety neurosis, absorbed in part into *dementia praecox,* and eventually came to rest in *folie circulaire* and its Anglo-American cousin, bipolar disorder.[40]

Like a series of nineteenth-century psychological states cum psychiatric diseases, the history of mental diagnosis and classification is the story of symptoms taken up into one term and folding into another. The effort to trace the "history" of the psychiatric diagnoses of epilepsy, schizophrenia, and depression—to name but a few psychopathological conditions that often carried legal implications—must therefore attend to changes in the prominence physicians and alienists gave to any particular symptom.[41] And thus with double—then multiple—personality, the diagnosis does not so much disappear as reappear in the form of hysteria, traced eventually to a traumatic psychological event. No longer considered a second personality, or even a delineated *état seconde,* the uncharacteristic moods, behavior, and attitudes could be conceptualized as a splitting of mental function—but not of personality—or the delayed emotion unexpressed at the moment of trauma. There was no longer a second self; there were only elements of the one self, split off.

Only in the 1970s—and primarily in North America—did a fully integrated and coherent second self emerge, but it did so with particular vengeance. In this case, it was the vengeance of the sexually abused child now adult, or rather *adults,* because there were no longer two but a multiplicity of inhabitants jockeying for priority in one psyche. As tales of repressed memory syndrome gained entrée into the courtroom—most noticeably, the criminal conviction of Paul Franklin based on his daughter's recovered memory of the killing of a childhood friend—American courts were forced to consider the ambiguity of memory and the possibility that there were events in one's past that were simply too painful to remember and that were consequently buried, like toxic waste sealed away but remaining forever potent.[42]

Without the media-generated publicity given to the specter of child sexual abuse and the hypothesized splitting thought to be its inevitable result, it is difficult to imagine how disparate elements of amnesia, identity confusion, unaccounted-for fears, and hostility could have become concretized into identifiable persons, known as "alters" to the court. Much like the nineteenth-century courtroom that found itself considering an expanded conception of consciousness owing to the newly enhanced role of the defense advocate and the consequent opening up of new areas for evidence and inquiry, the late-twentieth-century American courtroom found itself the hapless recipient of a profusion of new criminal defenses, derisively but aptly organized under the heading the "abuse excuse." As the creation of a multiple personality was seen as a way to cope with childhood sexual trauma—"I take his pain" (claims the abused child's alter personality)—the entry of alters into twentieth-century courtroom testimony represents only another in the series of phenomena associated with childhood sexual abuse.[43]

Criminal cases that make prominent use of the notion of multiple personality, however, do not emerge from the prosecution of the victim's abuser, or of those implicated in the victim's traumatic history, but rather from an array of crimes that have nothing to do with the actual abuse. If it is mentioned at all, family history might be invoked to account for the creation of the multiple. In crimes ranging from heroin possession to drunk driving, and from rape to baby stealing, the issue at trial is not a matter of sequestered psychic pain so much as the core issue of dividedness. Can the person on trial be held responsible for the actions of a second personality living within, whose existence the defendant knows nothing about and whose actions he cannot physically restrain?[44]

As there is no "typical" multiple personality patient, there is no typical multiple personality defendant, although the core issues of amnesia and unconsciousness—familiar since the mid-nineteenth-century trials of the "missing" defendants—unite the trials that surface repeatedly in late-twentieth-century medical and legal writings. Most often the defense attorney alleges an inability to control the actions of the alter, either because the defendant is unconscious (or asleep, or "not present") or because the second personality was simply too powerful. The defendant might wake up in his room and find unpurchased merchandise, or learn that the police had discovered a large cache of heroin that he did not purchase, or discover that a drunken alter had been driving his car at a time when the defendant was unconscious.[45] Cases in late-twentieth-century American jurisprudence feature alters committing murder to "put another alter away," as the defendant finds himself "utterly unable to resist" the alter's importunate demand to kill his wife. When forensic psychiatrists argue that such defendants meet the criteria established by the American Psychiatric Association for Multiple Personality Disorder, and the jury hears from the accused's neighbors that he or she has indeed displayed frequent examples of switching from

one personality to another, how is the court to respond to the most recent example of missing defendants?

At first glance it might appear that the presence of alternate selves
resident in the defendant's mind is sufficiently close to traditional notions of possession to qualify as a delusion and thus to fall within the
scope of an insanity plea. Indeed, some defense attorneys have tried to
invoke insanity provisions, especially as the two current criteria—an inability to understand the wrongfulness of one's acts and/or to conform
one's acts to the requirements of law—appear to fit particularly well the
case of a defendant missing at the time of the crime, or one unable to
subdue the "alter in control." The latter criterion, so graphic in courtroom testimony, bears an unfortunate resemblance to irresistible impulse and thus inherits the lingering suspicion that the impulse was
simply unresisted, the "host personality" voluntarily stepped aside for
the alter to do its work. In cases when a defendant claims to have been
unconscious and thus absent from the scene, some courts have advised
the jury to determine if the personality present at the time understood
what she was doing: if true, this finding would be sufficient to establish culpability.[46] As for "searching" for the real culprit in a purported
den of thieves, a Georgia court has memorably announced, "We will not
begin to parcel out responsibility among the various inhabitants of the
mind"—a ruling that has enjoyed wide application.[47]

Still, it would be wrong to conclude that the legal community has
contemptuously swept aside defenses based on multiple personality. In
the oft-cited case of Bridget Denny-Shaffer (1993), a delivery-room
nurse who stole a baby from a pediatric ward, a three-judge panel held
that the state's insanity defense provisions should favor Denny-Shaffer's
claim that "evidence that the host personality was unaware of or unable to control the behavior of the alter personalities would be sufficient
to warrant a finding of insanity." It is significant that the appeal panel
did not refer to "alter personalities" (explicitly), either in quotes or in
italics. The decision speaks to the issue of culpability, Applebaum and
Greer have pointed out, to the court's "perceived unfairness of convicting a host personality for behavior beyond his or her control."[48] Their
analysis helps to clarify why Multiple Personality Disorder invokes the
common law's unimpeachable grounds for acquittal: an unconscious
state of being.

The California Penal Code, to name only one state provision, maintains that "[a]ll persons are capable of committing crimes except . . . per-

sons who committed the act charged without being conscious thereof."[49]
A 1960 California appellate court ruling was even more prescriptive:
"[unconsciousness] is a 'complete defense' because it negates any capacity to commit any crime at all."[50] Although California's penal code
reflects the general disposition of state codes nationwide, and the ruling above enjoys wide citation, state courts vary regarding how "complete" they consider a defense of unconsciousness to be. What sort of
on-scene evidence, after all, permits this inference? How does one prove
unconsciousness? For that matter, how does one prove that he or she
was sleepwalking? Some courts consider automatism and unconsciousness to be separate from insanity; others find the inability to understand
the nature of the action to define both insanity and unconsciousness.
Still other states require the diagnosis of delirium or epilepsy before a
state of unconsciousness may be accepted. To say, therefore, that unconsciousness is a "complete defense" is to articulate a principle, not to
predict a verdict.

When states of lapsed or missing consciousness can be substanti-
ated, it is worth noting why the law excludes from culpability defendants so described: the act is "not the product of an individual's agency."
Criminal courts have traditionally considered action pursued while
sleepwalking or resulting from reflexes or seizure or in posthypnotic
suggestion to be involuntary, and thus to negate the second element of
essential culpability: the *actus rea*.[51] Multiple Personality Disorder
speaks most directly therefore to a defendant divided into parts, often
with no memory—let alone knowledge—of the actions taken when the
alters resurface. The failure to remember the alter's crime and any attendant circumstances also affects the defendant's competency to plead
and perhaps to stand trial, as well. A plea made in ignorance of the details of the surrounding events can hardly be termed "informed." A
sound defense strategy can hardly be fashioned when the defendant is
as much in the dark as the attorney.[52] That said, amnesia in and of itself has not rendered a person incompetent to stand trial, and for reasons that are not hard to comprehend. There is an obvious temptation
to forget one's barbarity, or at least to claim that the crime is all "just a
blank." Such claims to amnesia, similar to the claim of helplessness in
the face of a more powerful alter, are only that: claims.

A credible claim to involuntariness, dividedness, or unconsciousness
can be doubtless reinforced by forensic psychiatrists when diagnosis of
a discrete multiple personality will serve the defense strategy. But even

medicine's imprimatur on the alleged existence of a second and criminal self hidden inside the defendant, does not end the inquiry. As with insanity deliberations in general, the "finders of fact"—the judge or the jury—must make a determination regarding the significance of the diagnosed "condition" for the defendant's claim to lack responsibility for a particular crime. This was true when Eugène Azam, author of the chronicle of the first case of *dédoublement*, first queried jurists regarding the significance they would attribute to a diagnosis of doubled personality. Not surprisingly, he did not find a receptive audience. Like their brethren on the other side of the Channel, French judges were not keen to question their bedrock belief in free will, of "moral liberty." "Legal responsibility rests upon the principle of human liberty and consequently does not require the demonstration of a will in control of its actions." Similar to the unity of the person as a (legal) "given," human liberty is assumed since it sits at the center of "just desserts." Although they could imagine cases of lapsed memory that "could and should" result in exoneration, these judges found these to be rather "the exceptions which confirm the rule." Still, Azam's question regarding the legal implications of Félida's condition revealed that the memory component of double personality could be a salient forensic issue. "An absolute response" would be impossible, the jurists answered, for the "judge would have to consider the act in and of itself . . . and the incontrovertible evidence for the absence of memory."[53]

Regarding the particular features of the "act in and of itself," today's juror will likely hear nothing from the medical witness regarding the ultimate question before the court: What did this particular defendant understand about the nature of his acts? By virtue of the 1974 Insanity Defense Reform Act, the expert witness can serve only as a diagnostician; he may not state whether he believes a particular defendant possessed the mental condition requisite for committing a crime.[54] The effort observed in trials following McNaughtan to restrict the forensic psychiatric witness to the general features of extraordinary mental state therefore persists today, although, as in trials of the nineteenth century, an enterprising defense attorney and an articulate medical witness can try to tailor a general description of mental functioning to fit a particular defendant's criminal actions. That said, the courtroom remains, as always, a legal—not a clinical—forum; the distance to be bridged between medical category and legal determination is a considerable one. Possessing an anomalous personality trait—or indeed a trait of personalities—may provide for compelling courtroom testimony, but no juror is ever advised that diagnosis equals acquittal.

Instead, judicial instructions are likely to follow one of three formulas. There is first the "alter in control" advisory: whatever the condition of the defendant sitting before them, jurors are to consider the culpability of the alter who actually procured the drugs or drove the car while intoxicated. Alternatively, each alter may be examined by the court, and a collective sense of understanding—shared among the various personalities—may be gleaned. A third option is to focus on the host alone: what did he or she understand about the nature and quality (the consequences) of the act? Was the host able to appreciate that the act was wrong? Although this last courtroom strategy appears to treat Multiple Personality Disorder as delusion and thus represents no radical departure in courtroom jurisprudence, the reifying of alters into discrete, separate entities has led to burlesque courtroom antics.[55] A Wisconsin judge, for example, permitted a defendant to testify as a dog.

Persons or Personalities?

The larger problem encountered in asking juries to divine "which alter was in control," according to some medicolegal writers, is that personalities are being confused with whole individuals. Alter personalities are not persons, maintains Stephen Benhke; "only a person can form criminal intent." To elevate a personality to the status of an individual inevitably leads to an "unanswerable" question: whose mental state should the jury be considering? According to critics of the notion of Multiple Personality Disorder, both in and out of court, the diagnosis conveys the fatal misconception that these fragments of the host, split off from, or never initially integrated into, the self, constitute discrete entities or "personalities." In court, these "caricatures of wishes, feelings, needs and attitudes" assume the figure of a sentient, engaged person capable of forming criminal intent and acting upon it. But moods and unmet needs cannot form intent: only a person can act with resolve. The crime "belongs" to the patient diagnosed with Multiple Personality Disorder, not to one of these erroneously concretized attitudes conceived of as constituting a person.[56]

That a criminal defense founded upon Multiple Personality Disorder generates skepticism regarding both the defendant's claim and the testimony of the medical witness in the legal community and beyond should not surprise. "Have you not been here before," asked a judge in

1801 of a Dr. Luis Leo of Houndsditch, "as a Jew physician, to try to get someone off on the basis of insanity?"[57] Although one cannot be sure whether it was Dr. Leo's ethnicity or his professional efforts at the Old Bailey that raised suspicions, the judge's dismissal of the defense and contempt for the witness is clearly evident. As handy as a delusion or periodic lunacy might have been to plead nonresponsibility for nine-teenth-century crime, the presence of an "evil twin" is no less likely to seem a too-convenient ploy for today's transgressions.

But in a curious way, insanity posed much less of a threat to the common law's conception of criminal responsibility and the person than "dividedness" and the prospect of a missing defendant. As Radwin notes, the idea of multiple individuals "inhabiting the same body violates our sense of the person, and smacks of the crudest sort of demonology."[58] It is one's view of the individual as a "unified whole," as a morally and legally responsible person, that is at stake with the diagnosis of Multiple Personality Disorder. How could the essential element of legal responsibility—the capacity to choose—ever be attributed to a congeries of disparate selves?

Rejecting the notion of Multiple Personality Disorder on legal grounds alone reminds one of the forensic construction of the person that assumed human unity as a given, not as a proven commodity. One retained continuous consciousness and a capacity for remembering actions pursued because this was the only way responsibility could be ascribed. It is little wonder, then, that the prospect of a person constituted of relatively autonomous personalities invited derision and fierce opposition. But beyond the criticism of Multiple Personality Disorder for the damage it would do if widely accepted by the courts, there is a more thoroughgoing question concerning whether these disparate personalities are anything more than the unconscious motivations of a total person, emotional fragments that have found expression in the recognizable form of a discrete and separate identity.[59] This assertion reminds one of Hacking's point, referred to at the beginning of this chapter. Is the question one of what the diagnosed individual really "had," or is it a search for how contemporaries made sense of, interpreted, and applied the appropriate language to render the behavior "meaningful"? Therefore, the issue is not whether it is correct to make personalities out of unconscious hostile attitudes and unsavory wishes, but how this happened at all.

One finds mention in both historical and contemporary medical literature of a "looping effect": patients with ambiguous feelings of despair and unease seek treatment from a clinician who communicates to them—however subtly, or indirectly—the possible existence of an unknown self produced by an early trauma, whose existence will both confirm the trauma and retain the clinician's interest. The assertion that suggestible, nervous patients take their cue from the clinician dates at least to Mesmer and gained particular currency in the critical scrutiny to which hypnotism was subjected by various national medical committees.[60] But trial testimony—and courtroom behavior as well—offered graphic demonstration of dividedness and "identity amnesia" that suggested the existence of a second self inside.

Memory, the one constant element connecting the individual to his life, was also the one missing feature in defendants who found themselves unaccountably indicted. The failure to maintain a continuous consciousness of one's identity—the idea that surfaced most frequently in nineteenth-century trials that turned on missing or absent defendants—was precisely the conception of the mind most critical to legal fault-finding. Did the person retain the capacity to know what he was up to? Was he conscious that the act was wrong? The inability to remember distanced the defendant on trial from the malefactor whose criminal activity was described by the witnesses and the police. *That* defendant was the one who had killed a beloved child or friend, who remembered that it was wrong to poison, who knew that it was criminal to set a building ablaze. The question begged in all this is the human agency that actually lay behind the crimes. The defense attorney could argue that though his client's fingerprints were found on the weapon, the alter pulled the trigger.

Some force beyond sheer physical activity lay behind the crimes tried at the Old Bailey, crimes that revealed the ability to handle a weapon, to effect a getaway, to select the most propitious moment to strike. Hierarchies of "higher or lower functioning" and ideo-motor reflexes might inform results in the laboratory, but a trial in the courtroom required an intentional actor. The Old Bailey provided the first forum for autonomous yet hauntingly purposeful activity. When chroniclers of somnambulism wrote of "a new life . . . a new character [with] a separate consciousness," when the physical body could be depicted as accommodating "two souls" and animal magnetism described "[another] self emerging . . . an influential personality" capable of "transforming" the conventional self, contemporary medical and popular thought clearly embraced the notion of a second and dominant—though not at the moment present—self. In time, the frequency with which temperament took pride of place in describing the "doubly conscious" invited the substitution of personality for consciousness as the phenomenon that best captured the essence of a second self. It was not the uncharacteristic gaiety and intellectual curiosity that "broke out" at uneven intervals but the haunting evidence of violent and inexplicable deeds that first made their presence known in the courtroom. No Sybils were named or perhaps even envisioned in the years leading up to the "multiplicity." The only symptom language available to medical witnesses and lay jurors alike was the vocabulary of consciousness, of automatism, and of epileptic vertigo.

Nineteenth-century courtroom actors did not make sense of unaccountable, uncharacteristic criminality by envisioning a second self, and certainly not multiple selves. Instead, the language of memory and consciousness, of horror at learning of the deed and despair at learning of one's own contribution, distanced the mid-nineteenth-century defendant from the crime itself. A vocabulary that embraced somnambulism and absence, amnesia and possession, drew the courtroom defendant further away from the centuries-old conception of "the person": a consequences-perceiving, conscious, and remembering being. Here was ample evidence that actual courtroom persons were anything but a unity; not only might they be unconscious during the crime, they could not conceive of a reason why anyone would have contemplated that action. Although it would take a century for the diagnosis of Multiple Personality Disorder to enter medical nosology, and at least as long for the western legal system to be confronted with a number of cases stimulating medical and legal commentary, the Old Bailey cases of 1843 to 1876 illustrate the origins of the concept of dividedness and the common law's first efforts to articulate a response to unconscious criminality.

How did the courtroom respond? Tellingly, Old Bailey juries appeared willing to acknowledge that the defendant had indeed been "lost," but lost in a very particular way. One could be said to lose one's self; one could not be said to lose one's conscience. One could be possessed by another creature—even twenty thousand creatures; one could not be possessed by an idiosyncratic way of defining morality. In short, the court was quite willing to entertain the possibility that the defendant did not know he had assaulted his wife. It was not willing to accept the notion that the defendant did not know the assault to be wrong.

Beyond serving as a focal point for the evolving notion of double and then multiple personality, the trials at the Old Bailey that have structured this inquiry also informed a larger inquiry into clinical medicine's view of the person. One of the curious historical findings about Dewar's 1823 suggestion that double consciousness was more properly characterized as doubled personality is that this suggestion was essentially ignored for the next sixty years. Not until Azam published his description of Félida under the heading *dédoublement de la personnalité* was personality "doubled" once again.[61] Although missing in the contemporary medical literature, persons manifesting wildly disparate behavior and absence owing to unconsciousness were making their way into the courtroom and were the subject of increasing medical commentary and speculation. The Old Bailey, however, did not merely store the elements that defined double personality—amnesia, sleepwalking, and a "second self"—in anticipation of the day when Azam and other clinicians would take up the concept again to describe the notion of multiple personality. Courtroom inquiry in the form of questions from the attorney and judge, and witness-box testimony given by physicians and surgeons and also by the defendants themselves, provided weird and frightening evidence that the unconscious criminal activity belonged to someone of wildly discrepant temperament and wildly divergent moral sense from the defendant.

Although the relationship between psychiatry and forensic psychiatry is assumed to be an odyssey from the clinic to the courtroom, mental medicine's negotiation of unconscious criminality carried significance far beyond the Old Bailey. Here was evidence not only of an automatic and supposedly unconscious state of being but of a state of being that had meaning within the social web uniting victim and offender. Victimhood was not random, the mortal injury was not inflicted by accident, and the moment of the crime was not pure happenstance. In this so-called unconscious criminality were found the requisite elements of intention and resolve, but not in the person of the defendant facing the jury. It might take a Freud later in the century to connect the person with his hidden wishes, but it took only the Old Bailey sleepwalker to light the way.

APPENDIX

Table A.1. Offenses Featuring Aberrant Mental Condition as a Defense, 1843–1876

	Personal (%)	Property (%)	Other (%)	Total Offenses (N = 198)
1843–50	73	25	2	56
1851–60	74	19	7	57
1861–70	77	13	10	39
1871–76	80	11	9	46

Notes: Personal offenses include Assault, Manslaughter, Assault with Intent to Murder, and Murder. Property offenses include Stealing (predominantly), Breaking and Entering, Arson, Forgery and "Uttering" (counterfeiting). "Other" offenses include Libel and unspecified "Felonies" or "Misdemeanors."

Table A.2. Elements Mentioned as Causes of Derangement

Causal Element	Number of Trials*
Delusion	38
Womens' Problems**	25
Un/consciousness	22
Fits (including epilepsy)	19
Brain Fever / Concussion	12
Irresistible Impulse	7
Homicidal Mania	5
Melancholia	4
Monomania	3
Moral Insanity	3
Delirium	3
Paroxysm of Mania	2

Notes: Mentioned only once were Blood Disorders, "Erectomania," Kleptomania, Scrofula, "A Bad Fall," and "Absence."

  * The total number of trials for this array is 145. The 53 cases in which defendants were found unfit for trial do not yield any testimony regarding the nature of the accused's distraction since these hearings are not reported.

  ** These elements range from all possible behavioral changes attendant to pregnancy, delivery, "suppression of menses," and "the change of life."

Table A.3. Women's Offenses in Fifty-Six Cases of
Mental Aberration

Offense	Number
Willful Murder	32
of son	(10)
of daughter	(10)
of another's child	(4)
of "own infant"	(3)
of two children	(2)
of own child	(2)
of roommate	(1)
Assault/Wounding	14
of daughter	(7)
of son	(3)
of unspecified victim	(3)
of another's child	(1)
Stealing	7
Libel	2
Forgery	1

NOTES

Introduction

1. Norval Morris, "Somnambulistic Homicide: Ghosts, Spiders, and North Koreans," *Res Judicatae* 5 (1951): 29–33.

2. Elyn R. Saks and Stephen H. Behnke consider a number of these issues in *Jekyll on Trial: Multiple Personality Disorder and Criminal Law* (New York, 1997). The status of multiple personality defenses in the courtroom is taken up in the Conclusion.

3. The literature regarding splitting and "doubles" is vast. Among the most illuminating treatments are Ralph Tymms, *Doubles in Literary Psychology* (Cambridge, 1949); Jeremy Hawthorn, *Multiple Personality and the Disintegration of Literary Character: From Oliver Goldsmith to Sylvia Plath* (London, 1983); John Herdman, *The Double in Nineteenth-Century Fiction* (London, 1990); and Astrid Schmid, *The Fear of the Other: Approaches to English Stories of the Double, 1764–1910* (Berne, 1996).

4. The historical evolution and utility of the *Old Bailey Sessions Papers* (hereafter *OBSP*) are discussed in John H. Langbein's two comprehensive studies, "The Criminal Trial before the Lawyers," *University of Chicago Law Review* 45 (winter 1978): 263–316, and "Shaping the Eighteenth-Century Criminal Trial: A View from the Ryder Sources," *University of Chicago Law Review* 50 (winter 1983): 1–136. Although a priceless source for the history and sociology of law, the *OBSP* present a considerable challenge to the historian and sociologist who chooses to quote from lengthy testimony and to ground present-day interpretation in the language of an earlier day. Throughout this volume I have selected extracts from courtroom testimony and have tried to remain faithful to the punctuation and syntax that appeared in the *OBSP.* In the interest of coherence and intelligible reading, however, I have sometimes chosen forms of punctuation and presentation more in keeping with present usage. My primary concern was naturally to respect the integrity of the source while rendering comprehensible the courtroom dynamics.

5. J. M. Beattie, *Crime and the Courts in England, 1660–1800* (Oxford, 1986), 24. Although these trial narratives are not without their limitations—the pace, tone, and omissions in actual testimony can only be speculated upon—historians of law generally concede them to be "the most important source" for re-

constructing crime and justice in early modern England. For this most recent appraisal, see Peter King, *Crime, Justice and Discretion in England, 1740–1820* (Oxford, 2000), 221.

6. Joel Peter Eigen, *Witnessing Insanity: Madness and Mad-Doctors in the English Court* (New Haven, 1995).

7. The most comprehensive study of the McNaughtan trial may be found in Richard Moran, *Knowing Right from Wrong: The Insanity Defense of Daniel McNaughtan* (New York, 1981). Other historical treatments of McNaughtan's trial are included in Nigel Walker, *Crime and Insanity in England*, vol. 1, *The Historical Perspective* (Edinburgh, 1968), 84–103; and Eigen, *Witnessing Insanity*, 153–54.

8. *OBSP*, 1840, case 1877, 9th sess., 504–10. For a comprehensive study of the Oxford trial, see Richard Moran, "The Punitive Uses of the Insanity Defense: The Trial for Treason of Edward Oxford (1840)," *International Journal of Law and Psychiatry* 9 (1986): 171–90. See also Walker, *Crime and Insanity*, 186–87.

9. *OBSP*, 1842–43, case 874, 5th sess., 761–63.

10. Joel Peter Eigen, "Lesion of the Will: Medical Resolve and Criminal Responsibility in the Victorian Era," *Law and Society Review* 33 (1999): 425–60.

11. *OBSP*, 1840, case 1877, 9th sess., 505.

12. *OBSP*, 1846–47, case 2310, 12th sess., 1138.

13. Ibid., 1144.

14. The importance of delusion to the question of criminal culpability can be discerned from a variety of sources. Old Bailey judges often "cut through" medical testimony by asking preemptively, "Has he any delusion at all?" For examples, see *OBSP*, 1849–50, case 1300, 9th sess.; *OBSP*, 1851–52, case 572, 7th sess.; *OPSP*, 1866–67, case 912, 11th sess. The prominence of delusion was also apparent in the writing of James Fitzjames Stephen, a noted jurist: Delusion "may be evidence of a state of mind which prevented the person affected by it from knowing that his act was wrong . . . A man commits what on the face of it is a cruel and treacherous murder. It is proved that he laboured under an insane delusion that his little finger was made of glass. In itself such a delusion has no sort of tendency to excuse such a crime, and has no apparent connection with it, but if physicians of experience were to say that a fixed delusion on such a subject could arise only from a deep-seated disease affecting a man's whole view of the world in which he lived, falsifying his senses, rendering him inaccessible to reasoning of the simplest kind . . . I do not see why they should not be believed" (*A History of the Criminal Law of England*, vol. 2 [London, 1883], 161). Forensic author Alfred Swaine Taylor concluded, "The acts of the insane generally arise from motives based on delusion" (*The Principles and Practice of Medical Jurisprudence* [London, 1865], 1106). One measure of the growing legal unanimity regarding the centrality of delusion to criminal proceedings was the irritation this conviction sparked in medical circles. Writing in 1842, James

Cowles Prichard complained that it was "a settled doctrine of English Courts that there cannot be insanity without delusion" (*On the Different Forms of Insanity in Relation to Jurisprudence Designed for the Use of Persons Concerned in Legal Questions Regarding Unsoundness of Mind* [London, 1842], 16).

15. Prichard, *On the Different Forms*, 17.

16. These publications are explored in Chapter 1.

17. The most illuminating exposition of this innovative term is found in Jean-Pierre Falret, "De l'état mental des épileptiques," *Archives Générales de Médecine* 16, 5th series (1860–61): 661–97, 17: 461–91, 18: 423–43. Supplementary sources for other medical descriptions of *vertigé épileptique* are given in Chapter 6.

18. *OBSP,* 1875–76, case 413, 11th sess., 496–97.

19. Ibid., 497.

20. *OBSP,* 1876–77, case 246, 4th sess., 434–60.

21. I discuss McMurdo's prominence in nineteenth-century insanity trials in *Witnessing Insanity*, 129–31, 175–76.

22. Martin J. Wiener, "Judges v. Jurors: Courtroom Tensions in Murder Trials and the Law of Criminal Responsibility in Nineteenth Century England," *Law and History Review* 17 (1999): 467–506.

Chapter 1. Double Consciousness in the Nineteenth Century

1. The extent to which voluntary action could be stimulated by ideas introduced directly to nerve fibers, bypassing the subject's judgment and volition, was addressed in seminal nineteenth-century works in medical psychology. See, for example, James Braid, *Observation on Trance: Or, Human Hybernation* (London, 1850) and *Magic, Witchcraft, Animal Magnetism, Hypnotism, and Electro-Biology* (London, 1852); Thomas Laycock, "Reflex, Automatic, and Unconscious Cerebration: A History and a Criticism," *Journal of Mental Science* 21 (1876): 477–98; William B. Carpenter, *Principles of Human Physiology; With Their Chief Applications to Pathology, Hygiène, and Forensic Medicine* (London, 1842) and *The Doctrine of Human Automatism: A Lecture* (London, 1875); James Cowles Prichard, *Somnambulism and Animal Magnetism* (London, 1834). Secondary literature includes Roger Smith, *Trial by Medicine: Insanity and Responsibility in Victorian Trials* (Edinburgh, 1981); two works by Adam Crabtree, *Multiple Man: Explorations in Possession and Multiple Personality* (London, 1988) and *From Mesmer to Freud: Magnetic Sleep and the Roots of Psychological Healing* (New Haven, 1993); Henri F. Ellenberger, *The Discovery of the Unconscious: The History and Evolution of Dynamic Psychiatry* (New York, 1970); and most recently, Alison Winter, *Mesmerized: Powers of Mind in Victorian Britain* (Chicago, 1998).

2. A. P. W. Philip, *An Inquiry into the Nature of Sleep and Death* (London, 1834), 152. For a discussion of dreaming in relation to hallucinations and other psychological phenomena, see W. Griesinger, *Mental Pathology and Therapeutics*, trans. C. Lockhart Robertson and James Rutherford (London, 1867).

James Fitzjames Stephen considers the legal implications of the mental processes attendant to dreams and sleepwalking in *A General View of the Criminal Law of England* (London, 1863), 79.

3. One-time student of Mesmer and eventual professional rival, the Marquis de Puységur employed animal magnetism to precipitate a "perfect crisis"—a form of sleep he termed "artificial somnambulism." Accounts of his innovations in stimulating suspended sleep can be found in Ellenberger, *Discovery of the Unconscious*, 70–72, and Crabtree, *From Mesmer to Freud*, viii.

4. As Roger Smith explained, the words *mind* and *body* were increasingly replaced with *upper brain* and *central nervous system*, respectively, in medico-psychological writing, *Trial by Medicine*, 146–48.

5. For a comprehensive analysis of the concept of inhibition in nineteenth-century medical conceptualization, see Roger Smith, *Inhibition: History and Meaning in the Sciences of Mind and Brain* (Berkeley, 1992).

6. "[T]he contractile power of the uterus is altogether independent of volition" (Alfred Swaine Taylor, *The Principles and Practice of Medical Jurisprudence* [London, 1865], 765.) In court, medical witnesses in infanticide cases speculated whether the defendant was "conscious of her delivery." See, for example, *OBSP*, 1849–50, case 1893, 12th sess., 857.

7. Carpenter asserted that past mental activity left behind ideas in the mind that were capable of producing involuntary—that is, not consciously willed—muscular movement. "[T]he will is in abeyance . . . temporarily withdrawn from the control of his muscles by the state of abstraction to which his mind is given up" (quoted in Laycock, "Reflex, Automatic, and Unconscious Cerebration," 481.) See also Carpenter, *Doctrine of Human Automatism*, 25–28.

8. The specter of meeting one's double, in the form of either a homicidal Other or an increasingly grotesque portrait revealing one's character was also offered by eighteenth- and nineteenth-century fiction. A particularly illuminating literary analysis of the doppleganger and other forms of the double—either by duplication or division of its host into separable persons—is offered in Ralph Tymms, *Doubles in Literary Psychology* (Cambridge, 1949). Tymms is particularly keen to incorporate mesmeric observations of "unsuspected traits of character that emerged during the magnetic trance." Regarding somnambulism: "here unfamiliar impulses appeared, foreign to the patient's usual character, and as if revealing a second personality, which might even be the reverse of the first; and the investigators concluded that these incongruous characteristics had lain dormant in some part of the mind inaccessible to the rational consciousness" (26–27).

9. A.-J.-F. Bertrand described the sleepwalkers state as a "new life" with reference to the complete loss of memory of all that took place, only to be recalled in subsequent episodes of somnambulism (*Traité du somnambulisme et des différentes modifications qu'il présente* [Paris, 1823], 2). John Forbes also describes

somnambulists as revealing "a new character and a separate consciousness develop[ing]" in *Mesmerism True—Mesmerism False: A Critical Examination of the Facts, Claims, and Pretensions of Animal Magnetism* (London, 1845), 20.

10. Winter, *Mesmerized*, 71, 76.

11. Forbes, *Mesmerism True—Mesmerism False*, 20.

12. *The Lancet*, 26 May 1838, quoted in Winter, *Mesmerized*, 76.

13. Starkly contrasting temperaments were standard features in the tales of doubled consciousness. Specific case studies are given in the chapters that follow, but a comprehensive survey of the phenomenon of doubled consciousness can be found in Ian Hacking, "Double Consciousness in Britain, 1815–1875," *Dissociation* 4 (1991): 134–46.

14. Samuel L. Mitchill, "A Double Consciousness, or a Duality of Persön in the same Individual: From a Communication of Dr. Mitchill to the Reverend Dr. Nott, President of Union College. Dated January 16, 1816," in *The Medical Repository of Original Essays and Intelligence Relative to Physic, Surgery, Chemistry, and Natural History, etc.*, n.s., vol. 3 (18th from the beginning) (New York, 1817), 186.

15. Benjamin W. Dwight, "Facts Illustrative of the Powers and Operations of the Human Mind in a Diseased State," *American Journal of Science* 1 (1818): 431–33.

16. H. Dewar, "Report on a Communication of Dr. Dyce of Aberdeen, to the Royal Society of Edinburgh, 'On Uterine Irritation, and Its Effects on the Female Constitution,'" *Transactions of the Royal Society of Edinburgh* 9 (1823): 365–79.

17. Hacking, *Double Consciousness*, 136–37.

18. It is the presence of amnesia that defines the "switching" from one temperament to another as double consciousness and not as *la folie circulaire*, a precursor to what would become known as bipolar disorder. For a discussion of the distinguishing role of amnesia in these two diagnoses, see Hacking, *Double Consciousness*, 135–36.

19. J. Crichton Browne, "Personal Identity and Its Morbid Modifications," *Journal of Mental Science* 8 (1863): 537.

20. Ibid., 386.

21. Ibid., 542–43.

22. Whether they described the split in terms of "two different persons," "a person with two souls," or "[two] trains of thought dissevered from [each] other," Mitchill, Dwight, and Dewar respectively spoke of double consciousness in terms of persons, not moods or temperaments.

23. Eugène Azam, "Amnésie périodique, ou dédoublement de la vie," *Annales médico-psychologiques*, 5th series, vol. 16 (1876): 5–35.

24. Ibid. Reprinted and translated by James I. Tucker, "Periodical Amnesia; or, Double Consciousness," *Journal of Nervous and Mental Disease* 3 (1876): see esp. 600–602.

25. Tucker, "Periodical Amnesia," 595–96.

26. Ibid., 602. In another publication, Azam reports that he asked judges to gauge the likely significance of doubled personality regarding criminal responsibility. The answers are examined in Chapter 6.

27. The 1505 verdict was phrased, "It was found that at the time of the murder the felon was of unsound mind (de non saine memoire). Wherefore, it was decided that he should go free (qu'il ira quite)" (Nigel Walker, *Crime and Insanity in England*, vol. 1, *The Historical Perspective* [Edinburgh, 1968], 25–26). The phrase "unsound mind" would bedevil medical men of the eighteenth century for whom the term meant nothing in particular. They preferred to speak in the (medical) realm of delirium, delusion, or mania. This early difference between legal and medical preference for specific language to denote the essential character of derangement presaged the next two centuries' running dispute regarding the fit of medical diagnosis to legal criteria for a "sufficient" madness.

28. Joel Peter Eigen, *Witnessing Insanity: Madness and Mad-Doctors in the English Court* (New Haven, 1995), esp. 82–107.

29. Joel Peter Eigen, "Delusion in the Courtroom: The Role of Partial Insanity in Early Forensic Testimony," *Medical History* 35 (1991): 25–49.

30. *OBSP*, 1838, case 499, 4th sess., 412.

31. *OBSP*, 1842–43, case 874, 5th sess., 763.

32. Most of the law's contemptuous reaction to medical testimony concerned the diagnosis of moral insanity, which left those afflicted conscious of the crime they were committing but powerless to exert any self-control as they were carried into the crime by a passion or an impulse they could not resist. To one who failed to find such impairment credible, failure to curb a wicked passion was simply wickedness, and precisely the behavior the law was designed to deter if possible and to prosecute when necessary. Judge Baron Rolfe's 1848 comments to the jury in the trial of a juvenile poisoner (Chapter 5) are a good illustration of the law's concern that this sort of medical testimony was dangerous in the extreme. Other medicolegal flashpoints concerned the introduction of phrenology into courtroom testimony: "God forbid that doctrines like these [phrenology, lucid intervals] should ever be incorporated into the wholesome and just laws of the realm" (letter by attorney C. R. Bree in response to J. G. Davey's, "Plea of Insanity," *Association Medical Journal: Edited for the Provincial and Surgical Association* [London, 1854]: 930). When Davey replied that "lawyers should, on principle, defer to medical authority," he was not the only physician of his day to entertain this belief. Nor was Davey likely to have diverged from other medical writers' dislike for the term "mad-doctors," an eighteenth century sobriquet that continued into an era when asylum doctors and some clinicians frequently called to advise the court on matters of "mental" medicine believed that they constituted a mainstream medical specialty, no longer deserving the inherently derogatory label. "It is inconceivable that any

physician engaged in the management and the treatment of the insane would designate himself by so vulgar and contemptuous a title as 'mad doctor'" (Thomas Laycock, *The Antagonism of Law and Medicine in Insanity and Its Consequences: An Introductory Lecture* [Edinburgh, 1862], 14).

33. John Locke, *An Essay Concerning Human Understanding (1690)*, ed. Peter H. Nidditch (Oxford, 1975), bk. 2, ch. 27, 342.

34. Ibid., 335.

35. Ibid., 346.

36. Mary Douglas, "The Person in an Enterprise Culture," in Shaun Hargreaves Heap and Angus Ross, eds., *Understanding the Enterprise Culture: Themes in the Work of Mary Douglas* (Edinburgh, 1992), 49.

37. Locke, *An Essay*, 342–43. Emphasis in the original.

38. *OBSP,* 1842–43, case 874, 5th sess., 763.

39. Alfred Swaine Taylor, *A Manual of Medical Jurisprudence* (London, 1844), 657–58. That the "illusions of sleep" could continue into waking moments and may "give rise to extravagant, criminal, and dangerous acts" is discussed by A. Brierre de Boismont in *On Hallucinations: A History and Explanation of Apparitions, Visions, Dreams, Ecstasy, Magnetism, and Somnambulism,* trans. Robert T. Hulme (London, 1859), esp. 450–55.

40. Defendant's deposition given to Policeman Robert Sage, March 12, 1870. Public Records Office (hereafter, PRO), HO 144/26/63070, item 12.

41. The trial narrative is the *OBSP,* 1869–70, case 278, 5th sess., 370–86. The defendant's name is spelled Spinas in the letter at the PRO, but Spinasa in the *Old Bailey Sessions Papers.*

42. Ibid., 380–82.

43. Letter from Judge Baron Channell, dated March 12, to the Home Office, in which he refers "to the notes taken by me at the trial," PRO, HO 144/26/63070, item 12.

44. Ibid. Of the several petitions Spinasa wrote to the Home Office requesting release from prison, the letter written fifteen years after his incarceration repeats his assertion that this was "a crime of which I am unconscious." An anonymous note appended to his petition to the Home Office might explain why it took six further years for him to gain his release: "He was very nearly hanged for it, and I thought deserved it."

45. That is, he had no previous contact that the jury knew about. Spinasa's Home Office file contains letters from the Swiss Consul-General and a surgeon of the defendant's army battalion that attested to his hallucinations and general eccentricity. When in the throes of his visions, "several men could only hold him down with difficulty." Neither communication is mentioned in the Old Bailey narrative, although their existence in his file may explain why the defendant's sentence was reduced from death to penal servitude. Still, the proper moment to introduce these documents and to subpoena witnesses,

would have been *before* conviction, because they spoke directly to the violence
that attended the prisoner's hallucinations.

46. One of the reasons medical witnesses in particular disagreed with one
another may have had little to do with which side had hired their services. In
his commentary on the notorious trial of George Victor Townley, C. L. Robertson accounts for predictable differences in expert medical opinion when he
quotes [J. C.] Bucknill: "[M]edical witnesses may usually be divided into two
classes—those who know something of the prisoner and nothing of insanity,
and those who know something about insanity and nothing of the prisoner.
They generally succeed in neutralizing each other's evidence, and in bringing
the medical profession into contempt, at least among lawyers." The remedy, according to Lockhart, was "obvious, [medical witnesses should be] called by the
Court itself. In France, when a criminal is suspected to be insane, the Court
appoints a commission of medical men, or selects one man experienced in mental diseases, to examine into the case. By the adoption of some such plan, the
[English] Court could secure impartial and trustworthy evidence" (*Insanity and
Crime: A Medico-Legal Commentary on the Case of George Victor Townley* [Lon-
don, 1864], 46–47). For a comprehensive analysis of the French courts' employment of *chirurgiens jurés,* sworn to advise on matters medical and medico-
psychological, see Catherine Crawford, "The Emergence of English Forensic
Medicine: Medical Evidence in Common Law Courts, 1730–1830" (Ph.D. diss.,
Oxford, 1987). Further, one notes that Lockhart's remedy speaks to the number of medical witnesses to be called, not whether they should be in a court at
all. There were certainly members of the legal community who would have dis-
pensed with mad-doctors altogether. Speaking before a Select Committee for
the House of Commons, the Earl of Shaftsbury averred that "no professional
knowledge" was needed to determine if a man was incapable of managing his
own affairs. "My firm belief is that a sensible layman conversant with the world
and with mankind can give not only as good an opinion, but a better opinion
than all the medical men put together. I am fully convinced of it." In criminal
matters, judges could be just as dismissive. In an 1862 trial, a jury was instructed:
"You are not to be deprived (added the judge to the jury, proudly swelling with
the sense of their own sagacity and importance) of the exercise of your common sense, because a gentleman comes from London and tells you scientific
sense." Both Lord Shaftsbury's comment and the judge's instructions are
quoted in Thomas More Madden, *On Insanity and the Criminal Responsibility
of the Insane* (Dublin, 1866), 21.

47. The debate in the medical community regarding moral insanity was one
such conflict. Referring to the professionally combustible terms, homicidal
mania and moral insanity, the editors of the *Saturday Review of Politics, Literature, Science and Art* cautioned that the proffering of out-of-control impulses
"is a madness of [the medical man's] own making." According to the editors,

"Much of the medical evidence on which we have passed a running commentary affords a pitiable instance of the shallowness of so-called scientific education, even in a profession which takes its place in the learned triad. That any person merely repeating by rote the words, faculties, propensions, sentiments, moral, intellectual, delusions, and illusions, should think that he is giving an unimpugnable psychological and medical account of the human mind, and settling all the problems about choice, motive and responsibility, is a matter too melancholy to laugh at" (15 [21 March 1863]: 371).

48. Although conventionally called "schools," the various strands of professional belief among medical men who revealed a particular professional interest in mental deviation were likely to incorporate features of a range of psychological traditions. Followers of Pinel's school of *médecine mentale* argued for a nondelirious insanity; other practitioners and writers believed that Gall and Spurzheim's phrenology captured the essence of madness. Prichard and Conolly's faculty psychology attracted still others, and there remained medical men who simply affirmed the continuing legacy of eighteenth-century associationism. In addition, courtroom witnesses reflected a range of professional experiences with the deranged. Where pre-McNaughtan medical witnesses were likely to come from asylum practice or prison experience, medical men after 1843 represented a wider swath of the medical community, including specialists in "women's ailments" and practitioners well versed in epileptic convulsions. Their entrance appears to presage the beginning of neurological specialists testifying not as asylum superintendents but as general practitioners whose experiences extended to a noninsane state of unconsciousness. For an overview of the late-eighteenth- and early-nineteenth-century schools of medical psychology, and the institutional origins of medical witnesses before McNaughtan, see Eigen, *Witnessing Insanity,* esp. 63–79, 115–18, 216 n. 3, and 120–32, respectively.

49. Where medical and legal writers questioned the particular loyalties of forensic-psychiatric witnesses, it was not venality but penal philosophy that was thought to inform their judgment. Writing of medical testimony in insanity trials, forensic authority Alfred Swaine Taylor concludes, "A medical witness in these cases generally moulds his evidence to a foregone conclusion on the criminal responsibility of the accused, and thus he lays himself open to a remark from the judge that he must not encroach on the functions of the jury" (*Principles and Practice,* 1115). Of course, this supposed "encroachment" sat at the heart of legal disquiet with expert medical testimony. The court believed the medical witness's influence could be circumscribed by limiting him to "hypothetical" diagnostic comments surrounding the features of the disease. Still, it was not uncommon for a judge to ask a medical witness directly: "Do you believe him to be a responsible human being?"

50. For medical testimony in pre-McNaughtan insanity trials, see Eigen, *Witnessing Insanity,* esp. 136–60.

51. *OBSP,* 1859–60, case 169, 4th sess.; *OBSP,* 1871–72, case 117, 3rd sess.

52. *OBSP,* 1871–72, case 117, 3rd sess., 181.

53. Ibid.

54. The main feature of either of these two manias, as their names clearly suggest, is a purposefully destructive impulse the person cannot control. The assault victim was often the person of whom the prisoner was most fond. As a variation of "moral insanity," these two monomanias inherited the vociferous critics of any mental disease confined to deranged volition. In addition to lawyers, not a few physicians were audibly suspicious. For a comprehensive appraisal of these two forms of impulsive manias, see Taylor, *Principles and Practice,* esp. 1108–20; Alexander Morison, *Outlines of Lectures of the Nature, Causes and Treatment of Insanity* (London, 1848), 447–57. Thomas Mayo also explored the legal implications of a "moral insanity," in *Medical Testimony,* 75–90.

55. *OBSP,* 1849–50, case 1300, 9th sess., 387.

56. *OBSP,* 1849–50, case 1893, 12th sess.; *OBSP,* 1876–77, case 2310, 12th sess. A frequency distribution of reasons given for the criminal act is given in Appendix table A.2.

57. *OBSP,* 1876–77, case 246, 4th sess., 457.

58. *OBSP,* 1855–56, case 263, 4th sess., 476–77.

Chapter 2. "Do You Remember Cardiff?"

1. *The Cardiff and Merthyr Guardian,* 28 July 1854, *22,* 3. Although daily newspapers routinely reported summaries of criminal court proceedings, the attention given to this libel trial was remarkable. Included is the judge's characterization of Benyon's misdeed: "a filthy, degraded, disgusting, and black hearted libel, rendered more disgusting by the cant of religion, benevolence, and feeling for the public good, which [Benyon] mixed up with it" (*The Cardiff,* 3). Detailed testimony—and courtroom descriptions of the appearance and manner of the suit's participants and legal representation—are also offered in a second newspaper, *The Silurian; Cardiff, Merthyr, and Brecon Mercury,* 29 July 1854, *19,* 3.

2. *OBSP,* 1853–54, case 1122, 12th sess., 1561–71.

3. *Times of London,* 27 October 1854, 9b.

4. *OBSP,* 1853–54, case 1122, 12th sess., 1361.

5. Ibid., 1362–63.

6. McMurdo appeared at the trial of Daniel McNaughtan as one of nine witnesses who attested to the existence and consequence of the defendant's delusion. Although it was not unheard of for the prison-surgeon to support a plea of insanity, he usually asserted "no evidence of insanity at all." Sometimes this steadfast refusal could reach risible lengths, as in the trial of Noah Pease Folger, a ship's captain who, at the sound of the name of his arch nemesis, would tear off his clothes, break window panes with his bare fists, dance naked

on the broken glass, and complete the episode by jumping bareback on a passing whale. The narrative of these bizarre antics did not pierce the sang-froid of the Newgate medical man, who denied the existence "of any symptom which [Folger] has exhibited to make me come to the conclusion of his being of unsound mind" (*OBSP,* 1833, case 815, 4th sess., 402).

7. *OBSP,* 1853–54, case 1122, 12th sess., 1365; *Times of London,* 9c.

8. The Hadfield trial has been extensively examined in medico-historical literature. The most comprehensive treatment is found in Richard Moran, "The Origin of Insanity as a Special Verdict: The Trial for Treason of James Hadfield (1800)," *Law and Society Review* 19 (1985): 487–519. Further sources include Jacques M. Quen, "James Hadfield and Medical Jurisprudence of Insanity," *New York State Journal of Medicine* 69 (1969): 1221–26; Nigel Walker, *Crime and Insanity in England,* vol. 1, *The Historical Perspective* (Edinburgh, 1968), 74–81. See also the biography of James Hadfield by Joel Peter Eigen in *The Dictionary of National Biography* (Oxford, in press).

9. Hadfield's *actual* delusion was his belief that regicide would ensure his execution. Had he really wanted to ensure his death at the hands of the state there was only one crime to commit: counterfeiting. For an eighteenth-century trial of forgery in which an insanity plea—and a sought-for death—was put forward, see Joel Peter Eigen, *Witnessing Insanity: Madness and Mad-Doctors in the English Court* (New Haven, 1995), 47–48.

10. James Fitzjames Stephen, *A History of the Criminal Law of England,* vol. 2 (London, 1883), 159.

11. *OBSP,* 1853–54, case 1122, 12th sess., 1365–66. Although it was certainly unusual for a medical witness to be cross-examined by a putatively mad defendant, Willoughby's trial was not the first to feature such a remarkable dialogue at the Old Bailey. Forty years before Willoughby examined McMurdo, another defendant asked a medical witness to clarify the precise grounds for his inference of insanity. When the apothecary to St. Luke's answered, "From your action, and ideas, and your general conduct told me you were an improper person to be at liberty," the defendant countered, "You judge from ideas; you have good opinion of yourself" (*OBSP,* 1813, case 11, 1st sess., 14).

12. *OBSP,* 1853–54, case 1122, 12th sess., 1366–67.

13. Ibid., 1367–69.

14. For a discussion of the Victorian era's increasingly restrictive courtroom criteria for a defense based on provocation, see Martin J. Wiener, "Judges v. Jurors: Courtroom Tensions in Murder Trials and the Law of Criminal Responsibility in Nineteenth-Century England," *Law and History Review* 17 (1999): esp. 481–88.

15. *OBSP,* 1853–54, case 1122, 12th sess., 1369–71.

16. For an account of delusional ranters on the witness stand at the Old Bailey, see Eigen, *Witnessing Insanity,* esp. 174–78.

17. *Times of London,* 27 October 1854, 9c.

18. *OBSP,* 1859–60, case 120, 2nd sess., 157.

19. Ibid., 158–59.

20. Ibid., 159.

21. *Times of London,* 15 December 1859, 9c.

22. Wiener, "Judges v. Juries."

23. *OBSP,* 1854–55, case 464, 6th sess., 654.

24. Ibid., 658.

25. For a discussion of the Buranelli case in the medical literature, see *The Lancet,* parts 1 and 2, 1 (1855): 518–19, 540–41. A comprehensive description of the medical view of Buranelli's condition and a spirited defense of his innocence can be found in Forbes Winslow, *The Case of Luigi Buranelli: Medico-Legally Considered* (London, 1855).

26. John Locke, *An Essay Concerning Human Understanding (1690),* ed. Peter H. Nidditch (Oxford, 1975), bk. 2, ch. 27, 335–42.

Chapter 3. "I Mean She Was Quite Absent"

1. *Times of London,* 20 August 1847, 6c. The complete trial narrative is *OBSP,* 1846–47, case 1797, 10th sess., 653–82.

2. *OBSP,* 1846–47, case 1797, 10th sess., 660.

3. Ibid., 666–67.

4. Quoted in Elaine and English Showalter, "Victorian Women and Menstruation," in Martha Vicinus, ed., *Suffer and Be Still: Women in the Victorian Age,* (Bloomington, 1973): 40.

5. Surgeon Moat's testimony is given in *OBSP,* 1846–47, case 1797, 10th sess., 667–70.

6. Ibid., 670–72.

7. Ibid., 677.

8. Ibid., 679.

9. Ibid., 680–81.

10. *OBSP,* 1869–70, case 76, 1st sess., 89.

11. Of the five questions asked by the House of Lords of the judges who tried the McNaughtan case, only the last addressed the appropriate grounds for medical inference. As it turned out, this one issue would receive much less attention in subsequent legal commentary but much more attention in judicial observations offered in court. The McNaughtan trial prominently featured two medical witnesses who never met the defendant prior to the trial but offered their opinion based on testimony they had heard in court. Of all the anxieties surrounding the use of expert testimony, surely the gravest concerned the proffering of testimony based on nothing beyond evidence that the jury heard as well. Expert opinion enjoyed a long history in common-law courts, owing to the belief that persons of special skill, training, or experience might be called to advise the jury on issues where "factual" motive was in doubt. In mental med-

icine, this belief enabled the emerging specialty practiced by mad-doctors to be enlisted to inform the court of the clinician's experience with the accused as a neighbor, a patient, or upon visiting him or her in Newgate awaiting trial. In each case, the medical men's experience with the accused extended beyond the jury's familiarity, and one could defend the acceptance of specialist testimony as a way to endow the jury with enhanced insight.

Expert testimony based on courtroom testimony, though sanctioned indirectly by the McNaughtan Rules, could provoke vituperative judicial reaction, particularly because such opinion went to the heart of the debate about "facts" v. "opinion." In a memorable exchange between defense attorney and the bench, judicial dissatisfaction with McNaughtan provisions in general was evident. A defense attorney was about to ask Dr. Sutherland about the evidence he had just heard and began his questions with, "Having heard that evidence, in your judgment . . ." The judge interrupted, "I am of opinion that that question cannot be put." When the attorney objected, citing the decision in the McNaughtan case, the judge replied, "I am aware of that decision, and am quite sure it was wrong, and the sooner it is corrected the better. What are 'the facts proved?' Is Dr. Sutherland to be the Judge, or the Jury and I? It implies that the facts are proved, there are no facts proved at the present. I decide that the question cannot be put as a matter of right, and I do not think it ought as a matter of convenience" (*OBSP*, 1849–50, case 41, 1st sess., 49).

By not rejecting the court-specific testimony, the McNaughtan court added a further wrinkle to judicial anxiety regarding the expanding nature of the expert witness's testimony, and it is not surprising that this issue surfaced as one of the specific issues raised by the House of Lords. For an analysis of the range of associations between defendants and medical men leading to the appearance of mad-doctors in court, see Joel Peter Eigen, *Witnessing Insanity: Madness and Mad-Doctors in the English Court* (New Haven, 1995), esp. 120–30. The five questions asked by the House of Lords of the judges and their answers are given in *McNaughtan Case*, 10 Clark and Finnelly 203–14. Richard Moran provides a comprehensive account of the framing of the McNaughtan Rules, together with a dissenting and a majority opinion voiced by contemporary jurists in *Knowing Right from Wrong: The Insanity Defense of Daniel McNaughtan* (New York, 1981), esp. 168–75.

12. *OBSP*, 1846–47, case 1797, 10th sess., 681–82.

13. These specialized juries could be called in civil as well as criminal cases. In a comprehensive study of the Jury of Matrons, James C. Oldham points out that determining the pregnant status of a widow, for example, was of particular interest to the heirs of a recently deceased husband. No doubt criminal cases made the more dramatic use of these juries, but in either case, the practice of empaneling "wise women" in fact dates to the Roman Republic. The specific measures used to determine pregnancy remain a mystery.

Oldham traces the first English reference to the Jury of Matrons to de Bracton (1220) and the first actual criminal case in 1387. Registered medical practitioners replaced the Jury of Matrons by virtue of the criminal code of 1879 ("On Pleading the Belly: A History of the Jury of Matrons," *Criminal Justice History* 6 [1985]: 1–64).

14. Oldham, "On Pleading the Belly," 37–38.

15. Eigen, *Witnessing Insanity*, 18–23.

16. George Rudé, *Criminal and Victim: Crime and Society in Early Nine-teenth-Century England* (Oxford, 1985), esp. 50–64.

17. For a discussion of Robert Peel's efforts to consolidate capital statutes and to abolish execution for most forms of felony, see Leon Radzinowicz, *A History of the English Criminal Law and Its Administration from 1750*, vol. 1, *The Movement for Reform* (London, 1948), 567–607.

18. The difficulties attendant to prosecuting infanticide set these killings apart from the general category of homicide because in the latter there was no presumption that the victim had come to his death by natural means. In infant deaths, there was always the likelihood that the child had been stillborn, but with no witnesses at the scene this was a difficult argument to sustain. According to Nigel Walker, Englishwomen with dubious defenses of insanity were saved from the gallows by the jury's willingness to "grasp at any suggestion that the baby had been stillborn, or had died in the course of birth or had been accidentally killed" (*Crime and Insanity in England*, vol. 1, *The Historical Perspective* [Edinburgh, 1968], esp. 125–28).

19. Robert Burton, *The Anatomy of Melancholy (1621)*, ed. Floy Dell and Paul-John Smith (New York, 1927), 353.

20. Jordan's appearance in a seventeenth-century witchcraft trial is examined in Gilbert Geis and Ivan Bunn, *A Trial of Witches: A Seventeenth-Century Witchcraft Prosecution* (London, 1997), and also in Thomas Rogers Forbes, *Surgeons at the Bailey: English Forensic Medicine to 1878* (New Haven, 1985), 168–69.

21. Quoted in Vieda Skultans, *English Madness: Ideas on Insanity, 1580–1890* (London, 1979), 83.

22. For a discussion on the role of sexual difference in explaining nineteenth-century women's psychological functioning, see Thomas Laqueur, *Making Sex: Body and Gender from the Greeks to Freud* (Cambridge, 1990).

23. The discrepancy between medical writing and medical testimony is highlighted in Joel Peter Eigen, "Criminal Lunacy in Early Modern England: Did Gender Make a Difference?" *International Journal of Law and Psychiatry* 21 (1998): 409–19.

24. Roger Smith describes a filtering process that removed women suspected of infanticide from the criminal justice process at various stages up to the moment of sentencing, from the wink given to a terminated pregnancy, to the benefit of doubt regarding the birth itself, to the generous use of the in-

sanity plea. Few women faced a capital sentence for killing their children (*Trial by Medicine: Insanity and Responsibility in Victorian Trials* [Edinburgh, 1981], esp. 146–68).

25. Although mental exhaustion attendant to childbirth in particular and reproduction in general offered the jury a recognizable psychological ailment grounded in organic disturbance, acquittals were likely, but by no means guaranteed (Shelley Day, "Puerperal Insanity: The Historical Sociology of a Disease" [Ph.D. diss., Cambridge University, 1985]). Even if the woman was convicted, sentences in infanticide cases as early as the late sixteenth century could be commuted, one suspects because of the supposed mental state of the mother (121).

26. Rarely does the common law meet an impulse that is defined with reference to a particular crime. For the immediate legal significance of acknowledging such an impulse, see Walker, *Crime and Insanity*, 125–26.

27. On the changing legislation regarding infanticide and punishment, see George K. Behlmer, "Deadly Motherhood: Infanticide and Medical Opinion in Mid-Victorian England," *Journal of the History of Medicine and Allied Sciences* 34 (1979): 403–27. For a further look at the 1624 [1623] infanticide statute, see Mark Jackson, "Suspicious Infant Deaths: The Statute of 1624 and Medical Evidence at Coroners' Inquests," in Michael Clark and Catherine Crawford, eds., *Legal Medicine in History* (Cambridge, 1994), 64–86.

28. Walker, *Crime and Insanity*, 128.

29. Quoted in ibid.

30. *OBSP,* 1871–72, case 156, 3rd sess., 222.

31. Ibid., 222–23.

32. *OBSP,* 1844–45, case 1180, 7th sess., 165–71. See also Roger Smith's analysis of the Brixley case in *Trial by Medicine,* 155, and also comments in *London Medical Gazette,* n.s., vol. 1 (1845): 166–71.

33. *OBSP,* 1856–57, case 649, 7th sess., 138.

34. Alfred Swaine Taylor's comments about puerperal mania are found in *The Principles and Practice of Medical Jurisprudence* (London, 1865), 1121–23.

35. *OBSP,* 1869–70, case 36, 1st sess., 35–36.

36. *OBSP,* 1862–63, case 890, 9th sess., 350–53.

37. *OBSP,* 1864–65, case 915, 11th sess., 498.

38. *OBSP,* 1856–57, case 480, 6th sess., 722–23.

39. *OBSP,* 1855–56, case 386, 5th sess., 689.

40. *OBSP,* 1870–71, case 579, 10th sess., 350.

41. The fact that a desperate and distraught woman struck out against a target too weak to offer resistance should perhaps not come as a surprise. In some cases, the assault may indeed have been brought on by the mother's desire to save the child from a life of slow starvation and long-term deprivation. Medical writings that proffered the anatomical causes of child murder, however, explored few such situationally generated events.

42. *OBSP,* 1843–44, case 1013, 4th sess., 726–30.

43. Quoted in George K. Behlmer, "Deadly Motherhood," 406. For a contemporary treatment of infanticide—"In the quiet of the bedroom we raise the box lid, and the skeletons are there. In the calm of the evening walk we see in the distance the suspicious-looking bundle and the tangled infant is within. By the canal side, or in the water, we find the dead child."—see William Burke Ryan, *Infanticide: Its Law, Prevalence, Prevention, and History* (London, 1862), 45.

44. M. A. Baines, "A Few Thoughts Concerning Infanticide," *Journal of Social Science* 1 (1865–October 1866): esp. 536.

45. "The Jury of Matrons Revived," *London Medical Gazette, or Journal of Practical Medicine,* n.s. vol. 5 (1847): 597–98, 681, 861. Popular outrage at the forensic confidence invested in the Jury of Matrons was also the subject of contemporary newspapers. "What will the public say, when we tell them that the "forewoman" of this jury was the female turnkey [guard], who hands the female prisoners into the dock, and leads them from the prison to the gallows . . . [that] the prospect of earning a little gin and beer had brought them in voluntarily [to serve on the jury] . . . and this to determine a question that baffles the profoundest scientific knowledge!" (*Felix Farley's Bristol Journal, 9 October,* PRO, HO 45/9316/15682).

46. PRO 45/9316/15682 (25 August 1847).

47. Ibid., "Particulars of Mary Ann Hunt. Recommended for Conditional Pardon."

Chapter 4. The Princess and the Cherry Juice

1. In Comyns' *Digest,* Testamoigne Witness, A.1., "Who shall not be a witness,—1st, *non compos;* 2nd, infidel; 3rd, person convicted of treason or felony; 4th, any infamous man, and interested witnesses" (i.e., persons whose connection to the case might lead them to be unreliable courtroom witnesses). Regarding *non compos,* Chief Baron Comyns explained "every witness must be credible, and therefore a man of non-sane memory shall not be allowed as a witness, as an idiot, a lunatic during his lunacy; so one within age of discretion, so an infant who does not know the nature of an oath, but a lunatic may be a witness in 'lucidis intervallis'" (quoted by Attorney Collier in his appellate defense to the Court of Crown Cases Reserved, *Journal of Psychological Medicine and Mental Pathology* 4 [1851], 441–42).

2. "Medical Trials and Inquests: Alleged Death of a Lunatic From Violence in an Asylum—Competency of the Insane to Give Evidence," *London Medical Gazette, or Journal of Practical Medicine* 12 (1851): 168.

3. "Evidence of a Lunatic Taken in a Case of Manslaughter in a Lunatic Asylum," *Journal of Psychological Medicine and Mental Pathology* 4 (1851): 279.

4. Adam Crabtree, *Multiple Man: Explorations in Possession and Multiple Personality* (London, 1988), 353.

5. "Medical Trials and Inquests," 168–69.

6. *Times of London*, 2 February 1851, 7f.

7. *OBSP*, 1850–51, case 651, 4th sess., 626.

8. Ibid., 627.

9. *Dew v. Clark and Clark* (1826), 3 Addams' Ecclesiastical Reports 91. The relevance of this finding to the Donelly case will be discussed shortly.

10. *OBSP*, 1850–51, case 651, 4th sess., 628.

11. Ibid., 628–29.

12. "Evidence of a Lunatic," 283.

13. *Regina v. Samuel Hill* (1851), 2 Denison's Crown Cases 257.

14. "Evidence of a Lunatic," 283.

15. *Regina v. Samuel Hill*, 258.

16. "Evidence of a Lunatic," 283.

17. *OBSP*, 1850–51, case 651, 4th sess., 624–33.

18. Ibid., 631–33.

19. "Evidence of a Lunatic," 284.

20. "On the Admissibility of the Evidence of a Lunatic in a Court of Justice," *Journal of Psychological Medicine and Mental Pathology* 6 (1851): 437.

21. Ibid., 437–39.

22. Delusion, first as circumscribed belief and then acquiring a spur to action all its own, became the term of preference for medical witnesses appearing at the Old Bailey to support a plea of insanity. For the importance of delusion in the evolving professional voice of the mad-doctor in court, see Joel Peter Eigen, "Delusion in the Courtroom: The Role of Partial Insanity in Early Forensic Testimony," *Medical History* 35 (1991): 25–49. Collier's reference is to Francis Willis's *A Treatise on Mental Derangement*, most probably the second edition (London, 1843), although it is possible the attorney had access to the earlier printing, which appeared in 1822 as the Gulstonian Lectures.

23. *Dew v. Clark and Clark*, 91.

24. 40 George III, *State Trials*, 27: 1316–17. There is a John Monro, discharged at the Guildford Summer Assizes, 6 Geo. 3rd. 1766. PRO BT/165. (The noted mad-doctor and author William J. Battie is referred to in the court report as Dr. Battye.)

25. Franz Anton Mesmer, *Mémoire sur la découverte du magnétisme animal*, trans. G. Franklin [*Mesmerism; Being the First Translation to Appear in English*] (London, 1848). For a comprehensive study of Mesmer's role in the history of treatment and conceptualization of hysterical afflictions, the classic text remains Henri F. Ellenberger, *The Discovery of the Unconscious: The History and Evolution of Dynamic Psychiatry* (New York, 1970), esp. 57–81. For a recent illuminating appraisal of the fit between mesmerism and nineteenth-century English culture, see Alison Winter, *Mesmerized: Powers of Mind in Victorian Britain* (Chicago, 1998).

26. Ellenberger, *Discovery of the Unconscious*, 70–71.

27. Ibid., 82. For James Braid's full description of hypnotic marvels, see his *Magic, Witchcraft, Animal Magnetism, Hypnotism, and Electro-Biology* (London, 1852) and also *Observations on Trance: Or Human Hybernation* (London, 1850). See also Winter, *Mesmerized*, 185, and Ian Hacking's discussion of the place of hypnotism in the evolution of medical thinking regarding double consciousness in *Rewriting the Soul: Multiple Personality and the Sciences of Memory* (Princeton, 1995), esp. 144, 148–49.

28. Crabtree, *Multiple Man*, 350. For an illuminating discussion of the fit of classic cases of double consciousness and "identity amnesia," see pp. 60–66. The author's analysis of the changing role of possession, from intrusion to its manifestation in alter personalities, can be found in *From Mesmer to Freud: Magnetic Sleep and the Roots of Psychological Healing* (New Haven, 1993). Sleepwalkers also exemplified the phenomenon of the "unknown," someone having "no recollection of what transpired in the paroxysm" (L. W. Belden, *Somnambulism: The Extraordinary Case of Jane C. Rider, the Springfield Somnambulist* [London, 1834], 10). The lost memory of sleepwalking episodes is also discussed by Legrand du Saulle, "Le somnambulisme naturel: discussion médico-légale sur le crime et le suicide accomplis pendant le sommeil somnambulique," *Annales Médico-Psychologiques* (Paris, 1863); Robert MacNish, *The Philosophy of Sleep* (Glasgow, 1830); and Henry Maudsley, *Responsibility in Mental Disease* (London, 1876).

29. Crabtree, *Multiple Man*, 97, 354.

30. "On the Admissibility," 446–47.

31. Ibid., 442.

32. Collier had to address the question of lucid interval because Comyns' *Digest* makes an exception to peremptorily excluding lunatics from testifying, stipulating that this dictum need not apply in episodes when the afflicted *returned* to sanity. The possibility that lunatics might enjoy a lucid interval was a contentious issue among nineteenth-century medical men precisely because "surface calm" might reveal not a return to normality only that the florid delusion had yet to be touched upon. John Haslam, referred to by name in the trial regarding the *necessary* connection between faulty memory and insanity, also spoke no less unequivocally about the mistaken perception that lucid intervals were likely: "Ordinary persons have been much deceived by the temporary display of rational discourse . . . but let him protract the discourse . . . let him draw the hair-trigger which inflames the combustible materials of his disease, and he will be surprised if not alarmed by the explosion. . . . [T]he experienced will find that by some unaccountable association, even ordinary topics are linked to his darling delusions—the map of his mind will point out that the smallest rivulet flows into the great stream of his derangement" (*Medical Jurisprudence as It Relates to Insanity According to the Law of England* [London, 1817], 15–19).

In the same year as the Donelly case, J. G. Davey took issue with the concept of lucid intervals, speaking, as Haslam had also done, with reference to the sudden eruption of violence. "However quiet and comfortable such persons may usually be when protected from the anxieties and irritations of life, and when subject to the kind and considerate dictations of those under whose care they are placed, they are no sooner removed from such wholesome influences than the brain necessarily rebels with the stimuli offered to it" ("Plea of Insanity," *Association Medical Journal: Edited for the Provincial Medical and Surgical Association* [London, 1854], 880). Although both Haslam and Davey address the implications of "lucid intervals" for criminal rather than civil jurisdiction, their message is clear: surface rationality was ephemeral and never far from the consuming derangement lurking nearby. Donelly did not even reveal such "alternating" madness. As Collier would argue, there was never a moment when Donelly was lucid regarding the spirits who livid inside; this did not mean, however, that the judges could not find sufficient lucidity when the asylum patient affirmed that he knew what it meant to swear an oath.

33. Nineteenth-century criminal law and criminal-procedure reforms aimed to render the criminal trial a more professional forum by permitting the defense attorney a full advocacy role. The predictable effect of limiting the extraordinary range of judicial discretion—a staple courtroom feature in common-law courts—meant that courtroom evidence was for the first time coming under careful scrutiny. This issue, together with the larger question of changing patterns in the courtroom division of labor, is addressed in the concluding chapter.

34. "On the Admissibility," 447.

35. Further cases of asylum beatings are discussed in "The Prosecution of a Medical Superintendent for Manslaughter," *The Asylum Journal of Mental Science* 2 (1856): 517–23; "Conviction of Two Attendants at a Lunatic Asylum for the Manslaughter of a Lunatic," *London Medical Gazette, or Journal of Practical Medicine* 4 (1847): 919–20. For the removal of a madhouse license for the ill treatment of a pauper lunatic, see PRO, HO 45/5153. These cases reinforce the judges' opinion that without the testimony of asylum lunatics, their keepers would enjoy complete immunity from prosecution for the ill treatment or even death of inmates.

36. *OBSP,* 1850–51, case 1071, 7th sess., 21. Certification of the decision of these justices on 3 May 1851 can be found in the PRO, HO Crim 12/19.

Chapter 5. An Unconscious Poisoning

Epigraph: Alfred Swaine Taylor, "Arsenic. Symptoms of Acute Poisoning," *The Principles and Practice of Medical Jurisprudence* (London, 1865), 196–97.

1. The trial narrative is found in *OBSP,* 1847–48, case 290, 2nd sess., 280–94. Contemporary medical and legal commentary can be found in "The Plea of In-

sanity—Case of the Boy Allnutt," *London Medical Gazette, or Journal of Practical Medicine* n.s., vol. 6 (1848): 475–77; "Baron Rolfe's charge to the Jury in the case of the Boy Allnutt, who was tried at the Central Criminal Court for the Murder of his Grandfather, on the 15th of December, 1847," *Journal of Psychological Medicine and Mental Pathology* (1848): 193–219; *Times of London,* 26 November 1847, 3a, 16 December 1847, 7f, 8a and b.

2. *Moral insanity,* most often traced to Pinel's *manie sans délire,* is most frequently credited as James Cowles Prichard's contribution to the history of forensic psychopathology. Trained in Edinburgh, Prichard declared the emotions (or passions) to be "another class of phenomena distinct in their nature from ideas" (*A Review of the Doctrine of a Vital Principle as Maintained by Some Writers on Phrenology: With Observations on Physical and Animal Life* [London, 1829], 176). Moral insanity's "morbid perversion of the feelings" left the afflicted incapable of resisting the power of an emotion because the necessarily attached cultural prescription was missing: one either failed to understand why it was wrong or felt incapable of resisting the overwhelming force of the passion to injure, to acquire, to assault. To many a judicial mind—and Baron Rolfe's was one of them—surrendering to temptation is precisely the course the law was designed to thwart. To the bench, temptation was hardly a disease: it was the (standard) human condition. For an elaboration of Prichard's ideas on moral insanity, see his other works: *A Treatise on Insanity and Other Disorders Affecting the Mind* (London, 1835) and *On the Different Forms of Insanity in Relation to Jurisprudence, Designed for the Use of Persons Concerned in Legal Questions Regarding Unsoundness of Mind* (London, 1842).

3. *OBSP,* 1840, case 1877, 9th sess., 506.

4. Thomas Mayo, *Medical Testimony and Evidence in Cases of Lunacy; Being the Croonian Lectures* (London, 1854), 82. Impulses and instincts had immediate intelligibility in the nineteenth century when there was a special fascination with, and fear of, the automatic physiological functioning that underlay human behavior. *Homicidal orgasm,* a term encountered in medical literature but not in medical testimony (the *OBSP* did not even spell out *Buggery* in the court transcripts), similarly signified a descent into convulsive, involuntary behavior. Certainly the term itself implies something pleasurable, perhaps conveying its creator's wish to suggest at least an initial sensual indulgence.

5. A contemporary description of the diagnosis and effects of scrofula can be found in *The Lancet,* 2 (3 August 1850): 490–91.

6. *OBSP,* 1847–48, case 290, 2nd sess., 286. The mother's account, though here reported in the murder trial, was initially given at the police station in regard to the theft of her father's possessions. An association between the hearing of voices impelling the listener to crime and the "duality of the mind . . . two complete thinking organs in the skull" had been made a year before the Allnutt trial by A. L. Wigan. Although he wrote in terms of two hemispheres

rather than "double consciousness," Wigan's cases depicted the presence of a murderous "other" pressing the afflicted to unimaginable acts. "Something says to me 'Cut their throats,'" one patient at the Salpêtrière told him. "[I] would lose my life in defending [my children] from danger, even when I was in the act of killing them" (A. L. Wigan, "A Few More Words on the Duality of Mind and on Some of Its Corollaries" [London, 1847], 11).

7. An account of the police hearing investigating the boy's probable responsibility for the robbery can be found in the *Times of London,* 26 November, 1850, 3a and b.

8. *OBSP,* 1847–48, case 290, 2nd sess., 288.

9. Ibid., 287.

10. Ibid., 286.

11. Ibid., 289. Although the defense attorney does not refer to the title of Forbes Winslow's book, it was most likely *The Plea of Insanity in Criminal Cases* either in its second edition (London, 1843) or in its first printing, as the Gulstonian Lectures (London, 1822).

12. *OBSP,* 1847–48, case 290, 2nd sess., 291–92.

13. Ibid., 293. Duesbury's initial comment, "I am not prepared to answer," is clearly belied by the elaborate response he actually gives regarding the defendant's moral sense. Together with Alexander Morison's testimony in the Huggins trial, soon to follow, one suspects that these medical witnesses were showing exquisite sensitivity to the courtroom division of labor by the initial avowal of "I am not here to decide the question of responsibility of an insane person," only to speak directly to that one issue.

14. James Fitzjames Stephen, *A General View of the Criminal Law of England* (London, 1863), 95. Stephen's strong endorsement that such impulses may occur is cited two years later by Alfred Swaine Taylor, in *The Principles and Practice of Medical Jurisprudence* (London, 1865), 1102.

15. The classic works from Pinel's two star pupils are Jean-Etienne-Dominique Esquirol's *Mental Maladies: A Treatise on Insanity,* trans. E. K. Hunt (Philadelphia, 1845), and Etienne-Jean Georget's *De la folie: considérations sur cette maladie* (Paris, 1820) and *Discussion médico-légale sur la folie ou aliénation mentale: suivie de l'examen du procès criminel d'Henriette Cornier et de plusieurs autres procès* (Paris, 1826). Quote is from Georget, *De la folie,* 88. The most comprehensive analysis of the French school of *médecine mentale* can be found in Jan Goldstein, *Console and Classify: The French Psychiatric Profession in the Nineteenth Century* (Cambridge, 1987). Further discussion of the conceptual origin of "lesion of the will" specifically is offered in François Leuret, "Review of Elias Regnault, Degré de compétence," *Annales d'hygiène publique et de médecine légale* 1 (1829), and in two publications by Charles-Chrétien-Henri Marc: *Annales d'hygiène publique et de médecine légale* 10 (1833): 357–474, and *De la folie, considérée avec les questions médico-judiciares,* pt. 1 (Paris, 1840).

16. The term *monomanie homicide* originated with Georget. For a comprehensive review of the use of *monomanie* in the professional growth (and defensiveness) of French psychiatry, see Goldstein, *Console and Classify*, 155–89. For a review of Goldstein's interpretation, see Joel Peter Eigen, "A Mania for Diagnosis: Unraveling the Aims of Nineteenth-Century French Psychiatrists," *Journal of the History of the Human Sciences* 2 (1989): 41–51.

17. *OBSP,* 1847–48, case 290, 2nd sess., 293–94. Conolly was to be a frequent witness at the Old Bailey; indeed, he rivaled McMurdo not in the number of appearances but in having the knack of testifying in the most innovative defense cases. (The very model of a modern asylum superintendent, Conolly testified in the trials of John Ovenstone, James Huggins, and Luigi Buranelli, in addition to that of William Newton Allnutt to cite only the trials reported in this book.) As physician superintendent of Hanwell Lunatic Asylum with close to nine hundred patients under his care, Conolly cut a wide swath through Victorian London, although his courtroom appearances did not always yield the sort of public persona he would have esteemed.

18. When medical witnesses alleged a radical separation between Allnutt's capacity to understand the wrong he was committing and to *feel*—to appreciate—why it was wrong, they were describing a particular form of splitting that would be taken up by Eugen Bleuler early in the next century. In coining the term *schizophrenia*—or *dementia praecox*—Bleuler described the "splitting" of different psychic functions as one of schizophrenia's most important characteristics. Of course, historical nosology is frought with hazards, not least the priority of symptoms that any one classifier might adopt, but it seems fair to say that this seminal work in the history of psychiatric classification recognized the possibility of a split between affect and cognition, the peculiar and haunting specter of separation that Allnutt had, in fact, manifested. Eugen Bleuler, *Dementia Praecox or the Group of Schizophrenias,* trans. Joseph Zinkin (New York, 1950), esp. 7–9. Bleuler's relation of the "splitting" phenomenon to multiple states of being is discussed in Ian Hacking, *Rewriting the Soul: Multiple Personality and the Sciences of Memory* (Princeton, 1995), 128–34.

19. "Baron Rolfe's charge," 193.

20. *Times of London,* 16 December 1847, 9b.

21. "Baron Rolfe's charge," 215.

22. Ibid., 207.

23. *Times of London,* 16 December 1847, 9b.

24. Ibid.

25. This theme is developed in "Baron Rolfe's charge," 212–15.

26. "The Plea of Insanity."

27. *OBSP,* 1850–51, case 1502, 9th sess., 368–69. Conolly's colorful career was suitably public to have been lampooned in a contemporary best-seller, *Hard Cash,* by Charles Reade (London, 1864). In a biographical essay on Conolly's

career, Andrew Scull quotes Reade's characterization of the good doctor as "blinded by self interest . . . likely to find insanity wherever he looked" ("A Victorian Alienist: John Conolly, FRCP, DCL [1794–1866]," in W. F. Bynum, Roy Porter, and Michael Shepherd, eds., *The Anatomy of Madness: Essays in the History of Psychiatry*, vol. 1, *People and Ideas* [Tavistock, 1985]: 103–50).

28. Ten years earlier, at the trial of Edward Oxford, John Burt Davis was asked by the prosecuting attorney whether he appeared in court as a magistrate, a community member, or a physician. Davis answered simply but emphatically, "I answer as a physician." The significance of this assertion for the historical evolution of the forensic psychiatrist's unique professional voice is examined in Joel Peter Eigen, "I Answer as a Physician: Opinion as Fact in Pre-McNaughtan Insanity Trials," in Michael Clark and Catherine Crawford, eds., *Legal Medicine in History* (Cambridge, 1994), 167–99.

29. *OBSP,* 1850–51, case 1502, 9th sess., 370–71. Morison also did not interview Huggins directly. All his testimony is based on Conolly's cross-examination.

30. *Times of London,* 12 July 1851, 7f.

31. *OBSP,* 1861–62, case 745, 9th sess., 300–313.

32. Ibid., 307.

33. Ibid., 312.

34. Ibid., 312–13.

35. *Times of London,* 10 July 1862, 12b.

36. Ibid, 12c.

37. Dove's case was the subject of a full-length monograph by the seriously ruffled medical witness at the trial, Caleb Williams, M.D., *Observations on the Criminal Responsibility of the Insane. Founded upon the Trials of James Hill and William Dove* (London, 1856). Commentary is also found in a chapter written by James Fitzjames Stephen, "The Case of William Dove," in *A General View of the Criminal Law of England* (London, 1863), 391–402, and J. C. B. [presumably J. C. Bucknill], "Plea of Insanity—The Trial of William Dove," *Asylum Journal of Mental Science* 3 (1857): 125–34.

38. Williams, *Observations on Criminal Responsibility,* cxiii.

Chapter 6. Crimes of an Automaton

1. Although quoted in Alfred Swaine Taylor's classic text, *The Principles and Practice of Medical Jurisprudence* (London, 1865), 1131, Taylor's source for the hunters' story is William Mawdesley Best, *A Treatise on the Presumptions of Law and Fact with the Theory and Rules of Presumptive and Circumstantial Proof in Criminal Cases* (London, 1844), 282.

2. There were even tales of sleepwalkers who managed not to kill someone. Accounts of lethal and nonlethal sleepwalking regularly appeared in European publications, regardless of the country of their origin. Among the prominent

English sources are Taylor, *Principles and Practice,* and also his *A Manual of Medical Jurisprudence* (London, 1844), 657–58 (in *Principles and Practice,* Taylor mentions the Minchin case: "There was an absence of motive, but, as has been elsewhere stated, this alone does not create irresponsibility" [1132]); Alexander Morison, *Outlines of Lectures on the Nature, Causes and Treatment of Insanity* (London, 1848), 439–42; James Cowles Prichard, *Somnambulism and Animal Magnetism* (London, 1834); and J. C. Bucknill and D. Tuke, *A Manual of Psychological Medicine* (London, 1862), 213–14.

3. Quoted in Nigel Walker, *Crime and Insanity in England,* vol. 1, *The Historical Perspective* (Edinburgh, 1968), 167. Documentation of Culpeper's trial and the reprieve issued from the Palace are in the PRO SP 44/337, items 150 and 174.

4. *OBSP,* 1852–53, case 725, 8th sess., 215.

5. Ibid., 218.

6. *Times of London,* 17 June 1853, 7b and c.

7. Prichard, *Somnambulism,* 2.

8. Henry Maudsley, "States of Unconsciousness," *Journal of Psychological Medicine and Mental Pathology,* n.s., vol. 3, pt. 2 (1877): 189.

9. Silliman's description of a case concerning a New England woman, quoted in Prichard, *Somnambulism,* 8. Emphasis in the original.

10. James Fitzjames Stephen, *A General View of the Criminal Law of England* (London, 1863), 79.

11. François-Emmanuel Fodéré, for example, believed that the sleepwalker is responsible because it is *his* conscience that animates the action even in sleep. The conscience directs the crime, aiming perhaps to gratify revenge, revealing "during his sleep, the inmost recesses of his soul" (Alexander Morison, *Outlines of Lectures on the Nature, Causes, and Treatment of Insanity* [London, 1848], 439–40). A. A. Liébeault reports the story of a Caesar who tortured a man who dreamt of having assassinated him. The man must have entertained the treasonous plan in his diurnal moments, reasoned Caesar, to have dreamt of them at night: "Si tu n'avais pas pensé pendant le jour à m'assassiner, tu n'y aurais pas rêvé pendant le nuit,' lui dit l'implacable tyran" [If you had not thought of assassinating me during the day, you would not have dreamt it at night, the inflexible tyrant told him] (*Du sommeil et des états analogues: considérés surtout au point de vue de l'action du moral sur le physique* [Paris, 1866], 523).

12. *Regina v. Jackson* (1847), Liverpool Autumn Assizes. Quoted in Taylor, *Principles and Practice,* 1131–32.

13. William B. Carpenter, *The Doctrine of Human Automatism: A Lecture Delivered before the Sunday Lecture Society, 7 March 1875* (London, 1875), 23.

14. Although headless, this spunky invertebrate covered a lot of territory, making its presence known in Carpenter, *Doctrine,* 14, and in medical testimony in the trial of Elizabeth Carr, *OBSP,* 1875–76, case 413, 11th sess.

15. Writing of the remarkable states of somnambulism and mesmerism, Thomas Laycock observed, "We have found that a large number of vital phenomena are performed without consciousness; consequently, there must be a class of nerves to which the laws of consciousness are not applicable; and which must be the organs of physical sensation and involuntary motion" (*An Essay on Hysteria, Being an Analysis of Its Irregular and Aggravated Forms: Including Hysterical Hemorrhage, and Hysterical Ischuria* [Philadelphia, 1840], 171). For a fuller description of his views regarding the extent of involuntary muscular movements, see Laycock's "Reflex, Automatic, and Unconscious Cerebration: A History and a Criticism, *Journal of Mental Science* 21 (1876): 477–98.

16. Taylor, *Principles and Practice*, 1132.

17. Ibid., 1131; Taylor, *A Manual*, 657.

18. *Times of London*, 5 January 1859, 11d, continued on 19 January 1859, 11d.

19. It had implications most of all for the grand jury's relationship with the judiciary. An 1838 ruling held that a grand jury had "no authority by law to ignore a bill of murder, on the ground of insanity." Regardless of the testimony of witnesses, if the act committed would have amounted to murder in a sane man, "it is their duty to find the bill [i.e., to indict] otherwise the Court cannot order the detention of the party" (*Regina v. Hodges* [1838], 8 Carrington and Payne 195).

20. Walker, *Crime and Insanity*, 168–69. For Walker's original source, see J. C. Bucknill and David Tuke, *A Manual of Psychological Medicine* (London, 1862), 213–14.

21. For Morison's views on sleepwalking and criminal responsibility, see *Outlines of Lectures*, 439–42. Henry Maudsley's comments on the Griggs case and other sleepwalking assaults are given in *Responsibility in Mental Disease* (London, 1876), 249–53.

22. *HM Adv. v. Fraser* (1878), 4 Couper 78: pp. 70–78.

23. Ibid., 73.

24. Ibid. Dr. Yellowlees offered his complete view of Fraser's condition in "Homicide by a Somnambulist," *Journal of Mental Science* 24 (1878): 451–58.

25. *HM Adv. v. Fraser*, 73–75.

26. Ibid., 75.

27. Walker, *Crime and Insanity*, 169–70.

28. Before Parliament's passage of the 1800 Criminal Lunatics Act—which moved speedily toward ratification while Hadfield's trial was ongoing—no formal disposition attended prisoners acquitted on the ground of insanity. Indeed, there was no formal special verdict as such, either. Defendants were simply acquitted and discharged, like any prisoner found "not guilty." Occasionally one finds a note in the *OBSP* that a prisoner was put in the care of his or her family, but this was an infrequent and informal disposition. For a methodological jus-

tification for considering pre-1800 verdicts as "insanity acquittals," see Joel Peter Eigen, *Witnessing Insanity: Madness and Mad-Doctors in the English Court* (New Haven, 1995), 21–22.

29. Yellowlees, "Homicide," 458.

30. Prichard, *Somnambulism*, 18.

31. These fits could be associated with fainting dead away (*OBSP,* 1844–45, case 1061, 7th sess.), "You must have me confined; for I do not know what I do when these fits come on" (*OBSP,* 1847–48, case 948), or "when the fits are upon him he seems scarcely to know what he is about" (*OBSP,* 1849–50, case 1645, 11th sess.). Epileptic fits are mentioned by name beginning in 1850: The medical witness "could not undertake to say what period the prisoner was not conscious of. It was proved that she was subject to epileptic fits" (*OBSP,* 1849–50, case 1893, 12th sess.), "I especially lay stress upon the epileptic character of his appearance at the time the deed was committed, the staring eyes, the fixed expression, and afterward a sudden recovery" (*OBSP,* 1874–75, case 93, 2nd sess.).

32. *OBSP,* 1859–60, case 893, 12th sess. It should come as little surprise that a court in which poisoning could be seen as an impulsive crime could conceive of forgery to be effected in a fit.

33. Although Maudsley was not speaking with regard to these *OBSP* verdicts, his statement about the "success" of epilepsy as a defense is particularly apt: "Whenever such a suspension of present knowledge and of memory has been urged as explanatory or exculpatory of particular acts, the plea has either been rejected or accepted with grave suspicion . . . as the existence of such a state is doubted or disbelieved in by all, except psychologists" ("States of Unconsciousness," 198).

34. Stephen, *General View*, 78.

35. Ibid., 91.

36. Certainly the most widely quoted "general rule" of criminal responsibility regarding epilepsy, Zacchia's standard was not universally accepted by medicolegalists in the nineteenth century. Jean-Pierre Falret, for one, believed it far too general: it is the individual case that must be looked to—the existence of a reason for the crime, for example. Clearly, all medical writers believed that anyone in the midst of a grand mal seizure was perfectly blameless, but these moments were the exception. It was the ambiguous length of the *vertige,* the period of "absence," that invited medical caution regarding the assumed return to normalcy. For Falret's criticism of Zacchia, see "De l'état mental des épileptiques," *Archives Générales de Médecine* 16, vol. 2, 5th series (1860), esp. 428–30.

37. Trousseau (quoting Falret) believed that persons in a fit could not be held responsible for their "automatic" acts perpetrated during the short-lived delusion. Epileptics simply cannot know the nature of their acts (*Lectures on Clinical Medicine, delivered at the Hôtel-Dieu, Paris,* trans. P. Victor Bazire [London, 1867]). W. Griesinger countered that, with reference to "irresistible" im-

pulsive crimes, "few of the acts of the insane have the character of forced, purely automatic movements; in mania also, according to the testimony of individuals who have recovered, many of the wild desires could often be restrained; the criminal deeds of the insane are not generally instinctive" (*Mental Pathology and Therapeutics*, trans. C. Lockhart Robertson and James Rutherford [London, 1867], 77). Other opinion embraced a position parallel to the courtroom experience that had revealed mental derangement to carry no prescriptive influence on the jury. Falret, for example, wrote that it was difficult "to pronounce on the moral liberty of epileptics for their acts—because the same disease could account for some crimes and not others." Hinting at the notion that "even paranoids have enemies," the French physician averred, "The fact that a dark nature lay at the heart of an epileptic['s action] does not end the matter for the medical man." It is not the crime itself but an array of symptoms that allows one to assess moral liability ("De l'état mental," 18, vol. 2, 5th series [1861], 436).

38. See, for example, Joel Peter Eigen, "Delusion in the Courtroom: The Role of Partial Insanity in Early Forensic Testimony," *Medical History* 35 (1991): 25–49.

39. The literature on epilepsy as a psychological entity is vast. The most illuminating nineteenth-century studies include W. A. F. Browne, *Epileptics: Their Mental Condition* (London, 1865); Louis-Jean-François Delasiauve, *Traité de l'épilepsie: histoire, traitement, médecine légale* (Paris, 1854); Jean-Etienne-Dominique Esquirol, *Des maladies mentales, considérées sous les rapports medical, hygénique, et médico-légale* (Brussels, 1833); Edward H. Sieveking, *Analysis of Fifty-two Cases of Epilepsy Observed by the Author* (London, 1857); M. Gonzalez Echeverria, *On Epilepsy: Anatomo-Pathological and Clinical Notes* (New York, 1870) and "On the Relation of Epilepsy to Criminal Responsibility," *Journal of Mental Science* 23 (1877): 141–47; and works by Falret and Trousseau, cited above. For contemporary analysis of epilepsy in a historical context, see two works by G. E. Berrios: "Epilepsy and Insanity during the Early Nineteenth Century: A Conceptual History," *Archives of Neurology* 41 (1984): 978–81, and "Insanity and Epilepsy in the Nineteenth Century," in Martin Roth and Valerie Cowie, eds., *Psychiatry, Genetics and Pathography* (London, 1979), 161–71.

40. *Les vertiges* were the predominant focus of the French physicians cited above. Most illuminating among these sources are Falret, "De l'état mental," Trousseau, *Lectures on Clinical Medicine*, and Esquirol, *Des maladies mentales*. Additional material on epileptic vertigo can be found in W. A. F. Browne's experience with an individual who "passed many hours in a waking dream or trance—acting absurdly, spoke vaguely or menacingly, but . . . capable of willing and performing various complicated transactions" (*Epileptics: Their Mental Condition* [London, 1865], 14–15).

41. Falret, quoted in Browne, *Epileptics*, 14.

42. Trousseau, *Lectures on Clinical Medicine*, 56.

43. Ibid., 59.

44. Carpenter, *Doctrine*, 25.

45. Gonzalez Echeverria, *On Epilepsy*, 368–69. The quote originated with Trousseau, whose conception of *vertigé épileptique* is examined in his *Lectures on Criminal Medicine*, esp. 51–71.

46. *OBSP*, 1875–76, case 413, 11th sess., 495.

47. Ibid., 496–97.

48. This is a curiously emphatic statement from the coroner's jury, considering that the mother's action very clearly caused the child's death. As in the 1838 *Regina v. Hodges* ruling in which a specialized jury juxtaposed its judgment for that of the petit jury, the coroner's jury was indeed "acquitting on the ground of unconsciousness," as had the Old Bailey just days before (*Daily Telegraph*, 21 September 1876, 2).

49. *OBSP*, 1876–77, case 246, 4th sess., 435–38.

50. Ibid., 450–52.

51. Ibid., 445.

52. Ibid., 453–57.

53. Ibid., 456.

54. Ibid., 457–58.

55. Ibid., 458–59.

56. Ibid., 459–60.

57. *Times of London*, 9 February 1877, 5f.

58. Ibid.

59. Quoted in Browne, *Epileptics*, 7–8.

Conclusion

1. Ian Hacking, *Rewriting the Soul: Multiple Personality and the Sciences of Memory* (Princeton, 1995), 174.

2. Joel Peter Eigen, *Witnessing Insanity: Madness and Mad-Doctors in the English Court* (New Haven, 1995), esp. 106–7.

3. Hacking, *Rewriting the Soul*, 149.

4. *OBSP*, 1875–76, case 400, 8th sess., 154.

5. Pre-McNaughtan trials feature a host of defendants who used the "Prisoner's Defense" (the defendant's opportunity to make a statement at the conclusion of the trial) to describe the experience of derangement. When these accounts are analyzed one finds the frequent imagery of "[not] knowing right from wrong" as a formula for how defendants came to recognize that they were in fact deranged. Perhaps they were sitting in Newgate Prison with dog-eared copies of contemporary legal and medical texts, preparing their courtroom statements; perhaps the language of the courts had provided them with a name for their distress. The latter explanation would suggest that the social and legal context influenced the experience, not just the expression, of madness. Put another way,

one understood that one was mad precisely because no conscious purpose lay behind the act. An analysis of the expression and experience of the pre-McNaughtan insanity defendants is offered in Eigen, *Witnessing Insanity*, 161–81.

6. Medical men could occasionally find the courtroom a professionally abusive forum to announce their expertise. Certainly the comments of the judge in the Dove trial—"Experts in madness! Mad-doctors!"—would be difficult for any professional man to listen to, let alone to answer. As defense attorneys gained skills at cross-examination, witnesses in general faced the twisting of their words and the very real prospect of being reduced to ridicule; see, for example, J. M. Beattie, "Scales of Justice: Defense Counsel and the English Criminal Trial in the Eighteenth and Nineteenth Centuries," *Law and History Review* 9 (1991), esp. 236–44. The fear of embarrassment was particularly acute for some medical men specializing in insanity who warned their brethren what they could expect to find at the hands of a hostile bar. Prepare thoroughly for the courtroom, medical men were advised, offer opinion "so founded in experience and fortified by reason, that it may resist the blandishments of eloquence and the subtil [*sic*] underminings of cross-examination" (John Haslam, *Medical Jurisprudence as It Relates to Insanity According to the Law of England* [London, 1817], 4). For advice concerning possible answers medical witnesses might make to such cross examination, see George Edward Male, *Elements of Juridical or Forensic Medicine: For the Use of Medical Men, Coroners, and Barristers* (London, 1818).

7. But see Jan Goldstein's claim that "monomania" in France was used by forensic psychiatric witnesses to defend professionally grounded expertise in the first half of the nineteenth century, in *Control and Classify: The French Psychiatric Profession in the Nineteenth Century* (Cambridge, 1987). For an appraisal of some English jurists' views—"I abhor the traffic in testimony"—see Carol A. G. Jones, *Expert Witnesses: Science, Medicine, and the Practice of Law* (Oxford, 1994).

8. Robert K. Merton, *Social Theory and Social Structure* (New York, 1968), 73–138.

9. A comprehensive description of the reform of capital statutes is given in Leon Radzinowicz, *A History of the English Criminal Law and Its Administration from 1750*, vol. 1, *The Movement for Reform* (London, 1948). David J. A. Cairns provides a more recent analysis of the Bloody Code's domination of all facets of the eighteenth- and early-nineteenth-century capital prosecution system in *Advocacy and the Making of the Criminal Trial, 1800–1865* (Oxford, 1998), esp. 5–15.

10. The jury's effort to circumnavigate capital sentencing statutes is examined in Thomas Andrew Green, *Verdict According to Conscience: Perspectives on the English Criminal Trial, 1200–1800* (Chicago, 1985), esp. 378–83. The high rate of jury acquittals is also examined in Peter King, *Crime, Justice and Discretion in England, 1740–1820* (Oxford, 2000), esp. 238–46, and J. M. Beattie, *Crime and the Courts in England, 1660–1800* (Oxford, 1986).

11. For a particularly incisive analysis of Romilly's contribution, see Cairns, *Advocacy*, esp. 56–60.

12. These developments can in large part be attributed to the emergence of the defense attorney. By the end of the eighteenth century, approximately one in three Old Bailey defendants were represented (Beattie, *Scales of Justice*, 236). The presence of attorneys in the courtroom and the increasing frequency with which judges encouraged jurors to base their verdicts on guilt "beyond a reasonable doubt" doubtless focused the court's attention on the emerging standards of forensic proof. For an analysis of the philosophical thought guiding the evolving courtroom reasoning, see Barbara J. Shapiro, "'To a Moral Certainty': Theories of Knowledge and Anglo-American Juries, 1600–1850," *Hastings Law Journal* 38 (1986): 153–93.

13. John H. Langbein, "Historical Foundations of the Law of Evidence: A View from the Ryder Sources," *Columbia Law Review* 96 (1996): 1168–1202.

14. For historical appraisals of the judge's role at the Old Bailey, see John H. Langbein, "The Criminal Trial before the Lawyers," *University of Chicago Law Review* 45 (winter 1978): 263–316, and "Shaping the Eighteenth-Century Criminal Trial: A View from the Ryder Sources," *University of Chicago Law Review* 50 (winter 1983): 1–136; and Cairns, *Advocacy*, esp. 43–53.

15. That the defense attorney emerged at all is more a mystery than the question of why he arrived so late. Formally excluded by common law until the Treason Act of 1696, defense counsel was considered unnecessary at best and intrusive at worst, because "no one could speak more effectively for those accused of crimes than themselves." This stricture was relaxed in 1696 as the Whigs, now in prominence in Parliament, sought to redress their recent experience as the target of arbitrary political persecution by ensuring that defendants on trial for treasonous offences be permitted counsel. Early in the 1700s, some common-law judges continued to extend this privilege to persons charged with nontreasonous offenses—again, to redress a perceived imbalance. As individual judges permitted early-eighteenth-century prosecutors to avail themselves of legal representation, other members of the judiciary believed it only fair to do the same for the accused. By the 1730s, the participation of defense counsel was no longer anomalous. For the historical emergence of defense counsel in common-law courts, see Cairns, *Advocacy*; Beattie, *Scales of Justice*; and Langbein, *Historical Foundations*.

16. For an appraisal of Erskine's deft use of delusion in challenging the prevailing common-law assumption that only a total and complete insanity could support a defense of insanity, see Nigel Walker, *Crime and Insanity in England*, vol. 1, *The Historical Perspective* (Edinburgh, 1968), 74–81.

17. Literature concerning the pivotal role of the will for preserving a balance between the body and mind is vast, particularly the critical role of the will in restraining unruly passions. See, for example, Martin J. Wiener, *Recon-*

structing the Criminal: Culture, Law, and Policy in England, 1830–1914 (Cambridge, Mass., 1990); Bruce Haley, *The Healthy Body and Victorian Culture* (Cambridge, 1978), and, with specific reference to criminal defenses, Roger Smith, *Trial by Medicine: Insanity and Responsibility in Victorian Trials* (Edinburgh, 1981).

18. Martin Wiener, "Judges v. Jurors: Courtroom Tensions in Murder Trials and the Law of Criminal Responsibility in Nineteenth-Century England," *Law and History Review* 17 (1999): 467–506, and "The Sad Story of George Hall: Adultery, Murder, and the Politics of Mercy in Mid-Victorian England," *Social History* 24 (1999): 174–95.

19. For an analysis of the standard employed to pronounce "reasonableness" in matters bearing on criminal responsibility, see Bernard Brown, "The 'Ordinary Man' in Provocation: Anglo-Saxon Attitudes and 'Unreasonable Non-Englishmen,'" *International and Comparative Law Quarterly* 13 (1964): 203–35.

20. Roger Chadwick surmises that the growing willingness to accept insanity verdicts was encouraged by the opening of Broadmoor in 1863. Since 1800, persons who received the "special verdict" of insanity were detained, "awaiting the sovereign's pleasure." Incarceration, however, was unregulated, with no consistent administration supervising disposition. The construction of Broadmoor, according to Chadwick, "placed persons so acquitted firmly in the grasp of central government." Further, this centralization encouraged an enhanced partnership between the Home Office and medical specialists in insanity (*Bureaucratic Mercy: The Home Office and the Treatment of Capital Cases in Victorian Britain* [New York, 1992]).

21. Wiener, "Judges v. Jurors," esp. 497–505.

22. It is always important to keep in mind that the introduction of defense attorneys into the court did not necessarily alter the judge's conviction that he was, historically and perhaps even at present, the unofficial "counsel for the prisoner," although it may seem disingenuous to strike such a courtroom posture when the reality of an aggressive defense was in short supply. The fact remains that the judiciary was not viscerally disposed to bundle all prisoners off to Tyburn Tree. Even in insanity cases—trials likely to antagonize the bench if it suspected the defendant of feigning derangement—judges did not noticeably "lean against" the prisoner. In fact, they were capable of eliciting from medical witnesses the sort of evidence juries employed to acquit. Such solicitude had its limits, of course; comments regarding moral insanity could be sharp and dismissive. This attitude—ranging from doubt to outright contempt—can be traced from Oxford's 1840 trial through to Allnutt (1848) and Dove (1856).

23. Lawrence Rosen, "Intentionality and the Concept of the Person," in J. Roland Pennock and John W. Chapman, eds., *Criminal Justice*, Nomos 27 (New York, 1985), 52–77.

24. John Locke, *An Essay Concerning Human Understanding (1690)*, ed.

Peter H. Nidditch (Oxford, 1975), bk. 2, ch. 27. See also Nigel Walker's discussion of Locke's ideas on questions of criminal responsibility, *Aggravation, Mitigation, and Mercy in Criminal Justice* (Oxford, 1979), 208–9.

25. Mary Douglas, "The Person in an Enterprise Culture," in Shaun Hargreaves Heap and Angus Ross eds., *Understanding the Enterprise Culture: Themes in the Work of Mary Douglas* (Edinburgh, 1992), 41–62.

26. J. Crichton Browne, "Personal Identity and Its Morbid Modifications," *Journal of Mental Science* 8 (1863): 395.

27. Ibid., 386.

28. Samuel L. Mitchill, "A Double Consciousness, or a Duality of Person in the same Individual: From a Communication of Dr. MITCHILL to the Reverend Dr. NOTT, President of Union College. Dated January 16, 1816," in *The Medical Repository of Original Essays and Intelligence Relative to Physic, Surgeons, Chemistry, and Natural History, etc.*, n.s., vol. 3 (18th from the beginning) (New York, 1817), 186 (emphasis in the original). Bertrand also explored the nature of "heightened" memory—available to the person only in successive states of suspended consciousness—in *Traité du somnambulisme et des différentes modifications qu'il présente* (Paris, 1823), 97–109.

29. This alteration in memory was referred to as "identity amnesia," discussed in Chapter 4.

30. William Hamilton, *Lectures on Metaphysics and Logic*, ed. H. L. and John Veitch (Edinburgh, 1859), 347–48. I am indebted to Dr. Neil Manson's inspiring set of lectures on "The Unconscious before Freud" for alerting me to Hamilton's contribution to the literature on mental states held in abeyance.

31. Ibid., 339–41. But see his entire discussion of the varieties of unconscious mental activity, 311–79.

32. Ibid., 320.

33. *OBSP*, 1846–47, case 430, 3rd sess.; *OBSP*, 1864–65, case 667, 9th sess.

34. *OBSP*, 1845–46, case 1445, 9th sess.; *OBSP*, 1849–50, case 189, 3rd sess.

35. *OBSP*, 1847–48, case 2310, 12th sess.; *OBSP*, 1856–57, case 649, 7th sess.

36. *OBSP*, 1871–72, case 117, 3rd sess.

37. *OBSP*, 1872–73, case 516, 10th sess.

38. Locke, *An Essay*, 353.

39. Hacking, *Rewriting the Soul*, 128.

40. Ibid., 159–70.

41. G. E. Berrios makes this point repeatedly in his attempts to provide a conceptual history for a range of psychopathological phenomena. See, for example, "Epilepsy and Insanity during the Early 19th Century: A Conceptual History," *Archives of Neurology* 41 (1984): 978–81, and, with M. Gili, "Will and Its Disorders: A Conceptual History," *History of Psychiatry* 6 (1995): 87–104.

42. For a discussion of the Franklin case and a critical analysis of the phenomenon of repressed memory syndrome in court, see Elizabeth F. Loftus,

"The Reality of Repressed Memories," *American Psychologist* 48 (1993): 518–37. A highly critical appraisal of the role of repressed and recovered memory in courtroom testimony is offered by Frederick Crews in "The Revenge of the Repressed," *New York Review of Books*, pt. 1: 17 November 1994, 54–60; pt. 2: 2 December 1994, 49–58. Further discussion of the legal issues raised in trials of multiple persons is offered in Elyn R. Saks, with Stephen H. Behnke, *Jekyll on Trial: Multiple Personality Disorder and Criminal Law* (New York, 1997); Ralph B. Allison, "Difficulties Diagnosing the Multiple Personality Syndrome in a Death Penalty Case," *International Journal of Clinical and Experimental Hypnosis* 32 (1984): 102–17; Alfred P. French and Bryan R. Shechmeister, "The Multiple Personality Syndrome and Criminal Defense," *Bulletin of the American Academy of Psychiatry and Law* 11 (1983): 17–25; Paul S. Applebaum and Alexander Greer, "Who's on Trial? Multiple Personalities and the Insanity Defense," *Hospital and Community Psychiatry* 45 (1994): 965–66; Elyn R. Saks, "Does Multiple Personality Disorder Exist? The Beliefs, the Data, and the Law," *International Journal of Law and Psychiatry* 17 (1994): 43–78; Irwin N. Perr, "Crime and Multiple Personality Disorder: A Case History and Discussion," *Bulletin of the American Academy of Psychiatry and the Law* 19 (1991): 203–14; Stanley Abrams, "The Multiple Personality: A Legal Defense," *American Journal of Clinical Hypnosis* 25 (1983): 225–31; and Martin T. Orne, David F. Dinges, and Emily Carota Orne, "On the Differential Diagnosis of Multiple Personality in the Forensic Context," *International Journal of Clinical and Experimental Hypnosis* 32 (1984): 118–69.

43. Hacking provides an excellent appraisal of a confluence of cultural forces—feminism, child sexual abuse activism, an activist defense bar—in his study of the historical moment that witnessed the emergence of Multiple Personality Disorder in the popular imagination, clinical theorizing, and the criminal courtroom, *Rewriting the Soul*, esp. 39–68, 113–27. The phenomenon of adults using recovered memories to bring their alleged abusers to court is explored in Hollida Wakefield and Ralph Underwager, "Recovered Memories of Alleged Sexual Abuse: Lawsuits Against Parents," *Behavioral Sciences and the Law* 10 (1992): 483–507.

44. Jennifer Radden presents a comprehensive analysis of the legal implications of dividedness for Lockean conceptions of the forensic person in *Divided Minds and Successive Selves: Ethical Issues in Disorders of Identity and Personality* (Cambridge, Mass., 1996), esp. 34–107.

45. The most frequently cited cases in the medicolegal literature relate to each of these offenses. For legal issues raised in prosecuting a "multiple" in a case of baby stealing, see *United States v. Denny-Shaffer*, 2 F3d 999 (10th In Cir 1993); of drunk driving, *State v. Grimsley*, 444 NE2d 1071 (Ohio Ct App 1982); of drug possession, *Commonwealth v. Roman*, 606 NE2d 1333 (Mass 1993); of rape, *State v. Milligan*, 530 NE2d 965 (Ohio Ct App 1988). The trial most prominent in the literature is doubtless the Hillside Strangler Case, discussed

by a participating forensic psychiatric witness, in Allison, "Difficulties Diagnosing," 102–17. The ambiguity of the defendant's mental state is also discussed in John G. Watkins, "The Bianchi (L.A. Hillside Strangler) Case: Sociopath or Multiple Personality?" *International Journal of Clinical and Experimental Hypnosis* 32 (1984): 67–101. A popular treatment of the phenomenon of multiple personality can be found in Daniel Keyes, *The Minds of Billy Milligan* (New York, 1981).

46. *State v. Grimsley*, 444 NE2d 1071 (Ohio Ct App 1982). The original ruling had rejected the insanity defense, affirming that the courtroom evidence "fail[ed] to establish that [the alter personality] was either unconscious or acting involuntarily. There was only one person driving the car, the only one accused of drunk driving. It is immaterial whether she was in one state of consciousness or another so long as the personality then controlling her behavior . . . was conscious, and her actions were a product of her own volition."

47. *Kirkland v. State*, 304 SE2d 561 (Ga Ct App 1983).

48. Applebaum and Greer, "Who's on Trial," 966.

49. California Penal Code, Section 26.

50. *People v. Newton*, 3 3d 357, 377 (Cal App 1960).

51. Stephen H. Behnke distinguishes involuntariness as a defect in the physical act of doing, rather than the mental contemplation of the act, the *mens rea*. Among the acts that have been considered to suggest involuntariness, he includes sleepwalking, reflexes, seizures, and posthypnotic suggestion. See his "Assessing the Criminal Responsibility of Individuals with Multiple Personality Disorder: Legal Cases, Legal Theory," *Journal of the American Academy of Psychiatry and Law* 25 (1997): 392. See also a discussion of voluntary conduct and culpability in J. W. C. Turner, "The Mental Element in Crimes at Common Law," in P. H. Winfield, ed., *The Modern Approach to Criminal Law, Collected Essays* (London, 1945), 195–261. "If it be established that the accused person's conduct was involuntary he will have the valid defence that he is not responsible for the *actus*, and possibly [for] an act done under hypnotic suggestion or when sleepwalking or by pure accident" (204).

52. For the significance of MPD on issues concerning competency to plead, particularly, see Dorothy Otnow Lewis and Jennifer S. Bard, "Multiple Personality and Forensic Issues," *Psychiatric Clinics of North America* 14 (1991): 741–56; and French and Shechmeister, "Multiple Personality Syndrome," 20.

53. Eugène Azam, "La double conscience," *Revue scientifique*, 2nd series, 8 (1878): 185–86. For a more comprehensive look into thinking about Félida, see his text, *Hypnotisme, double conscience, et altérations de la personnalité* (Paris, 1887).

54. Jill O. Radwin, "The Multiple Personality Disorder: Has This Trendy Alibi Lost Its Way?" *Law and Psychology Review* 15 (1991): 367–69. See also French and Shechmeister, "Multiple Personality Syndrome," 22.

55. The various approaches courts have employed to prosecute defendants claiming MPD are examined in Behnke, "Assessing the Criminal Responsibility," 393–94. Beyond the strategies of how to treat the defendant, Radden surveys the courts' response to dissociative disorders in *Divided Minds*. In addition to pointing out the similarities to defenses of unconsciousness and insanity, she examines the fit of dissociation with the concept of diminished capacity, "suspended personhood," and simple, unadorned guilty convictions, esp. 120–38.

56. A considerable body of medicolegal opinion has despaired of the attempt to present the defendant claiming MPD as a series of successive selves, rather than as separate and possibly discrete moods and hostilities. See, for example, Behnke, "Assessing the Criminal Responsibility," 394–96.

57. *OBSP,* 1800–1801, case 446, 5th sess., 319–20.

58. Quoted in Radwin, "Multiple Personality Disorder," 355.

59. Seymour Halleck, "Dissociative Phenomena and the Question of Responsibility," *International Journal of Clinical and Experimental Hypnosis* 38 (1990): 307. Lewis and Bard are also unequivocal in asserting that, far from being whole individuals, people with MPD are "rather, the unconscious creations of the mind of a single individual in his or her struggle to cope with intolerable pain." The authors' treatment of MPD is diffused through a lens that proffers child sexual abuse as the core etiological factor in dissociation. See their "Multiple Personality," 746.

60. The belief that patients have cooked up alter personalities to entertain and intrigue their therapists has characterized much of the debate about the actual existence of multiple personality. While the willingness of clinician and patient to share this fantasy has at times been referred to as a *folie à deux,* Ian Hacking suggests employing the term *folie à combien,* to reflect the numerous selves suggested by the first case of multiple personality in France (*Rewriting the Soul,* 173). Regarding the plausible charge that MPD is particularly likely to be iatrogenically inspired, Halleck points to the clinician's tendency to consider seriously the claims of a patient who desperately craves attention. In his less charitable moments, Halleck believes that the therapist's desire for the "long-term patient" may be driving the discovery of this admittedly intriguing mental aberration ("Dissociative Phenomena," 300–303). But beyond looking for long-term clients, the clinician may conceive of the therapeutic role as part of a study of sexual trauma. Judith Herman, author of *Trauma and Recovery* writes that "advances in the [study of sexual trauma] occur only when they are supported by a political movement powerful enough to legitimate an alliance between investigators and patients and to counteract the ordinary social processes of silencing and denial" ([New York, 1994], 9). When a therapist encounters a tale of child sexual abuse, Herman asserts, "your job is not to be a detective, your job is not to be a fact finder, your job is not to be a judge or a jury . . . your

job is to help the patient make sense out of her life . . . to help make meaning out of her experience" ("Divided Memories," *Frontline,* Documentary Consortium of Public Television Stations, 1992). Not all clinicians, however, assume the "ally in healing" posture, at least to the point of relinquishing the role of detective. Speaking on the same program, Dr. Michael Yapko characterized the uncritical acceptance of patients' stories as "the narrative truth perspective: if the patient believes it, it may as well be true."

61. Ian Hacking, "Double Consciousness in Britain, 1815–1875," *Dissociation* 4 (1991): 136.

INDEX

219